Cinema 1 *The Movement-Image*

Cinema 1
The Movement-Image

Gilles Deleuze
Translated by Hugh Tomlinson
and Barbara Habberjam

 University of Minnesota Press
Minneapolis

Copyright © 1986 The Athlone Press

First published in France by Les Editions de Minuit
as Cinéma 1. L'Image-Mouvement
Copyright © 1983 by Les Editions de Minuit

Published by the University of Minnesota Press
111 Third Avenue South, Suite 290, Minneapolis, MN 55401-2520
http://www.upress.umn.edu
Printed in the United States of America on acid-free paper

Eleventh printing 2017

Library of Congress Cataloging-in-Publication Data
Deleuze, Gilles.
 Cinema.

 Translation of: Cinéma 1. L'Image-Mouvement
 Bibliography:
 Includes index.
 1. Moving-pictures—Philosophy. I. Title.
PN1995.D39313 1986   791.43'01   85-28898
ISBN 0-8166-1399-0 (v. 1)
ISBN 0-8166-1400-8 (pbk.: v. 1)

The University of Minnesota is an equal-opportunity
educator and employer.

Contents

Preface to the English edition

This book does not set out to produce a history of the cinema but to isolate certain cinematographic concepts. These concepts are not technical (such as the various kinds of shot or the different camera movements) or critical (for example the great genres, the Western, the detective film, the historical film, etc.). Neither are they linguistic, in the sense in which it has been said that the cinema was the universal language, or in the sense in which it has been said that the cinema is a language. The cinema seems to us to be a composition of images and of signs, that is, a pre-verbal intelligible content (*pure semiotics*), whilst semiology of a linguistic inspiration abolishes the image and tends to dispense with the sign. What we call cinematographic concepts are therefore the types of images and the signs which correspond to each type. The image of the cinema being, therefore, 'automatic' and presented primarily as movement-image, we have considered under what conditions it is specifically defined into different types. These types are, principally, the perception-image, the affection-image and the action-image. Their distribution certainly does determine a representation of time, but it must be noted that time remains the object of an indirect representation in so far as it depends on montage and derives from movement-images.

It is possible that, since the war, a direct time-image has been formed and imposed on the cinema. We do not wish to say that there will no longer be any movement, but that – just as happened a very long time ago in philosophy – a reversal has happened in the movement-time relationship; it is no longer time which is related to movement, it is the anomalies of movement which are dependent on time. Instead of an indirect representation of time which derives from movement, it is the direct time-image which derives from movement, it is the direct time-image which commands the *false movement*.[1] Why did the war make possible this reversal, this emergence of a cinema of time, with Welles, with neo-realism, with the new wave . . .? Here again, it will be necessary to discover which types of images correspond to the new time-image and which signs combine with these types. Everything perhaps suddenly appears in a shattering of the sensory-motor schema: this schema, which had linked perceptions, affections and actions, does not enter a profound crisis without the general regime of the image being changed. In any case, the cinema has undergone a much more important change here than the one which happened with the talkie.

It is not a matter of saying that the modern cinema of the time-image is 'more valuable' than the classical cinema of the movement-image. We are talking only of masterpieces to which no hierarchy of value applies. The cinema is always as perfect as it can be, taking into account the images and signs which it invents and which it has at its disposal at a given moment. This is why this study must interweave concrete analyses of images and signs with the 'monographs' of the great directors who have created or renewed them.

The first volume deals with the movement-image. The second will deal with the time image. If, at the end of this first volume, we try to understand the full importance of Hitchcock - one of the greatest English film-makers - it is because we think he invented an extraordinary type of image: the image of mental relations. Relations, as external to their terms, have always been the subject of English philosophical thought. When a relation terminates or changes, what happens to its terms? Thus Hitchcock asks in *Mr and Mrs Smith*, a minor comedy, what happens to a man and a woman who suddenly learn that, as their marriage is not legal, they have never been married? Hitchcock produces a cinema of relation, just as English philosophy produced a philosophy of relation. In this sense he is, perhaps, at the juncture of the two cinemas, the classical that he perfects and the modern that he prepares. In all these respects, it is not sufficient to compare the great directors of the cinema with painters, architects or even musicians. They must also be compared with thinkers. The question of a crisis of the cinema is often raised - under the pressure of television, then of the electronic image. But the creative capacities of both are inseparable from what the great directors of the cinema contribute to them. Rather like Varese in music, they lay claim to the new materials and means that the future makes possible.

Gilles Deleuze

Note

1 *Faux Mouvement* (false movement) is the French title of Wim Wenders' film *Falsche Bewegung*, usually known as *Wrong Move* in English.

Translators' introduction

This is Gilles Deleuze's first book on film, published in France in
October 1983. It is an illustration and exemplification of Deleuze's
radical view of philosophy developed in a series of major works, from
Différence et Répétition to *Mille Plateaux*.

Thus, in one sense, it is a work of philosophy. 'Philosophy in the
traditional sense of the word', the creation of concepts.[1] Beginning
from an analysis of Bergson, the book puts forward a view of the
image which is radically different from that which dominated
classical philosophy. This account is combined with an interpretation
of the classification of types of signs advanced by Peirce to provide a
powerful typology with which to approach images of all types.

On the other hand, this is plainly a book 'about' the cinema. Not
only does it discuss a large number of images from particular films,
but it also advances a series of general views about the 'types' to
which particular films belong. This may lead the reader to classify it
as a work of 'film theory', in the traditional sense. This would be a
mistake.

For Deleuze, philosophy cannot be a reflection on something else.
It is, as we have said, a creation of concepts. But concepts, for Deleuze,
are thought of in a new way. They are no longer 'concepts of',
understood by reference to their external object. They are 'exactly
like sounds, colours or images, they are intensities which either suit
you or don't, which work or don't'.[2] Concepts are the images of
thought.

The function and purpose of philosophy itself changes. 'Philosophy
is not in a state of external reflection on other domains, but in a state
of active and internal alliance with them, and it is neither more
abstract nor more difficult.'[3] Therefore, 'It is not a question of
reflecting on the cinema, it is normal that philosophy produces
concepts which are in resonance with the pictorial images of today or
with cinemamatographic images, etc.'[4] Thus Deleuze is engaged in
the work of concept creation 'alongside' the cinema. New concepts
are invented, on the basis of some well-known philosophical themes,
and then put to work in the cinema.

This Deleuzian approach will seem strange to those schooled in
more traditional philosophical themes. It will perhaps seem less
strange to those who work in the cinema and are constantly involved
in processes of creation of their own. One startling by-product of

Deleuze's way of working is that the usual boundaries between disciplines lose their relevance and sense as new 'assemblages' are created. Who would have thought that the historical films of Cecil B. de Mille could be brought into productive relationship with Nietzsche's essay on nineteenth-century German historiography? Finally, these conjunctions between particular themes illustrate a broader conjunction between philosophy and the cinema, one which makes a work of this type particularly productive. For what is interesting in philosophy is that it proposes a cutting [*découpage*] of things, a new cutting: it groups under a single concept things that one would have thought were different, and it separates from it others which one would have thought very close. Now, the cinema by itself is also a cutting of visual and sound images. There are modes of cutting which can converge.[5]

The book can, therefore, be seen as a kind of intercutting of cinema and philosophy. As such, it brings together a whole range of terms from each sphere, many of which may be unfamiliar to readers more at home in the other. We have therefore tried, in the remainder of this Introduction, to provide some preliminary explanations of some of the terms used in the hope that these might be of some assistance in the reading of this rich but difficult book. We would like to thank Tom Milne for his invaluable explanations of the technical film terms.

The French word for 'shot' is '*plan*', which also means 'plane'. Deleuze occasionally plays on the two senses of the French word and we have sometimes translated it as 'plane'. The two senses of the word should be borne in mind whenever the word 'shot', in any of its many variants, appears in the translation. The phrase '*champ-contrechamp*' has been translated 'shot-reverse shot'; it could also have been rendered 'shot-reaction shot' or even, in some contexts, 'cross-cutting'.

In the first chapter, Deleuze uses the term '*pose*' in two senses: in its literal sense (as in English) of a sustained position; and in a cinematographic sense, as in '*photo de pose*', where it has been rendered as 'long-exposure photo' to differentiate it from the 'snapshot' (*instantané*) with which Deleuze contrasts it.

We have left the word '*photogramme*' untranslated, it denotes a single frame of exposed film or still taken directly from such a frame (a 'frame still'). We have rendered the notoriously difficult term '*découpage*' as 'cutting' throughout. It can be taken in a more general sense as a 'cutting style' or even, by extension, the 'way the film is put together'.

Deleuze draws a systematic distinction between the terms *'tout'* and *'ensemble'* which we have rendered as 'whole' and 'set' respectively. In French the two words can be used interchangeably in many contexts and the keeping of the words distinct in English is sometimes artificial. We have occasionally translated *'ensemble'* as 'whole' and have then placed the French word in brackets. In general, however, we have sought to keep the two words distinct in English in line with the philosophical distinction in the original.

We have translated Deleuze's term *'Englobant'* as 'Encompasser'. The verb *'englober'* has the sense of 'to include, embody, bring together into a whole'. Following Deleuze's use, in his recent work, of a systematic distinction between the 'major' and 'minor' modes we have translated *'majorer'* and *'minorer'* as 'to major' and 'to minor'. The former is usually rendered as 'to raise (a price)', or 'to over-value'.

We have included further explanations of Deleuze's terms in translator's footnotes which are indicated by an asterisk (*). A glossary of technical terms is also included. We would like to thank all those who have given us advice and assistance in preparing this translation, including Meaghan Morris and everyone at New Court.

Hugh Tomlinson
Barbara Habberjam

Notes

1 Interview with Cathérine Clément, *L'Arc 49 (Deleuze)*, second edition, 1980, p. 99.
2 Gilles Deleuze and Claire Parnet, *Dialogues*, 1977, p. 10 (English edition forthcoming from The Athlone Press).
3 Interview with Herve Guibert, *Le Monde*, 6 October 1983.
4 *Ibid.*
5 *Ibid.*

Preface to the French edition

This study is not a history of the cinema. It is a taxonomy, an attempt at the classification of images and signs. But this first volume has to content itself with determining the elements, and the elements of only one part of the classification.

We will frequently be referring to the American logician Peirce (1839-1914), because he established a general classification of images and signs, which is undoubtedly the most complete and the most varied. It can be compared with Linnaeus's classifications in natural history, or even more with Mendeleev's table in chemistry.

Another comparison is no less necessary. Bergson was writing *Matter and Memory* in 1896: it was the diagnosis of a crisis in psychology. Movement, as physical reality in the external world, and the image, as psychic reality in consciousness, could no longer be opposed. The Bergsonian discovery of a movement-image, and more profoundly, of a time-image, still retains such richness today that it is not certain that all its consequences have been drawn. Despite the rather overhasty critique of the cinema that Bergson produced shortly afterwards, nothing can prevent an encounter between the movement-image, as he considers it, and the cinematographic image.

In this first part, we will deal with the movement-image and its varieties. The time-image will be the subject of a second part. The great directors of the cinema may be compared, in our view, not merely with painters, architects and musicians, but also with thinkers. They think with movement-images and time-images instead of concepts. One cannot object by pointing to the vast proportion of rubbish in cinematographic production – it is no worse than anywhere else, although it does have unparalleled economic and industrial consequences. The great cinema directors are hence merely more vulnerable – it is infinitely easier to prevent them from doing their work. The history of the cinema is a long martyrology. Nevertheless, the cinema still forms part of art and part of thought, in the irreplaceable, autonomous forms which these directors were able to invent and get screened, in spite of everything.

We are not providing any reproductions as illustrations to our text, as it is in fact our text alone which aspires to be an illustration of the great films, of which each of us retains to a greater or lesser extent a memory, emotion or perception.

Gilles Deleuze

1 Theses on movement
First commentary on Bergson

1 First thesis: movement and instant

Bergson does not just put forward one thesis on movement, but three. The first is the most famous, and threatens to obscure the other two. It is, however, only an introduction to the others. According to the first thesis, movement is distinct from the space covered. Space covered is past, movement is present, the act of covering. The space covered is divisible, indeed infinitely divisible, whilst movement is indivisible, or cannot be divided without changing qualitatively each time it is divided. This already presupposes a more complex idea: the spaces covered all belong to a single, identical, homogeneous space, while the movements are heterogeneous, irreducible among themselves.

But, before being developed, the first thesis contains another proposition: you cannot reconstitute movement with positions in space or instants in time: that is, with immobile sections [coupes]. You can only achieve this reconstitution by adding to the positions, or to the instants, the abstract idea of a succession, of a time which is mechanical, homogeneous, universal and copied from space, identical for all movements. And thus you miss the movement in two ways. On the one hand, you can bring two instants or two positions together to infinity; but movement will always occur in the interval between the two, in other words behind your back. On the other hand, however much you divide and subdivide time, movement will always occur in a concrete duration [durée]; thus each movement will have its own qualitative duration. Hence we oppose two irreducible formulas: 'real movement → concrete duration', and 'immobile sections + abstract time'.

In 1907, in *Creative Evolution*, Bergson gives the incorrect formula a name: the cinematographic illusion. Cinema, in fact, works with two complementary givens: instantaneous sections which are called images; and a movement or a time which is impersonal, uniform, abstract, invisible, or imperceptible, which is 'in' the apparatus, and 'with' which the images are made to pass consecutively.[1] Cinema thus gives us a false movement – it is the typical example of false movement. But it is strange that Bergson should give the oldest illusion such a modern and recent name ('cinematographic'). In fact,

says Bergson, when the cinema reconstitutes movement with mobile
sections, it is merely doing what was already being done by the most
ancient thought (Zeno's paradoxes), or what natural perception does.
In this respect, Bergson's position differs from that of phenomenology,
which instead saw the cinema as breaking with the conditions of
natural perception. 'We take snapshots, as it were, of the passing
reality, and, as these are characteristics of the reality, we have only to
string them on a becoming abstract, uniform and invisible, situated
at the back of the apparatus of knowledge. . . . Perception, intellection,
language so proceed in general. Whether we would think becoming,
or express it, or even perceive it, we hardly do anything else than set
going a kind of cinematograph inside us.[2] Does this mean that for
Bergson the cinema is only the projection, the reproduction of a
constant, universal illusion? As though we had always had cinema
without realising it? But then a whole range of problems arises.

Firstly, is not the reproduction of the illusion in a certain sense also
its correction? Can we conclude that the result is artificial because the
means are artificial? Cinema proceeds with photogrammes – that is,
with immobile sections – twenty-four images per second (or eighteen
at the outset). But it has often been noted that what it gives us is not
the photogramme: it is an intermediate image, to which movement is
not appended or added; the movement on the contrary belongs to the
intermediate image as immediate given. It might be said that the
position of natural perception is the same. But there the illusion is
corrected 'above' perception by the conditions which make perception
possible in the subject. In the cinema, however, it is corrected at the
same time as the image appears for a spectator without conditions (in
this respect, as we will see, phenomenology is right in assuming that
natural perception and cinematographic perception are qualitatively
different). In short, cinema does not give us an image to which
movement is added, it immediately gives us a movement-image. It
does give us a section, but a section which is mobile, not an immobile
section + abstract movement. Now what is again very odd is that
Bergson was perfectly aware of the existence of mobile sections or
movement-images. This happened before *Creative Evolution*, before
the official birth of the cinema: it was set out in *Matter and Memory* in
1896. The discovery of the movement-image, beyond the conditions
of natural perception, was the extraordinary invention of the first
chapter of *Matter and Memory*. Had Bergson forgotten it ten years
later?

Or did he fall victim to another illusion which affects everything in
its initial stages? We know that things and people are always forced to

conceal themselves, have to conceal themselves when they begin. What else could they do? They come into being within a set which no longer includes them and, in order not to be rejected, have to project the characteristics which they retain in common with the set. The essence of a thing never appears at the outset, but in the middle, in the course of its development, when its strength is assured. Having transformed philosophy by posing the question of the 'new' instead of that of eternity (how are the production and appearance of something new possible?), Bergson knew this better than anyone. For example, he said that the novelty of life could not appear when it began, since when it began life was forced to imitate matter. . . . Is it not the same with the cinema? Is not cinema at the outset forced to imitate natural perception? And, what is more, what *was* cinema's position at the outset? On the one hand, the view point [*prise de vue*] was fixed, the shot was therefore spatial and strictly immobile; on the other hand, the apparatus for shooting [*appareil de prise de vue*] was combined with the apparatus for projection, endowed with a uniform abstract time. The evolution of the cinema, the conquest of its own essence or novelty, was to take place through montage, the mobile camera and the emancipation of the view point, which became separate from projection. The shot would then stop being a spatial category and become a temporal one, and the section would no longer be immobile, but mobile. The cinema would rediscover that very movement-image of the first chapter of *Matter and Memory*.

We must conclude that Bergson's first thesis on movement is more complex than it initially seemed. On the one hand there is a critique of all attempts to reconstitute movement with the space covered, that is, by adding together instantaneous immobile sections and abstract time. On the other hand there is the critique of the cinema, which is condemned as one of these illusory attempts, as the attempt which is the culmination of the illusion. But there is also the thesis of *Matter and Memory*, mobile sections, temporal planes [*plans*] which prefigure the future or the essence of the cinema.

2   Second thesis: privileged instants and any-instant-whatevers

Now *Creative Evolution* advances a second thesis, which, instead of reducing everything to the same illusion about movement, distinguishes at least two very different illusions. The error remains the same – that of reconstituting movement from instants or positions – but there are two ways of doing this: the ancient and the modern. For antiquity, movement refers to intelligible elements, Forms or Ideas which are themselves eternal and immobile. Of course, in order to reconstitute movement, these forms will be grasped as close as possible to their actualisation in a matter-flux. These are potentialities which can only be acted out by being embodied in matter. But, conversely, movement merely expresses a 'dialectic' of forms, an ideal synthesis which gives it order and measure. Movement, conceived in this way, will thus be the regulated transition from one form to another, that is, an order of *poses* or privileged instants, as in a dance. The forms or ideas

> are supposed [. . .] to characterise a period of which they express the quintessence, all the rest of this period being filled by the transition, of no interest in itself, from one form to another form [. . . .] They noted, then, the final term or culminating point (telos, acmè), and set it up as the essential moment: this moment, that language has retained in order to express the whole of the fact, sufficed also for science to characterise it.[3]

The modern scientific revolution has consisted in relating movement not to privileged instants, but to any-instant-whatever. Although movement was still recomposed, *it was no longer recomposed from formal transcendental elements (poses), but from immanent material elements (sections).* Instead of producing an intelligible synthesis of movement, a sensible analysis was derived from it. In this way, modern astronomy was formed, by determining a relation between an orbit and the time needed to traverse it (Kepler); modern physics, by linking the space covered to the time taken by a body to fall (Galileo); modern geometry, by working out the equation of a flat curve, that is, the position of a point on a moving straight line at any moment in its course (Descartes); and lastly differential and integral calculus, once they had the idea of examining sections which could be brought infinitely closer together (Newton and Leibniz). Everywhere the mechanical succession of instants replaced the dialectical order of poses: 'Modern science must be defined pre-eminently by its aspiration to take time as an independent variable.'[4]

Cinema seems to be the last descendant of this lineage which Bergson traced. One might conceive of a series of means of translation (train, car aeroplane . . .) and, in parallel, a series of means of expression (diagram, photo, cinema). The camera would then appear as an exchanger or, rather, as a generalised equivalent of the movements of translation. And this is how it appears in Wenders's films. When we think about the prehistory of the cinema, we always end up confused, because we do not know where its technological lineage begins, or how to define this lineage. We can always refer to shadow puppets, or the very earliest projection systems. But, in fact, the determining conditions of the cinema are the following,: not merely the photo, but the snapshot (the long-exposure photo [*photo de pose*] belongs to the other lineage); the equidistance of snapshots; the transfer of this equidistance on to a framework which constitutes the 'film' (it was Edison and Dickson who perforated the film in the camera); a mechanism for moving on images (Lumière's claws). It is in this sense that the cinema is the system which reproduces movement as a function of any-instant-whatever that is, as a function of equidistant instants, selected so as to create an impression of continuity. Any other system which reproduces movement through an order of exposures [*poses*] projected in such a way that they pass into one another, or are 'transformed', is foreign to the cinema. This is clear when one attempts to define the cartoon film; if it belongs fully to the cinema, this is because the drawing no longer constitutes a pose or a completed figure, but the description of a figure which is always in the process of being formed or dissolving through the movement of lines and points taken at any-instant-whatevers of their course. The cartoon film is related not to a Euclidean, but to a Cartesian geometry. It does not give us a figure described in a unique moment, but the continuity of the movement which describes the figure.

Nevertheless, the cinema seems to thrive on privileged instants. It is often said that Eisenstein extracted from movements or developments certain moments of crisis, which he made the subject of the cinema par excellence. This is precisely what he called the 'pathetic': he picks out peaks and shouts, he pushes scenes to their climax and brings them into collision. But this is definitely not an objection. Let us return to the cinema's prehistory, and to the famous example of the horse's gallop: this could only be dissected exactly by Marey's graphic recordings and Muybridge's equidistant snapshots, which relate the organised whole of the canter to any-point-whatever. If the equidistant points are chosen well, one inevitably comes across remarkable occasions; that is, the moments when the horse has one hoof on the ground, then three, two, one. These may be called privileged instants, but not in the sense of the poses or generalised postures which marked the gallop in the old forms. These instants have nothing in common with long-exposures [*poses*], and would even be formally impossible as long-exposures. If these are privileged instants, it is as remarkable or singular points which belong to movement, and not as the moments of actualisation of a transcendent form. The meaning of the notion has completely changed. The privileged instants of Eisenstein, or of any other director, are still any-instant-whatevers: to put it simply, the any-instant-whatever can be regular *or* singular, ordinary *or* remarkable. If Eisenstein picks out remarkable instants, this does not prevent him deriving from them an immanent analysis of movement, and not a transcendental synthesis. The remarkable or singular instant remains any-instant-whatever among the others. This is indeed the difference between the modern dialectic, to which Eisenstein appeals, and the old dialectic. The latter is the order of transcendental forms which are actualised in a movement, while the former is the production and confrontation of the singular points which are immanent to movement. Now this production of singularities (the qualitative leap) is achieved by the accumulation of banalities (quantitative process), so that the singular is taken from the any-whatever, and is itself an any-whatever which is simply non-ordinary and non-regular. Eisenstein himself made it clear that 'the pathetic' presupposed 'the organic' as the organised set of any-instant-whatevers through which the cuts [*coupures*] have to pass.[5]

The any-instant-whatever is the instant which is equidistant from another. We can therefore define the cinema as the system which reproduces movement by relating it to the any-instant-whatever. But it is here that the difficulty arises. What is the interest of such a system? From the point of view of science, it is very slight. For the scientific revolution was one of analysis. And, if movement had to be related to the any-instant-whatever in order to analyse it, it was hard to see any interest in a synthesis or reconstitution based on the same principle, except a vague interest of confirmation. This is why neither Marey nor Lumière held out much hope for the invention of the cinema. Did it at least have artistic interest? This did not seem likely either, since art seemed to uphold the claims of a higher synthesis of movement, and to remain linked to the poses and forms that science had rejected. We have reached the very heart of cinema's ambiguous position as 'industrial art': it was neither an art nor a science.

Contemporaries, however, might have been sensitive to a development at work in the arts, which was changing the status of movement, even in painting. To an even greater degree, dance, ballet and mime were abandoning figures and poses to release values which were not posed, not measured, which related movement to the any-instant-whatever. In this way, art, ballet and mime became actions capable of responding to accidents of the environment; that is, to the distribution of the points of a space, or of the moments of an event. All this served the same end as the cinema. From the time of the talkie, the cinema was able to make the musical comedy one of its principal genres, with Fred Astaire's 'action dance' which takes place in any-location-whatever: in the street, surrounded by cars, along a pavement.[6] But even in silent films, Chaplin had divorced mime from the art of poses to make it an action-mime. Mitry answered complaints that Charlie used the cinema, rather than serving it, by arguing that he gave mime a new model, a function of space and time, a continuity constructed at each instant, which now only allowed itself to be decomposed into its prominent immanent elements, instead of being related to prior forms which it was to embody.[7]

Bergson forcefully demonstrates that the cinema fully belongs to this modern conception of movement. But, from this point, he seems to hesitate between two paths, one of which leads him back to his first thesis, the other instead opening up a new question. According to the first path, although the two conceptions may be different from the scientific point of view, they nevertheless have a more or less identical result. In fact, to recompose movement with *eternal poses* or with *immobile sections* comes to the same thing: in both cases, one misses the movement because one constructs a Whole, one assumes that 'all is given', whilst movement only occurs if the whole is neither given nor giveable. As soon as a whole is given to one in the eternal order of forms or poses, or in the set of any-instant-whatevers, then either time is no more than the image of eternity, or it is the consequence of the set; there is no longer room for real movement.[8] Another path, however, seemed open to Bergson. For, if the ancient conception corresponds closely to ancient philosophy, which aims to think the eternal, then the modern conception, modern science, calls upon *another* philosophy. When one relates movement to any-moment-whatevers, one must be capable of thinking the production of the new, that is, of the remarkable and the singular, at any one of these moments: this is a complete conversion of philosophy. It is what Bergson ultimately aims to do: to give modern science the metaphysic which corresponds to it, which it lacks as one half lacks the other.[9] But can we stop once we have set out on this path? Can we deny that the arts must also go through this conversion or that the cinema is an essential factor in this, and that it has a role to play in the birth and formation of this new thought, this new way of thinking? This is why Bergson is no longer content merely to corroborate his first thesis on movement. Bergson's second thesis – although it stops half way – makes possible another way of looking at the cinema, a way in which it would no longer be just the perfected apparatus of the oldest illusion, but, on the contrary, the organ for perfecting the new reality.

3   *Third thesis: movement and change*

And this is Bergson's third thesis, which is also contained in *Creative Evolution*. If we tried to reduce it to a bare formula, it would be this: not only is the instant an immobile section of movement, but movement is a mobile section of duration, that is, of the Whole, or of a whole. Which implies that movement expresses something more profound, which is the change in duration or in the whole. To say that duration is change is part of its definition: it changes and does not stop changing. For example, matter moves, but does not change. Now movement expresses a change in duration or in the whole. What *is* a problem is on the one hand this expression, and on the other, this whole-duration identification.

Movement is a translation in space. Now each time there is a translation of parts in space, there is also a qualitative change in a whole. Bergson gave numerous examples of this in *Matter and Memory*. An animal moves, but this is for a purpose: to feed, migrate, etc. It might be said that movement presupposes a difference of potential, and aims to fill it. If I consider parts or places abstractly – A and B – I cannot understand the movement which goes from one to the other. But imagine I am starving at A, and at B there is something to eat. When I have reached B and had something to eat, what has changed is not only my state, but the state of the whole which encompassed B, A, and all that was between them. When Achilles overtakes the tortoise, what changes is the state of the whole which encompassed the tortoise, Achilles, and the distance between the two. Movement always relates to a change, migration to a seasonal variation. And this is equally true of bodies: the fall of a body presupposes another one which attracts it, and expresses a change in the whole which encompasses them both. If we think of pure atoms, their movements, which testify to a reciprocal action of all the parts of the substance, necessarily express modifications, disturbances, changes of energy in the whole. What Bergson discovers beyond translation is vibration, radiation. Our error lies in believing that it is the any-element-whatevers, external to qualities which move. But the qualities themselves are pure vibrations which change at the same time as the alleged elements move.[10]

In *Creative Evolution*, Bergson gives an example which is so famous that it no longer surprises us. Putting some sugar in a glass of water, he says that 'I must, willy-nilly, wait until the sugar melts'.[11] This is slightly strange, since Bergson seems to have forgotten that stirring with a spoon can help it to dissolve. But what is his main point? That the movement of translation which detaches the sugar particles and suspends them in the water itself expresses a change in the whole, that is, in the content of the glass; a qualitative transition from water which contains a sugar lump to the state of sugared water. If I stir with the spoon, I speed up the movement, but I also change the whole, which now encompasses the spoon, and the accelerated movement continues to express the change of the whole. 'The wholly superficial displacements of masses and molecules studied in physics and chemistry would become, by relation to that inner vital movement (which is transformation and not translation) what the position of a moving object is to the movement of that object in space.'[12] Thus, in his third thesis, Bergson puts forward the following analogy:

$$\frac{\text{immobile sections}}{\text{movement}} = \frac{\text{movement as mobile section}}{\text{qualitative change}}$$

The only difference is this: the ratio on the left-hand side expresses an illusion; and that on the right-hand side, a reality.

Above all, what Bergson wants to say using the glass of sugared water is that my waiting, whatever it be, expresses a duration as mental, spiritual reality. But why does this spiritual duration bear witness, not only for me who wait, but for a whole which changes? According to Bergson the whole is neither given nor giveable (and the error of modern science, like that of ancient science, lay in taking the whole as given, in two different ways). Many philosophers had already said that the whole was neither given nor giveable: they simply concluded from this that the whole was a meaningless notion. Bergson's conclusion is very different: if the whole is not giveable, it is because it is the Open, and because its nature is to change constantly, or to give rise to something new, in short, to endure. 'The duration of the universe must therefore be one with the latitude of creation which can find place in it.'[13] So that each time we find ourselves confronted with a duration, or in a duration, we may conclude that there exists somewhere a whole which is changing, and which is open somewhere. It is widely known that Bergson initially

discovered duration as identical to consciousness. But further study
of consciousness led him to demonstrate that it only existed in so far
as it opened itself upon a whole, by coinciding with the opening up of
a whole. Similarly for the living being: in comparing the living being
to a whole, or to the whole of the universe, Bergson seems to be
reviving the most ancient simile.[14] However, he completely reverses
its terms. For, if the living being is a whole and, therefore,
comparable to the whole of the universe, this is not because it is a
microcosm as closed as the whole is assumed to be, but, on the
contrary, because it is open upon a world, and the world, the
universe, is itself the Open. 'Wherever anything lives, there is, open
somewhere, a register in which time is being inscribed.'[15]

If one had to define the whole, it would be defined by Relation.
Relation is not a property of objects, it is always external to its terms.
It is also inseparable from the open, and displays a spiritual or mental
existence. Relations do not belong to objects, but to the whole, on
condition that this is not confused with a closed set of objects.[16] By
movement in space, the objects of a set change their respective
positions. But, through relations, the whole is transformed or
changes qualitatively. We can say of duration itself or of time, that it
is the whole of relations.

The whole and the 'wholes' must not be confused with *sets*. Sets
are closed, and everything which is closed is artificially closed. Sets
are always sets of parts. But a whole is not closed, it is open; and it has
no parts except in a very special sense, since it cannot be divided
without changing qualitatively at each stage of the division. 'The real
whole might well be, we conceive, an indivisible continuity.'[17] The
whole is not a closed set, but on the contrary that by virtue of which
the set is never absolutely closed, never completely sheltered, that
which keeps it open somewhere as if by the finest thread which
attaches it to the rest of the universe. The glass of water is indeed a
closed set containing the parts, the water, the sugar, perhaps the
spoon; but that is not the whole. The whole creates itself, and
constantly creates itself in another dimension without parts – like that
which carries along the set of one qualitative state to another, like the
pure ceaseless becoming which passes through these states. It is in this
sense that it is spiritual or mental. 'The glass of water, the sugar, and
the process of the sugar's melting in the water are abstractions and
. . . the whole within which they have been cut out by my senses and
understanding progresses, it may be, in the manner of a consciousness.'[18]
In any case, this artificial division of a set or a closed system is not a
pure illusion. It is well founded and, if it is impossible to break the

link of each thing with the whole (this paradoxical link, which ties it to the open), it can at least be drawn out, stretched to infinity, made finer and finer. The organisation of matter makes possible the closed systems or the determinate sets of parts; and the deployment of space makes them necessary. But the point is that the sets are in space, and the whole, the wholes are in duration, are duration itself, in so far as it does not stop changing. So that the two formulas which corresponded to Bergson's first thesis now take on a much more rigorous status; 'immobile sections + abstract time' refers to closed sets whose parts are in fact immobile sections, and whose successive states are calculated on an abstract time; while 'real movement → concrete duration' refers to the opening up of a whole which endures, and whose movements are so many mobile sections crossing the closed systems.

The upshot of this third thesis is that we find ourselves on three levels: (1) the sets or closed systems which are defined by discernible objects or distinct parts; (2) the movement of translation which is established between these objects and modifies their respective positions; (3) the duration or the whole, a spiritual reality which constantly changes according to its own relations.

Thus in a sense movement has two aspects. On one hand, that which happens between objects or parts; on the other hand that which expresses the duration or the whole. The result is that duration, by changing qualitatively, is divided up in objects, and objects, by gaining depth, by losing their contours, are united in duration. We can therefore say that movement relates the objects of a closed system to open duration, and duration to the objects of the system which it forces to open up. Movement relates the objects between which it is established to the changing whole which it expresses, and vice versa. Through movement the whole is divided up into objects, and objects are re-united in the whole, and indeed between the two 'the whole' changes. We can consider the objects or parts of a set as *immobile sections*; but movement is established between these sections, and relates the objects or parts to the duration of a whole which changes, and thus expresses the changing of the whole in relation to the objects and is itself a *mobile section* of duration. Now we are equipped to understand the profound thesis of the first chapter of *Matter and Memory*: (1) there are not only instantaneous images, that is, immobile sections of movement; (2) there are movement-images which are mobile sections of duration; (3) there are, finally, time-images, that is, duration-images, change-images, relation-images, volume-images which are beyond movement itself. . . .

2 Frame and shot, framing and cutting

1 The first level: frame, set or closed system

We will start with very simple definitions, even though they may
have to be corrected later. We will call *the determination of a closed
system, a relatively closed system which includes everything which is
present in the image* – sets, characters and props – *framing*. The frame
therefore forms a set which has a great number of parts, that is of
elements, which themselves form sub-sets. It can be broken down.
Obviously these parts are themselves in image [*en image*]. This is
why Jakobson calls them object-signs, and Pasolini 'cinemes'.
However this terminology suggests comparisons with language
(cinemes would be very like phonemes, and the shot would be like a
moneme) which do not seem necessary.[1] For, if the frame has an
analogue, it is to be found in an information system rather than a
linguistic one. The elements are the data [*données*], which are
sometimes very numerous, sometimes of limited number. The frame
is therefore inseparable from two tendencies: towards saturation or
towards rarefaction. The big screen and depth of field in particular have allowed the multiplication of independent data, to the
point where a secondary scene appears in the foreground while the
main one happens in the background (Wyler), or where you can no
longer even distinguish between the principal and the secondary
(Altman). On the other hand, rarefied images are produced, either
when the whole accent is placed on a single object (in Hitchcock, the
glass of milk lit from the inside, in *Suspicion*; the glowing cigarette
end in the black rectangle of the window in *Rear Window*) or when
the set is emptied of certain sub-sets (Antonioni's deserted landscapes;
Ozu's vacant interiors). The highest degree of rarefaction seems to be
attained with the empty set, when the screen becomes completely
black or completely white. Hitchcock gives an example of this in
Spellbound, when another glass of milk invades the screen, leaving
only an empty white image. But, from either side – whether
rarefaction or saturation – the frame teaches us that the image is not
just given to be seen. It is legible as well as visible. The frame has the
implicit function of recording not merely sound information, but also
visual information. If we see very few things in an image, this is

because we do not know how to read it properly; we evaluate its rarefaction as badly as its saturation. There is a pedagogy of the image, especially with Godard, when this function is made explicit, when the frame serves as an opaque surface of information, sometimes blurred by saturation, sometimes reduced to the empty set, to the white or black screen.[2]

In the second place, the frame has always been geometrical *or* physical, depending on whether it constitutes the closed system in relation to chosen coordinates or in relation to selected variables. The frame is therefore sometimes conceived of as a spatial composition of parallels and diagonals, the constitution of a receptacle such that the blocs [*masses*] and the lines of the image which come to occupy it will find an equilibrium and their movements will find an invariant. It is often like this in Dreyer; Antonioni seems to go to the limit of this geometric conception of the frame which preexists that which is going to be inserted within it (*Eclipse*).[3] Sometimes the frame is conceived as a dynamic construction in act [*en acte*], which is closely linked to the scene, the image, the characters and the objects which fill it. The iris method in Griffith, which isolates a face first of all, then opens and shows the surroundings; Eisenstein's researches inspired by Japanese drawing, which adapt the frame to the theme; Gance's variable screen which opens and closes 'according to the dramatic necessities', and like a 'visual accordion' – from the very beginning attempts were made to test dynamic variations of the frame. In any case framing is limitation.[4] But, depending on the concept itself the limits can be conceived in two ways, mathematically or dynamically: either as preliminary to the existence of the bodies whose essence they fix, or going as far as the power of existing bodies goes. For ancient philosophy, this was one of the principal features of the opposition between the Platonists and the Stoics.

The frame is also geometric or physical in another way – in relation to the parts of the system that it both separates and brings together. In the first case, the frame is inseparable from rigid geometric distinctions. A very fine image in Griffith's *Intolerance* cuts the screen along a vertical which corresponds to a wall of the ramparts of Babylon; whilst on the right one sees the king advancing on a higher horizontal, a high walk on the ramparts; on the left the chariots enter and leave, on a lower horizontal, through the gates of the city. Eisenstein studied the effects of the golden section on cinematographic imagery; Dreyer explored horizontals and verticals, symmetries, the high and the low, alternations of black and white; the Expressionists developed diagonals and counter-diagonals, pyramidal or triangular

figures which agglomerate bodies, crowds, places, the collision of
these masses, a whole paving of the frame 'which takes on a form like
the black and white squares of a chess-board' (Lang's *The Nibelungen*
and *Metropolis*).[5] Even light is the subject of a geometrical optic,
when it is organised with shadows into two halves, or into
alternating rays, as is done by one Expressionist tendency (Wiene,
Lang). The lines separating the great elements of Nature obviously
play a fundamental role, as in Ford's skies: the separation of earth and
sky, the earth pushed down to the base of the screen. But it also
involves water and earth, or the slender line which separates air and
water, when water hides an escapee in its depths, or drowns a victim at
the limit of the surface (Le Roy's *I am a Fugitive from a Chain Gang*
and Newman's *Sometimes a Great Notion*). As a general rule, the
powers of Nature are not framed in the same way as people or things,
and individuals are not framed in the same way as crowds, and sub-
elements are not framed in the same way as terms, so that there are
many different frames in the frame. Doors, windows, box office
windows, skylights, car windows, mirrors, are all frames in
frames. The great directors have particular affinities with particular
secondary, tertiary, etc. frames. And it is by this dovetailing of
frames that the parts of the set or of the closed system are separated,
but also converge and are reunited.

On the other hand, the physical or dynamic conception of the
frame produces imprecise sets which are now only divided into zones
or bands. The frame is no longer the object of geometric divisions,
but of physical gradations. The parts of the set are now intensive
parts, and the set itself is a mixture which is transmitted through all
the parts, through all the degrees of shadow and of light, through the
whole light-darkness scale (Wegener, Murnau). This was the
Expressionist optic's other tendency, although some directors, both
inside and outside Expressionism, participate in both. It is the hour
when it is no longer possible to distinguish between sunrise and
sunset, air and water, water and earth, in the great mixture of a marsh
or a tempest.[6] Here, it is by degrees of mixing that the parts become
distinct or confused in a continual transformation of values. The set
cannot divide into parts without qualitatively changing each time: it
is neither divisible nor indivisible, but 'dividual' [*dividuel*]. Admittedly
this was already the case in the geometric conception – there the
dovetailing of frames indicated the qualitative changes. The cinematographic image is always dividual. This is because, in the final
analysis, the screen, as the frame of frames, gives a common standard
of measurement to things which do not have one – long shots of

countryside and close-ups of the face, an astronomical system and a single drop of water – parts which do not have the same denominator of distance, relief or light. In all these senses the frame ensures a deterritorialisation of the image.

In the fourth place, the frame is related to an angle of framing. This is because the closed set is itself an optical system which refers to a point of view on the set of parts. Of course, the point of view can be – or appear to be – bizarre or paradoxical: the cinema shows extraordinary points of view – at ground level, or from high to low, from low to high, etc. But they seem to be subject to a pragmatic rule which is not just valid for the narrative cinema: to avoid falling into an empty aestheticism they must be explained, they must be revealed as normal and regular – either from the point of view of a more comprehensive set which includes the first, or from the point of view of an initially unseen, not given, element of the first set. In Jean Mitry we find a description of a sequence which is exemplary here (Lubitsch's *The Man I Killed*); the camera, in a lateral mid-height travelling shot, shows a row of spectators seen from behind and tries to glide to the front, then stops at a one-legged man whose missing leg provides a vista on the scene – a passing military parade. It thus frames the good leg, the crutch, and, under the stump, the parade. Here we have an eminently bizarre angle of framing. But another shot shows another cripple behind the first, one with no legs at all, who sees the parade in precisely this way, and who actualises or accomplishes the preceding point of view.[7] It can therefore be said that the angle of framing was justified. However, this pragmatic rule is not always valid, or even when it is valid, it is not the whole story. Bonitzer has constructed the interesting concept of 'deframing' [*décadrage*] in order to designate these abnormal points of view which are not the same as an oblique perspective or a paradoxical angle, and refer to another dimension of the image.[8] We find examples of this in Dreyer's cutting frames; faces cut by the edge of the screen in *The Passion of Joan of Arc*. But, we see it even more in empty spaces like those of Ozu, which frame a dead zone, or in disconnected spaces as in Bresson, whose parts are not connected and are beyond all narrative or more generally pragmatic justification, perhaps tending to confirm that the visual image has a legible function beyond its visible function.

There remains the out-of-field [*hors-champ*]. This is not a negation; neither is it sufficient to define it by the non-coincidence between two frames, one visual and the other sound (for example, in Bresson, when the sound testifies to what is not seen, and 'relays' the visual instead of duplicating it).[9] The out-of-field refers to what is neither seen nor understood, but is nevertheless perfectly present. This presence is indeed a problem and itself refers to two new conceptions of framing. If we return to Bazin's alternative of mask or frame, we see that sometimes the frame works like a mobile mask according to which every set is extended into a larger homogeneous set with which it communicates, and sometimes it works as a pictorial frame which isolates a system and neutralises its environment. This duality is most clearly expressed in Renoir and Hitchcock; in the former space and action always go beyond the limits of the frame which only takes elements from an area; in the latter the frame 'confines all the components', and acts as a frame for a tapestry rather than one for a picture or a play. But, if a partial set only communicates formally with its out-of-field through the positive characteristics of the frame and the reframing, it is none the less true that a system which is closed – even one which is very closed up – only apparently suppresses the out-of-field, and in its own way gives it an even more decisive importance.[10] All framing determines an out-of-field. There are not two types of frame only one of which would refer to the out-of-field; there are rather two very different aspects of the out-of-field, each of which refers to a mode of framing.

The divisibility of content means that the parts belong to various sets, which constantly subdivide into sub-sets or are themselves the sub-set of a larger set, on to infinity. This is why content is defined both by the tendency to constitute closed systems and by the fact that this tendency never reaches completion. Every closed system also communicates. There is always a thread to link the glass of sugared water to the solar system, and any set whatever to a larger set. This is the first sense of what we call the out-of-field: when a set is framed, therefore seen, there is always a larger set, or another set with which the first forms a larger one, and which can in turn be seen, on condition that it gives rise to a new out-of-field, etc. The set of all these sets forms a homogeneous continuity, a universe or a plane [*plan*] of genuinely unlimited content. But it is certainly not a 'whole' although this plane or these larger and larger sets necessarily have an indirect relationship with the whole. We know the insoluble contradictions we fall into when we treat the set of all sets as a whole. It is not because the notion of the whole is devoid of sense; but it is not a set and does not have parts. It is rather that which prevents each set, however big it is, from closing in on itself, and that which forces it to extend itself into a larger set. The whole is therefore like thread which traverses sets and gives each one the possibility, which is necessarily realised, of communicating with another, to infinity. Thus the whole is the Open, and relates back to time or even to spirit rather than to content and to space. Whatever their relationship, one should therefore not confuse the extension of sets into each other with the opening of the whole which passes into each one. A closed system is never absolutely closed; but on the one hand it is connected in space to other systems by a more or less 'fine' thread, and on the other hand it is integrated or reintegrated into a whole which transmits a duration to it along this thread.[11] Hence, it is perhaps not sufficient to distinguish, with Burch, a concrete space from an imaginary space in the out-of-field, the imaginary becoming concrete when it in turn passes into a field, when it thus ceases to be out-of-field. In itself, or as such, the out-of-field already has two qualitatively different aspects: a relative aspect by means of which a closed system refers in space to a set which is not seen, and which can in turn be seen, even if this gives rise to a new unseen set, on to infinity; and an absolute aspect by which the closed system opens on to a duration which is immanent to the whole universe, which is no longer a set and does not belong to the order of the visible.[12] *Deframings [décadrages] which are not 'pragmatically' justified refer to precisely this second aspect as their raison d'être.*

In one case, the out-of-field designates that which exists elsewhere, to one side or around; in the other case, the out-of-field testifies to a more disturbing presence, one which cannot even be said to exist, but rather to 'insist' or 'subsist', a more radical Elsewhere, outside homogeneous space and time. Undoubtedly these two aspects of the out-of-field intermingle constantly. But, when we consider a framed image as a closed system, we can say that one aspect prevails over the other, depending on the nature of the 'thread'. The thicker the thread which links the seen set to other unseen sets the better the out-of-field fulfils its first function, which is the adding of space to space. But, when the thread is very fine, it is not content to reinforce the closure of the frame or to eliminate the relation with the outside. It certainly does not bring about a complete isolation of the relatively closed system, which would be impossible. But, the finer it is – the further duration descends into the system like a spider – the more effectively the out-of-field fulfils its other function which is that of introducing the transspatial and the spiritual into the system which is never perfectly closed. Dreyer made this into an ascetic method: the more the image is spatially closed, even reduced to two dimensions, the greater is its capacity to *open itself* on to a fourth dimension which is time, and on to a fifth which is Spirit, the spiritual decision of Jeanne or Gertrud.[13] When Claude Ollier defines Antonioni's geometric frame, he not only says that the awaited character is not yet visible (the first function of the out-of-field) but also that he is momentarily in a zone of emptiness, 'white on white which is impossible to film', and truly invisible (the second function). And, in another way, Hitchcock's frames are not content to neutralise the environment, to push the closed system as far as possible and to enclose the maximum number of components in the image; at the same time they make the image into a *mental image*, open (as we will see) on to a play of relations which are purely thought and which weave a whole. This is why we said that there is always out-of-field, even in the most closed image. And that there are always simultaneously the two aspects of the out-of-field: the actualisable relation with other sets, and the virtual relation with the whole. But in the one case the second relation – the most mysterious – is reached indirectly, on to infinity, through the intermediary and the extension of the first, in the succession of images; in the other case it is reached more directly, in the image itself, and by limitation and neutralisation of the first.

Let us summarise the results of this analysis of the frame. Framing is the art of choosing the parts of all kinds which became part of a set. This set is a closed system, relatively and artificially closed. The closed system determined by the frame can be considered in relation to the data that it communicates to the spectators: it is 'informatic', and saturated or rarefied. Considered in itself and as limitation, it is geometric or dynamic-physical. Considered in the nature of its parts, it is still geometric or physical and dynamic. It is an optical system when it is considered in relation to the point of view, to the angle of framing: it is then pragmatically justified, or lays claim to a higher justification. Finally, it determines an out-of-field, sometimes in the form of a larger set which extends it, sometimes in the form of a whole into which it is integrated.

2 *The second level: shot and movement*

Cutting [découpage] is the determination of the shot, and the shot, the determination of the movement which is established in the closed system, between elements or parts of the set. But we have seen that movement also concerns a whole which is qualitatively different from the set. The whole is that which changes – it is the open or duration. Movement thus expresses a change of the whole, or a stage, an aspect of this change, a duration or an articulation of duration.

Thus movement has two facets, as inseparable as the inside and the outside, as the two sides of a coin: *it is the relationship between parts and it is the state [affection] of the whole*. On the one hand it modifies the respective positions of the parts of a set, which are like its sections [*coupes*], each one immobile in itself; on the other it is itself the mobile section of a whole whose change it expresses. From one point of view, it is called relative; from the other, it is called absolute. Take a fixed shot where the characters move: they modify their respective positions in a framed set; but this modification would be completely arbitrary if it did not also express something in the course of changing, a qualitative alteration, even a minute one, in the whole which passes through this set. Take a shot where the camera moves: it can go from one set to another, modifying the respective position of sets. All this is necessary only if relative modification expresses an absolute change of the whole which is transmitted through these sets. For example, the camera follows a man and a woman who climb a staircase and arrive at a door that the man opens; then the camera leaves them, and draws back in a single shot. It runs along the external wall of the apartment, comes back to the staircase that it descends backwards, coming out on to the pavement, and rises up the exterior up to the opaque window of the apartment seen from outside. This movement, which modifies the relative position of immobile sets, is only necessary if it expresses something in the course of happening, a change in the whole which is itself transmitted through these modifications: the woman is being murdered. She went in free, but cannot expect any help – the murder is inexorable. We could say that this example (Hitchcock's *Frenzy*) is a case of ellipsis in the narration. But, whether there is ellipsis or not, or even whether there is narration or not, does not matter for the moment. What counts in these examples is that the shot, of whatever kind, has as it were two poles: in relation to the sets in space where it introduces relative modifications between elements or sub-sets; in relation to a whole whose absolute change in duration it expresses. This whole is never content to be elliptical, nor narrative, though it can be. But the shot, of whatever kind, always has these two aspects: it presents modifications of relative position in a set or some sets. It expresses absolute changes in a whole or in the whole. The shot in general has one face turned towards the set, the modifications of whose parts it translates, and another face turned towards the whole, of which it expresses the – or at least a – change. Hence the situation of the shot, which can be defined abstractly as the intermediary between the framing of the set and the montage of the whole, sometimes tending towards the pole of framing, sometimes tending towards the pole of montage. The shot is movement considered from this dual point of view: the translation of the parts of a set which spreads out in space, the change of a whole which is transformed in duration.

This is not merely an abstract determination of the shot. For the shot finds its concrete determination in so far as it continually brings about the transition from one aspect to the other, the apportionment or distribution of the two aspects, their perpetual conversion. Let us return to the three Bergsonian levels: the sets and their parts; the whole which fuses with the Open or change in duration and the movement which is established between parts or sets, but which also expresses duration, that is – the change of the whole. The shot is like the movement which continuously ensures conversion, circulation. It divides and subdivides duration according to the objects which make up the set; it reunites objects and sets into a single identical duration. It continuously divides duration into subdurations which are themselves heterogeneous, and reunites these into a duration which is immanent to the whole of the universe. Given that it is a consciousness which carries out these divisions and reunions, we can say of the shot that it acts like a consciousness. But the sole cinematographic consciousness is not us, the spectator, nor the hero; it is the camera – sometimes human, sometimes inhuman or superhuman. Take, for example, the movement of water, that of a bird in the distance, and that of a person on a boat: they are blended into a single perception, a peaceful whole of humanised Nature. But then the bird, an ordinary seagull, swoops down and wounds the person: the three fluxes are divided and become external to each other. The whole will be reformed, but it will have changed: it will have become the single consciousness or the perception of a whole of birds, testifying to an entirely bird-centred Nature; turned against Man in infinite anticipation. It will be redivided again when the birds attack, depending on the modes, places and victims of their attack. It will be reformed again to bring about a truce, when the human and the inhuman enter into an uncertain relationship (Hitchcock's *The Birds*). One could say that either the division is between two wholes, or the whole between two divisions.[14] The shot, that is to say consciousness, traces a movement which means that the things between which it arises are continuously reuniting into a whole, and the whole is continuously dividing between things (the Dividual).

It is movement itself which is decomposed and recomposed. It is decomposed according to the elements between which it plays in a set: those which remain fixed, those to which movement is attributed, those which produce or undergo such simple or divisible movement. . . . But it is also recomposed into a great complex indivisible movement according to the whole whose change it expresses. Certain great movements are like a director's signature, which characterise the whole of a film, or even the whole of an oeuvre, but resonate with the relative movement of a particular signed image, or a particular detail in the image. In an exemplary study of Murnau's *Faust*, Eric Rohmer showed how the movements of expansion and contraction were apportioned between people and objects in a 'pictorial space', but also expressed genuine Ideas in the 'filmic space' – Good and Evil, God and Satan.[15] Orson Welles often describes two movements which are formed, one of which is like a horizontal linear flight in a kind of elongated, striated cage, lattice-worked, and the other a circular sweep whose vertical axis performs a high or a low angle shot from a height: these movements are those which had already inspired Kafka's literary work and we can infer that Welles has an affinity with Kafka which goes beyond the film of *The Trial*, explaining why Welles needed to confront Kafka directly. These movements are rediscovered and are profoundly combined in Reed's *The Third Man* and we can conclude either that Welles was more than an actor in this film and was closely involved in its construction, or that Reed was an inspired disciple of Welles. In many of his films, Kurosawa has a signature which resembles a fictitious Japanese character: a thick vertical stroke goes down the screen from top to bottom whilst two thinner lateral movements cross it from left to right and right to left; such a complex movement relates to the whole of the film, as we will see, to a way of conceiving the whole of a film. Analysing certain Hitchcock films François Regnault identifies a global movement for each one, or a 'principal geometric or dynamic form', which can appear in the pure state in the credits: 'the spirals of *Vertigo*, the broken lines and the contrasting black and white structure of *Psycho*, the arrowing Cartesian coordinates of *North by Northwest*. . . .' And perhaps the general movements of these films are in turn the components of a still more general movement which would express the whole of Hitchcock's work, and the way in which this work evolved and changed. But no less interesting is the other direction where a general movement – turned towards a changing whole – is decomposed into relative movements, into local forms turned towards the respective positions of the parts of a set, the attributions to persons or objects, the distributions between elements. Regnault studies it in Hitchcock (thus in *Vertigo* the great spiral can become the vertigo of the hero, but also the circuit he maps out in his car, or the curl in the heroine's hair).[16] But this type of analysis is desirable for every director. It is the necessary research programme for all director-analysis – what could be called a stylistic: the movement which is established between the parts of a set in a frame, or between one set and another in a reframing; the movement which expresses a whole in a film or in an oeuvre; the correspondence between the two, the way in which they echo each other, in which they pass from one to the other. Because it is the same movement, sometimes composing, sometimes decomposing; these are the two aspects of the same movement. And this movement is the shot, the concrete intermediary between a whole which has changes and a set which has parts, and which constantly converts the one into the other according to its two facets.

The shot is the movement-image. In so far as it relates movement to a whole which changes, it is the mobile section of a duration. Describing the image of a street demonstration Pudovkin says: it is as if you climbed on a roof to see it, then you climb down to the first floor window to read the placards, then you mix with the crowd. . . .[17] It is only 'as if'; for natural perception introduces halts, moorings, fixed points or separated points of view, moving bodies or even distinct vehicles, whilst cinematographic perception works continuously, in a single movement whose very halts are an integral part of it and are only a vibration on to itself. Take, for example, the famous shot in King Vidor's *The Crowd*, what Mitry called 'one of the most beautiful tracking shots in the whole silent cinema': the camera advances into the crowd, against the flow, makes its way towards a skyscraper, climbs up to the twentieth floor, frames one of the windows, discovers a hall full of desks, goes in to arrive at a desk where the hero is sitting. Or take the famous shot in Murnau's *The Last Laugh*; the camera on a bicycle is put first of all in the lift, descends with it and takes in the entrance hall of a grand hotel through the glass of the window, performing constant decompositions and recompositions, then 'goes through the vestibule and through the enormous revolving door in a single and perfect tracking shot'. Here the camera involves two movements, two moving bodies or two vehicles, the lift and the bicycle. It can show the one, which is part of the image, and hide the other (it can also in certain cases show a camera itself in the image). But this is not what counts. What counts is that the mobile camera is like a *general equivalent* of all the means of locomotion that it shows or that it makes use of – aeroplane, car, boat, bicycle, foot, metro. . . . Wenders was to make this equivalence the soul of two of his films, *Kings of the Road* and *Alice in the Cities*, thus introducing into the cinema a particularly concrete reflection on the cinema. In other words, the essence of the cinematographic movement-image lies in extracting from vehicles or moving bodies the movement which is their common substance, or extracting from movements the mobility which is their essence. This was what Bergson wanted: beginning from the body or moving thing to which our natural perception attaches movement as if it were a vehicle, to extract a simple coloured 'spot', the movement-image, which 'is reduced in itself to a series of extremely rapid oscillations' and 'is in reality only a movement of movements'.[18] Now, because Bergson only considered what happened in the apparatus (the homogeneous abstract movement of the procession of images) he believed the cinema to be incapable of that which the apparatus is in fact most capable, eminently capable of: the movement image – that is, pure movement extracted from bodies or moving things. This is not an abstraction, but an emancipation. It is always a great moment in the cinema, as for example in Renoir, when the camera leaves a character, and even turns its back on him, following its own movement at the end of which it will rediscover him.[19]

By producing in this way a mobile section of movements, the shot is not content to express the duration of a whole which changes, but constantly puts bodies, parts, aspects, dimensions, distances and the respective positions of the bodies which make up a set in the image into variation. The one comes about through the other. It is because pure movement varies the elements of the set by dividing them up into fractions with different denominators – because it decomposes and recomposes the set – that it also relates to a fundamentally open whole, whose essence is constantly to 'become' or to change, to endure; and vice versa. Epstein has the most deeply and poetically extracted this nature of the shot as pure movement, comparing it to a cubist or simultaneist painting: 'All the surfaces are divided, truncated, decomposed, broken, as one imagines that they are in the thousand-faceted eyes of the insect – descriptive geometry whose canvas is the limit shot. Instead of submitting to perspective, this painter splits it, enters it. . . . For the perspective of the outside he thus substitutes the *perspective of the inside*, a multiple perspective, shimmering, sinuous, variable and contractile, like the hair of a hygrometer. It is not the same to the right as it is to the left, nor above as it is below. That is, the fractions of reality which the painter presents do not have the same denominators of distance – of relief or of light.' The cinema, even more directly than painting, conveys a relief in time, a perspective in time: it expresses time itself as perspective or relief.[20] This is why time essentially takes on the power to contract or dilate, as movement takes on the power to slow down or accelerate. Epstein comes closest to the concept of the shot: it is a mobile section, that is, a *temporal perspective or a modulation*. The difference between the cinematographic image and the photographic image follows from this. Photography is a kind of 'moulding': the mould organises the internal forces of the thing in such a way that they reach a state of equilibrium at a certain instant (immobile section). However, modulation does not stop when equilibrium is reached, and constantly modifies the mould, constitutes a variable, continuous, temporal mould.[21] This is the movement-image that Bazin contrasts from this point of view with the photo: 'The photographer proceeds, via the intermediary of the lens, to a point where he literally takes a luminous imprint, a cast. . . . [But] the cinema realises the paradox of moulding itself on the time of the object and of taking the imprint of its duration as well.'[22]

3   Mobility: *montage and movement of the camera*

What happened when the camera was fixed? The situation has often been described. In the first place, the frame is defined by a unique and frontal point of view which is that of the spectator on an invariable set: there is therefore no communication of mutually referring variable sets. In the second place, the shot is a uniquely spatial determination, indicating a 'slice of space' at a particular distance from the camera, from close-up to long shot (immobile sections): movement is therefore not extracted for itself and remains attached to elements, characters and things which serve as its moving body or vehicle. Finally, the whole is identical to the set in depth, such that the moving body goes through it in passing from one spatial shot/plane [*plan*] to another, from one parallel slice to another, each having its independence or its focus. There is therefore neither change nor duration properly speaking, in as much as duration implies a completely different conception of depth, which mixes up and dislocates parallel zones instead of superimposing them. We can therefore define a primitive state of the cinema where the image is in movement rather than being movement-image. It was at this primitive state that the Bergsonian critique was directed.

But if we ask how the movement-image is constituted, or how movement is extracted from persons and things, we see that it is in two different forms, and in both cases imperceptibly. On the one hand of course, through the mobility of the camera, the shot becoming mobile itself; but on the other by montage, that is, by the continuous connecting of shots, each one, or the majority of which, could perfectly well remain fixed. This method allows the achievement of a pure mobility extracted from the movements of characters, with very little camera movement: indeed this was the most common practice, and notably was still used by Murnau in *Faust* – the mobile camera being reserved for exceptional scenes or remarkable movements. Now, at the outset these two methods were in some sense obliged to conceal themselves; not only had the connections of montage to be imperceptible (for example, connections along the axis) but also the camera movements, in so far as they concerned ordinary moments or banal scenes (movements which are so slow as to be close to the threshold of perception).[23] The two forms or means only intervened to realise a potential contained in the fixed primitive image, that is in movement when it was still attached to people or things. This movement was already characteristic of the cinema, and demanded a kind of emancipation, incapable of being satisifed within the limits set by the primitive conditions – so that the so-called primitive image, the image in movement, was defined less by its state than by its tendency. The spatial and fixed shot tended to produce a pure movement-image, a tendency which imperceptibly came to be acted out [*passait à l'acte*] by the mobilisation of the camera in space, or by montage in time of mobile or simply fixed shots. As Bergson says, although he had not seen its application to cinema, things are never defined by their primitive state, but by the tendency concealed in this state.

The word 'shot' can be reserved for fixed spatial determinations, slices of space or distances in relation to the camera. This is the way Jean Mitry defined it, not only when he condemned the expression 'sequence shot', which according to him was incomprehensible, but with more justification, when he saw the tracking shot not as a shot but as a sequence of shots. It is then the sequence of shots which inherits the movement and the duration. But since this is not an adequately determinate notion, it is necessary to create more precise concepts to identify the unities of movement and duration: we see this in Christian Metz's 'syntagms' and Raymond Bellour's 'segments'. But from our point of view for the moment, the notion of shot [*plan*] has sufficient unity and extension if it is given its full projective, perspectival or temporal sense. In fact a unity is always that of an act which includes as such a multiplicity of passive or acted elements.[24] *Shots*, as immobile spatial determinations, are perfectly capable of being, in this sense, the multiplicity which corresponds to the unity *of the* shot, as mobile section or temporal perspective. The unity will vary according to the multiplicity that it contains, but will be no less the unity of this correlative multiplicity.

We can distinguish several cases here. In the first case, the continuous movement of the camera which defines the shot, whatever the changes of angle and of multiple points of view (for example, a tracking shot). In a second case, the continuity of connection constitutes the unity of the shot, although this unity has as its 'content' two or more successive shots which can moreover be fixed. Mobile shots can also owe their distinction to material constraints alone, and form a perfect unity as a function of the nature of their connection: thus in Orson Welles, the two high-angle shots of *Citizen Kane* where the camera literally goes through a window pane and penetrates into the interior of a great room, sometimes by means of the rain which crashes against the window pane and mists it up, sometimes by means of the storm and of a clap of thunder which breaks it. In a third case, we are confronted with a long-duration fixed or mobile shot, a 'sequence shot', with depths of field: such a shot includes within itself all the slices of space at once, from close-up to long distance shot, but nevertheless has a unity which permits it to be defined as a shot. Depth is no longer conceived, in the manner of the 'primitive' cinema, as a superimposition of parallel slices each of which is self-sufficient, all of them merely traversed by a single moving body. On the contrary, in Renoir or in Welles, the set of movements is distributed in depth in such a way as to establish liaisons, actions and reactions, which never develop one beside the other, in a single shot, but are spaced out at different distances, and from one shot to the next. The unity of the shot is produced here by the direct liaison between elements caught in the multiplicity of superimposed shots which can no longer be separated: the relationship of near and distant parts produces the unity. The same evolution appears in the history of painting between the sixteenth and the seventeenth centuries: a superimposition of planes each of which is occupied by a specific scene and where characters meet side by side is replaced by a completely different vision of depth, where characters meet obliquely and summon each other from one plane to the other, where the elements of a plane act and react on the elements of another plane, where no form, no colour is restricted to a single plane, where the dimensions of the foreground are abnormally enlarged in order to enter directly into relationship with the background by an abrupt reduction in sizes.[25] In a fourth case, the sequence-shot (for it has many types) no longer involves any depth, nor superimposition, nor drawing back: on the contrary, it brings all the spatial shots back to a single fore-shot [*avant plan*] which passes through different frames, in such a way that the unity of the shot refers back to the perfect planeness [*planitude*] of the image, whilst the correlative multiplicity is that of reframings. This was true for Dreyer in his sequence shots which were analogous to uniform tints [*aplats*] renouncing all distinction between different spatial planes [*plans*], making movement pass through a series of reframings which are substituted for change of shot [*plan*] (*Ordet*; *Gertrud*).[26] Images without depth or with little depth form a type of flowing and sliding shot, which is opposed to the volume of deep images.

In all these senses, the shot indeed has a unity. It is a unity of movement, and it embraces a correlative multiplicity which does not contradict it.[27] At the very most it can be said that this unity is caught between two demands: of the whole whose change it expresses throughout the film; of the parts whose displacements within each set and from one set to another it determines. Pasolini has expressed this dual requirement very clearly. On the one hand, the cinematographic whole would be one single analytic sequence shot, by rights unlimited, theoretically continuous; on the other, the parts of the film would in fact be discontinuous, dispersed, disseminated shots, without any assignable link. Therefore the whole must renounce its ideality, and become the synthetic whole of the film which is realised in the montage of the parts; and, conversely, the parts must be selected, coordinated, enter into connections and liaisons which, through montage, reconstitute the virtual sequence shot or the analytic whole of the cinema.[28]

But there is no such division between the shot 'in fact' and the shot as it ought, 'by right', to be (which leads to Pasolini's great aversion to the sequence-shot, which is always maintained in virtuality). There are two aspects which are equally of 'fact' and 'right', and which manifest the tension of the shot as unity. On the one hand the parts and their sets enter into relative continuities, by imperceptible connections, by camera movements, by sequence-shots of fact, with or without depth of field. But there will always be breaks and ruptures, which show clearly enough that the whole is not here, even if continuity is re-established afterwards. The whole intervenes elsewhere and in another order, as that which prevents sets from closing in on themselves or on each other – that which testifies to an opening which is irreducible to continuities as well as to their ruptures. It appears in the dimension of a duration which changes and never ceases to change. It appears in *false continuities* [*faux raccords*] as an essential pole of the cinema. False continuities can come into play in a set (Eisenstein) or in the passage from one set to another, between two sequence-shots (Dreyer). This is indeed why the sequence-shot does not merely interiorise montage in the shooting: on the contrary, it poses specific problems of montage. In a conversation on montage, Narboni, Sylvie Pierre and Rivette ask: where did *Gertrud* happen, where did Dreyer make it happen? And the answer that they give is: it happened in the splicing [*collure*].[29] False continuity is neither a connection of continuity, nor a rupture or a discontinuity in the connection. False continuity is in its own right a dimension of the Open, which escapes sets and their parts. It realises the other power of the out-of-field, this elsewhere or this empty zone, this 'white on white which is impossible to film'. Gertrud happened in what Dreyer called the fourth dimension. Far from breaking up the whole, false continuities are the act of the whole, the hallmark that they impress on sets and their parts, just as true continuities represent the opposite tendency: that of the parts and the sets to rejoin a whole which escapes them.

3 Montage

1 The third level: the whole, the composition of movement images and the indirect image of time

Montage is the determination of the whole (the third Bergsonian level) by means of continuities, cutting and false continuities. Eisenstein continually reminds us that montage is the whole of the film, the Idea. But why *should* the whole be the object of montage? Between the beginning and the end of a film something changes, something has changed. But this whole which changes, this time or duration, only seems to be capable of being apprehended indirectly, in relation to the movement-images which express it. Montage is the operation which bears on the movement-images to release the whole from them, that is, the image *of* time. It is a necessarily indirect image, since it is deduced from movement-images and their relationships. Montage does not come afterwards, for all that. Indeed, it is necessary that the whole should be primary in a certain way, that it should be presupposed. Particularly since, as we have seen, in Griffith's time and after, the movement-image in itself only rarely relates to the mobility of the camera, but arises more frequently from a succession of fixed shots which presupposes montage. If we consider the three levels – that of the determination of closed systems, that of the movement which is established between the parts of a system, and that of the changing whole which is expressed in movement – there is a circulation between the three which enables each to contain or prefigure the others. Some directors are therefore able to 'insert' the montage into the shot or even into the frame, and thus attach little importance to montage in itself. But the specificity of the three operations nevertheless survives, even in their mutual interiority. What amounts to montage, in itself or in something else, is the indirect image of time, of duration. Not a homogeneous time or a spatialised duration like that which Bergson attacks, but an effective duration and time which flow from the articulation of the movement-images, as they appear in Bergson's earlier texts. We must leave aside for the moment the task of ascertaining whether there are, in addition, direct images which might be called time-images, to what extent they would be separate from movement-images, and to what extent, conversely, they would be based on certain unknown aspects of these images.

Montage is composition, the assemblage [*agencement*] of movement-images as constituting an indirect image of time. Now, since the most ancient philosophy, there have been many different ways in which time can be conceived as a function of movement, in relation to movement, in various arrangements. We are likely to come across this variety again in the different 'schools' of montage. If we give to Griffith the distinction, not of having invented montage, but of having raised it to the level of a specific dimension, it seems that four main trends can be distinguished: the organic trend of the American school; the dialectic trend of the Soviet school; the quantitative trend of the pre-war French school; and the intensive trend of the German Expressionist school. In each case the directors may be very different; however, they have a community of themes, problems and preoccupations: in short, an ideal community which is all that is needed, in the cinema as elsewhere, to found concepts of schools or trends. We will now describe briefly each of these four schools of montage.

Griffith conceived of the composition of movement-images as an organisation, an organism, a great organic unity. This was his discovery. The organism is, firstly, unity in diversity, that is, a set of differentiated parts; there are men and women, rich and poor, town and country, North and South, interiors and exteriors, etc. These parts are taken in binary relationships which constitute a *parallel alternate montage*, the image of one part succeeding another according to a rhythm. But the part and the set must also necessarily enter into a relationship, exchange their relative dimensions. *The insertion of the close-up* in this sense does not merely involve the enlargement of a detail, but produces a miniaturisation of the set, a reduction of the scene (to the scale of a child, for example, like the baby who is present during the action of *The Massacre*). And, more generally, by showing the way in which the characters live the scene of which they form part, the close-up endows the objective set with a subjectivity which equals or even surpasses it (not just the close-ups of soldiers which alternate with the long shots of the battle, or the terrified close-ups of the young girl chased by a Negro in *Birth of a Nation*, but also the close-up of the young woman who identifies with the images of her thought in *Enoch Arden*).[1] Finally, the parts must necessarily act and react on each other in order to show how they simultaneously enter into conflict and threaten the unity of the organic set, and how they overcome the conflict or restore the unity. From some parts actions arise which oppose good and bad, but from other parts convergent actions arise which come to the aid of the good: through all these actions the form of a duel develops and passes through different stages. Indeed, it is in the nature of the organic set that it should continually be threatened: the accusation raised against the Negroes in *Birth of a Nation* is that of wanting to shatter the newly-won unity of the United States by using the South's defeat to their own advantage. . . . The convergent actions tend towards a single end, reaching the site of the duel to reverse its outcome, to save innocence or reconstitute the compromised unity – like the gallop of the horsemen who come to the rescue of the besieged, or the advance of the rescuer who recovers the girl on the thawing ice (*Orphans of the Storm*). It is the third aspect of montage, *concurrent or convergent montage*, which alternates the moments of two actions which will come back together again. And the more the actions converge, the closer the junction approaches, the more rapid the alternation becomes (accelerated montage). Admittedly, in Griffith, the junction does not always take place, and the innocent young girl is often condemned, almost sadistically, because she could only find her place and salvation in an 'inorganic' abnormal union: the Chinese opium-addict arrives too late in *Broken Blossoms*. This time it is a perverse acceleration which forestalls convergence.

These are the three forms of montage, or of rhythmic alternation; the alternation of differentiated parts, that of relative dimensions, and that of convergent actions. A powerful organic representation produces the set and the parts in this way. The American cinema draws from it its most solid form; from the general situation to the re-established or transformed situation through the intermediary of a duel, of a convergence of actions. American montage is organico-active. It is wrong to criticise it as being subordinate to the narration; it is the reverse, for the narrativity flows from this conception of montage. In *Intolerance*, Griffith discovers that the organic representation can be immense, encompassing not merely families and a society, but different epochs and civilisations. The parts thrown together by parallel montage are the civilisations themselves. The relative dimensions which are interchanged range from the king's city to the capitalist's office. And the convergent actions are not just the duels proper to each civilisation – the chariot-race in the Babylonian episode, the race between the car and the train in the modern episode – but the two races themselves converge through the centuries in an accelerated montage which superimposes Babylon and America. Never again will such an organic unity be achieved, by means of rhythm, from parts which are so different and actions which are so distant.

Whenever time has been considered in relation to movement,

whenever it has been defined as the measure of movement, two aspects of time have been discovered, which are chronosigns: on the one hand, time as whole, as great circle or spiral, which draws together the set of movement in the universe; on the other, time as interval, which indicates the smallest unit of movement or action. Time as whole, the set of movement in the universe, is the bird which hovers, continually increasing its circle. But the numerical unit of movement is the beating of a wing, the continually diminishing interval between two movements or two actions. Time as interval is the accelerated variable present, and time as whole is the spiral open at both ends, the immensity of past and future. Infinitely dilated, the present would become the whole itself: infinitely contracted, the whole would happen in the interval. What originates from montage, or from the composition of movement-images is the Idea, that indirect image of time: the whole which winds up and unwinds the set of the parts in the famous wellspring of *Intolerance*, and the interval between actions which gets smaller and smaller in the accelerated montage of the races.

2   *The Soviet school*

While he fully acknowledges his debt to Griffith, Eisenstein nevertheless makes two objections. Firstly, it might be said that the differentiated parts of the set are given of themselves, as independent phenomena. Just like bacon, with its alternation of lean meat and fat, there are rich and poor, good and bad, Whites and Blacks, etc. Thus when the representatives of these parts confront each other, it must be in the form of individual duels where narrowly personal motifs (for example, a love story, the melodramatic element) are hidden beneath collective motivations. It is like parallel lines which pursue each other, and indeed meet at infinity, but only collide here below when a secant brings together a particular point on the one and a particular point on the other. Griffith is oblivious to the fact that rich and poor are not given as independent phenomena, but are dependent on a single general cause, which is social exploitation. . . . These objections which condemn Griffith's 'bourgeois' view do not merely relate to his way of telling a story or of understanding History. They relate directly to parallel (and also convergent) montage.[2] Eisenstein criticises Griffith for having a thoroughly empirical conception of the organism, without a law of genesis or development – for having conceived of its unity in a completely extrinsic way as a unity of

collection, the gathering together of juxtaposed parts, and not as a
unity of production, a *cell* which produces its own parts by division,
differentiation; for having interpreted opposition as an accident
and not as the internal motive force by which the divided unity forms
a new unity on another level. It will be noted that Eisenstein retains
Griffith's idea of an organic composition or assemblage of movement-
images: from the general situation [*situation d'ensemble*] to the
transformed situation, through the development and transcendence
of the oppositions. But is *is* true that Griffith did not see the dialectical
nature of the organism and its composition. The organic is indeed a
great spiral, but the spiral should be conceived of 'scientifically' and
not empirically, in terms of a law of genesis, growth and development.
Eisenstein judged that he had mastered his method in *Battleship
Potemkin*, and it is in his commentary on this film that he puts forward
the new conception of the organic.[3]

The organic spiral finds its internal law in the golden section,
which marks a caesura-point and divides the set into two great parts
which may be opposed, but which are unequal (this is the moment of
sorrow where a transition is made from the ship to the town, and
where the movement is reversed). But it is also each twist of the
spiral, or segment, which divides up in its turn into two unequal
opposing parts. And there are many kinds of opposition: quantitative
(one-many, one man-many men, a single shot-a salvo, one ship-a
fleet); qualitative (sea-land); intensive (dark-light); dynamic (movement upwards and downwards, from left to right and vice versa).
Moreover, if one starts off from the end of the spiral rather than its
beginning, the golden section determines another caesura, the highest
point of reversal instead of the lowest, which gives rise to other
divisions and other oppositions. Thus the spiral progresses by
growing through oppositions or contradictions. But what is
expressed in this way is the movement of the One, which divides
itself in two and recreates a new unity. Indeed, if the opposable parts
are related to the origin O (or to the end), from the standpoint of
genesis they enter into a proportion which is that of the golden
section, according to which the smallest part must be to the largest
what the largest is to the set:

$$\frac{OA}{OB} = \frac{OB}{OC} = \frac{OC}{OD} \ldots = m$$

The opposition serves the dialectical unity whose progression from
the initial to the final situation it marks. It is in this sense that the set is

reflected in each part and each part or twist of the spiral reproduces the set. And this applies not only to the sequence, but to each image which also contains its caesuras, its oppositions, its origin and its end. Each image not only has the unity of an element which may be juxtaposed to others, but the genetic unity of a 'cell', which may be divided into others. Eisenstein says that the movement-image is the cell of montage, and not simply an element of montage. In short, *montage of opposition* takes the place of parallel montage, under the dialectical law of the One which divides itself in order to form the new, higher unity.

We are only outlining the theoretical skeleton of Eisenstein's commentary, which closely follows the concrete images (the Odessa steps, for example). This dialectical composition may be seen in *Ivan the Terrible*, in particular with the two caesuras which correspond to Ivan's two moments of doubt – first, when he examines his conscience beside his wife's coffin, and then when he pleads with the monk. The first marks the end of the first twist of the spiral, the first stage of the struggle against the boyars; the other marks the beginning of the second stage and, between the two, the retreat from Moscow. Official Soviet criticism attacked Eisenstein for having conceived the second stage as a personal duel between Ivan and his aunt. Eisenstein does indeed reject the anachronistic view of an Ivan who united himself with the people. From start to finish, Ivan merely uses the people as a tool, as is appropriate to the historical conditions of the period. Nevertheless within these conditions he develops his opposition to the boyars, which does not become a personal duel in the manner of Griffith, but evolves from political compromise to physical and social extermination.

Eisenstein calls upon science, mathematics and the natural sciences in his defence. This does not detract from art, since – like painting – the cinema must invent the spiral which suits the theme, and choose the caesura points well. We can already see from this standpoint of genesis and growth that Eisenstein's method essentially involves the determination of remarkable points or privileged instants. But they do not, as in Griffith, express an accidental element or the contingency of the individual. On the contrary, they belong fully to the regular construction of the organic spiral. This is even clearer if we consider a new dimension which Eisenstein presents, sometimes adding itself to those of the organic, sometimes perfecting them. The composition, the dialectical assemblage, involves not only the organic – that is, genesis and growth – but also the *pathetic* or the 'development'. The pathetic should not be confused with the organic. The point is that from one point to another on the spiral one can extend vectors which are like the strings of a bow, or the spans of the twist of a spiral. It is no longer a case of the formation and progression of the oppositions themselves, following the twists of the spiral, but of the transition from one opposite to the other, or rather into the other, along the spans: the leap into the opposite. There is not simply the opposition of earth and water, of the one and the many; there is the transition of the one into the other, and the sudden upsurge of the other out of the one. There is not simply the organic unity of opposites, but the pathetic passage of the opposite into its contrary. There is not simply an organic link between two instants, but a pathetic jump, in which the second instant gains a new power, since the first has passed into it. From sadness to anger, from doubt to certainty, from resignation to revolt. . . . The pathetic, for its part, involves these two aspects: it is simultaneously the transition from one term to another, from one quality to another, and the sudden upsurge of the new quality which is born from the transition which has been accomplished. It is both 'compression' and 'explosion'.[4] *The General Line* divides its spiral into two opposed parts, 'the Old' and 'the New', and reproduces its division, redistributes its oppositions on one side and the other: this is the organic. But in the famous scene of the creamer, we witness the transition from one moment to the other, from suspicion and hope to triumph, from the empty tube to the first drop, a transition which accelerates as the new quality, the triumphant drop, approaches; this is the pathetic, the jump or qualitative leap. The organic was the bow, the collection of bows; but the pathetic is both the string and the arrow, the change in quality and the sudden upsurge of the new quality, its squaring, its raising to the power two.

The pathetic therefore implies a change not merely in the content of the image, but also in the form. The image must, effectively, change its power, pass to a higher power. This is what Eisenstein calls 'absolute change of dimension', in contrast to Griffith's merely relative changes. By absolute change, we must understand that the qualitative leap is as much formal as material. In Eisenstein, the insertion of the close-up marks just such a formal leap – an absolute change, that is, the 'squaring' of the image. In comparison with Griffith, this is a completely new function of the close-up.[5] And if it includes a subjectivity, it is in the sense that consciousness is also a passage into a new dimension, a raising to the power two (which can be achieved through 'a series of enlarging close-ups', but which may equally make use of other techniques). In any case, consciousness is the pathetic, the transition from Nature to man and the quality which is born from the transition which has been accomplished. It is at once the dawn of consciousness and consciousness attained, revolutionary consciousness attained, at least to a certain degree: which may be the very limited degree of Ivan, or the merely anticipatory degree of _Battleship Potemkin_, or the culminating degree of _October_. If the pathetic is development, it is because it is the development of consciousness itself: it is the leap of the organic which produces an external consciousness of society and its history, of the social organism from one moment to the next. And there are yet other leaps – in variable relationships with those of consciousness – all expressing new dimensions, formal and absolute changes, raisings to yet higher powers. It is the leap into colour, like the red flag of _Battleship Potemkin_, or Ivan's red banquet. With sound and the talkie, Eisenstein was to discover still further raisings of power.[6] But, to confine ourselves to silent films, the qualitative leap can attain formal or absolute changes which already constitute powers to the 'nth degree': the stream of milk in _The General Line_ gives way to jets of water (passage to scintillation), then to a firework (passage to colour) and finally to zigzags of figures (passage from the visible to the legible). From this standpoint, Eisenstein's difficult concept of 'montage of attractions' – which can certainly not be reduced to the bringing into play of comparisons or even of metaphors – becomes much more comprehensible.[7] In our view the 'attractions' consist sometimes in theatrical or circus representations (Ivan's red banquet), sometimes in plastic representations (the statues and sculptures in _Battleship Potemkin_ and particularly in _October_) which intervene to prolong or replace the image. The jets of fire and water in _The General Line_ are of the same type. Of course, attraction must firstly be understood in its spectacular sense. Then also in an associative sense: the association of images as a Newtonian law of attraction. But, furthermore, what Eisenstein calls 'attractional calculus' marks this dialectical yearning of the image to gain new dimensions, that is, to leap formally from one power into another. The jets of water and fire raise the drop of milk to a properly cosmic dimension. And it is consciousness which becomes cosmic at the same time as it becomes revolutionary – having reunited in a final leap of pathos the whole of the organic in itself – earth, air, fire and water. We will see later how, in this way, montage of attractions constantly makes the organic and the pathetic communicate with one another.

Eisenstein substitutes a montage of opposition for Griffith's parallel montage, and a montage of qualitative leaps ('jumping montage') for convergent or concurrent montage. All kinds of new aspects of montage are brought together at this point – or rather flow from it – in a grand creation both of practical operations and theoretical concepts: a new conception of the close-up, a new conception of accelerated montage, vertical montage, montage of attractions, intellectual or consciousness montage. . . . We believe in the coherence of this organic-pathetic set. And this is indeed the key point of Eisenstein's revolution: he gives the dialectic a properly cinematographic meaning, he tears rhythm away from the purely empirical or aesthetic value which it had, for example, in Griffith, he reaches an essentially dialectical conception of the organism. Time remains an indirect image which is born from the organic composition of movement-images, *but the interval, as well as the whole [tout] takes on a new meaning.* The interval, the variable present, has become the qualitative leap which reaches the raised power of the instant. As for the whole as immensity, this is no longer a totality of reuniting which subsumes the independent parts on the sole condition that they exist for each other, and which can always be enlarged if one adds parts to the conditioned set [*ensemble*], or if one relates two independent sets to the idea of an identical end. It is a totality which has become concrete or existing, in which the parts are produced by each other in their set and the set is reproduced in the parts, so that this reciprocal causality refers back to the whole as cause of the set *and* of its parts, according to an internal finality. The spiral open at both ends is no longer a way of assembling an empirical reality from outside, but the way in which dialectical reality constantly produces itself and grows. Things truly plunge *into* time and become immense because they occupy there an infinitely greater position than the parts have in the set or the set in itself. The set and the parts of *Battleship Potemkin* – forty-eight hours – or of *October* – ten days – occupy in time, that is, in the whole [*tout*] an immeasurably prolonged period. And, far from being added, or compared from the outside, the attractions *are* this very prolongation, or this internal existence in the whole. In Eisenstein the dialectical conception of the organism and of montage combines the ever-open spiral and the perpetually-leaping instant.

The dialectic, as is well-known, is defined by many laws. There is the law of the quantitative process and the qualitative leap: the passage from one quality to another and the sudden upsurge of the new quality. There is the law of the whole, of the set and of the parts. There is also the law of the One and the opposition, on which – it is said – the two other laws depend: the One which becomes two to

attain a new unity. If we can speak of a Soviet school of montage, it is
not because its directors are similar but because within the dialectical
conception which they share they in fact differ, each having an
affinity with one or other of the laws which his inspiration recreates.
Pudovkin is clearly mainly interested in the progression of consciousness, in the qualitative leaps of a dawn of consciousness: it is
from this viewpoint that *Mother*, *The End of St Petersburg* and *Storm
over Asia* form a great trilogy. Nature is there, in its splendour and
theatricality – the Neva carrying along its ice-floes, the Mongolian
plains – but as the linear thrust which subtends the moments of
dawning consciousness; that of the mother, the peasant, or the
Mongol. And Pudovkin's most profound art lies in disclosing the set
of a situation through the consciousness which a character gains of it,
and in prolonging it to the point where consciousness can expand and
act (the mother watching over the father who wants to steal the
weights of a clock, or, in *The End of St Petersburg*, the woman who
sums up in a glance the elements of the situation; the policeman, the
glass of tea on the table, the smoking candle, the boots of the arriving
husband).[8] Dovzhenko is a dialectician in another way, obsessed
with the triadic relation of the parts, the set and the whole. If there
was ever a director who knew how to make a set and the parts plunge
into a whole which gives them a depth and extension disproportionate
to their proper limits, it was Dovzhenko to a far greater extent than
Eisenstein. This is the source of the fantasy and enchantment in
Dovzhenko. Sometimes scenes can be static parts or disjointed
fragments, like the images of poverty at the beginning of *Arsenal* – the
prostrate woman, the immobile mother, the muzhik, the woman
sowing, the gassed corpses (or, on the other hand, the joyous images
of *Earth* – the couples who are immobile, seated, standing or
recumbent). Sometimes a dynamic and continuous set [*ensemble*] can
form at a particular place, at a particular moment, for example in the
'taiga' of *Aerograd*. Each time, we can be sure that a plunge into the
whole will connect the images with a millenial past, like that of the
Ukrainian mountain and the treasure of the Scythians in *Zvenigora*,
and with a planetary future where aeroplanes bring the builders of the
new city from all points of the horizon. Amengual used to speak of
'the abstraction of montage' which, through the set or the fragments,
gave the director the 'power to speak outside real time and space'.[9]
But this outside is also the Earth, or the true interiority of time, that is
the whole which changes, and which by changing perspective,
constantly gives real beings that infinite space which enables them to
touch the most distant past and the depths of the future simultaneously,

and to participate in the movement of its own 'revolution': for instance, the grandfather who dies peacefully at the start of *Earth*, or the one in *Zvenigora* who frequents the inside of time. What Dovzhenko gives to his peasants, and to *Shchors*, as 'legendary beings of a fabulous epoch' is what Proust describes as the giants' stature which men assume in time, which separates the parts as much as it prolongs the set.

In a certain respect, Eisenstein could consider himself leader of the school – in relation to Pudovkin and Dovzhenko – because he was imbued with the third law of the dialectic, the one which seemed to contain the other two: the One which becomes two and gives it a new unity, reuniting the organic whole and the pathetic interval. In fact, there were three ways of conceiving a dialectical montage, of which none was destined to please Stalinist criticism. But all three had in common the idea that materialism was primarily historical, and that Nature was only dialectical because always integrated into a human totality. Hence the name which Eisenstein gave to Nature: the 'non-indifferent'. Vertov's originality, on the contrary, is the radical affirmation of a dialectic of matter in itself. This is like a fourth law, breaking with the other three.[10] To be sure, what Vertov was showing was man present in Nature, his actions, his passions, his life. But, if he worked through documentaries and newsreels, if he violently challenged the filming of Nature and the construction of the action, this was for a profound reason. Whether there were machines, landscapes, buildings or men was of little consequence: each – even the most charming peasant woman or the most touching child – was presented as a material system in perpetual interaction. They were catalysts, converters, transformers, which received and re-emitted movements, whose speed, direction, order, they changed, making matter evolve towards less 'probable' states, bringing about changes out of all proportion to their own dimensions. It is not that Vertov considered beings to be machines, but rather machines which had a 'heart' and which 'revolved, trembled, jolted about and threw out flashes of lightning', as man could also do, using other movements and under other conditions, but always in interaction with each other. What Vertov discovered in contemporary life was the molecular child, the molecular woman, the material woman and child, as much as systems which are called mechanisms or machines. Most important were all the (communist) transitions from an order which is being undone to an order which is being constructed. But between two systems or two orders, between two movements, there is necessarily the variable interval. In Vertov the interval of movement is perception, the glance, the eye. But the eye is not the too-immobile human eye; it is the eye of the camera, that is an eye in matter, a perception such as it is in matter, as it extends from a point where an action begins to the limit of the reaction, as it fills the interval between the two, crossing the universe and beating in time to its intervals. The correlation between a non-human matter and a superhuman eye is the dialectic itself, because it is also the identity of a community of matter and a communism of man. And montage itself constantly adapts the transformations of movements in the material universe to the interval of movement in the eye of the camera: rhythm. Montage, it must be said, was already everywhere in the two preceding moments. It precedes the filming, in the choice of material, that is, the portions of matter which are to enter into interaction, sometimes very distant or far apart (life as it is). It enters into the filming, in the intervals occupied by the camera-eye (the cameraman who follows, runs, enters, exits: in short, life in the film). It comes after the filming, in the editing-room, where material and filming are evaluated against one another (the life of the film), and in the audience, who compare life in the film and life as it is. These are the three levels which are explicitly shown to co-exist in *Man with a Movie-Camera*, but which had already inspired all his previous work.

Dialectic was not just a word for Soviet film-makers. It was both the practice and the theory of montage. But, while the three other great directors used the dialectic to transform the organic composition of movement-images, Vertov found in it the means of breaking with this composition. He criticised his rivals for being carried along in Griffith's wake, for imitating the American cinema, or for a bourgeois idealism. In his view, the dialectic should break with a Nature which was still too organic, and with a man still too readily pathetic. The result in his work was that the whole merges with the infinite set of matter, and the interval merges with an eye in matter, Camera. He would no longer be understood by official criticism. But he would have taken to its limit a debate within the dialectic which Eisenstein knew very well how to summarise when he was not content with polemic. Vertov opposes to the 'Nature–man', 'Nature–fist', 'Nature–punch' pair (organic–pathetic) a 'matter–eye' pair.[11]

3   The pre-war French school

In the pre-war French school (whose recognised leader, in certain respects, was Gance) we also witness a break with the principle of organic composition. This, however, was not a case of Vertovism, even of a moderated form. Should we call it Impressionism in order to contrast it with German Expressionism? The French school might be better defined by a sort of Cartesianism: these directors were primarily interested in the *quantity of movement* and in the metrical relations which allow us to define it. They have a debt as great as the Soviets to Griffith, and also want to go beyond what remains empirical in Griffith to a more scientific conception, as long as it serves the inspiration of the cinema and even the unity of the arts (this is the same concern for 'science' that one finds in painting at that time). Now the French turned away from organic composition, and similarly avoided a dialectical composition, but built up a vast mechanical composition of movement-images. This, however, was an ambiguous formula. Take, for example, a number of scenes which have become part of the anthology of French cinema: Epstein's travelling fair (*Coeur fidèle*), L'Herbier's ball (*El Dorado*), Grémillon's farandoles (from *Maldone* onwards). In a group dance, there is certainly an organic composition of the dancers and a dialectical composition of their movements, not merely fast and slow, but also linear and circular, etc. But, even while recognising these movements, one can extract or abstract from them a single body which might be 'the' dancer, the single body of all these dancers, and a single movement which might be 'the' fandango of L'Herbier, the movement of all possible fandangos made visible.[12] One goes beyond the moving bodies to extract a maximum quantity of movement in a given space. Thus Grémillon films his first farandole in a closed space which releases a maximum of movement. Furthermore we should not describe other farandoles in his later films as others, but rather always as *the* farandole, whose mystery – that is, the quantity of movement – Grémillon never tires of extracting, rather as Monet never stops painting *the* Water-Lily.

Taken to extremes, the dance might be a machine, with dancers as its components. In fact, French cinema uses the machine to attain a mechanical composition of movement-images in two ways. A first type of machine is the automaton, a simple machine or clock mechanism, a geometrical configuration of parts which combine, superimpose or transform movements in homogeneous space, according to the relationships through which they pass. The automaton does not – as in German Expressionism – illustrate another menacing life which threatens to plunge into darkness. Rather, it illustrates a clear mechanical movement as law of the maximum for a set of images which brings together things and living beings, the inanimate and the animate, by making them the same. The puppets, the passers-by, the reflections of puppets, the shadows of passers-by, enter into very subtle relationships of reduplication, alternation, periodical return and chain reaction, which constitute the set to which the mechanical movement must be attributed. This can be said of the young woman's flight in Vigo's *L'Atalante*, but it can also be applied to Renoir; from *The Little Match-Girl's* dream to the great composition of *La Règle du jeu*. It is obviously René Clair who gives this formula its greatest poetic generality, and animates geometrical abstractions in a space which is homogeneous, luminous and grey, without depth.[13] The concrete object, the object of desire, appears as a motor or spring acting in time, *primum movens*, which triggers off a mechanical movement, towards which an increasing number of characters contribute, appearing in turn in space, like the parts of an expanding mechanised set (*The Italian Straw Hat, Le Million*). Individualism is the essential element throughout: the individual holds himself behind the object, or rather himself plays the role of spring or motor developing its effects in time; ghost, illusionist, devil or mad scientist, destined to be wiped out when the movement which he determines has reached its maximum or overtaken him. Then everything will return to a state of order. In short, an automatic ballet, whose motor itself circulates, through the movement. The other type of machine is the engine which runs on steam or fire, the powerful energy machine which produces movement out of something else, and constantly affirms a heterogeneity whose terms it links – the mechanical and the living, the inside and the outside, the engineer and the force – in a process of internal resonance or amplifying communication. An epic or tragic element is substituted for the comic or dramatic element. In this the French school distinguishes itself from the Soviets, who incessantly filmed great energy machines (not just Eisenstein and Vertov, but also Tourin's masterpiece *Turksib*). For them, man and machine formed an active dialectical unity, which transcended the opposition between mechanical work and human worker, whereas the French conceived the kinetic unity of the quantity of movement in a machine and the direction of movement in a soul, positing this unity as a Passion which had to lead to death. The states through which the new motor and the mechanical movement pass are enlarged to the scale of the cosmos, just as in this other union of man and machine the states through which the new individual and the human groups [*ensembles*] pass are raised to the scale of a world-soul. This is why it is futile to try to sort out two kinds of images in Gance's *La Roue*: those of mechanical movement, which have kept their beauty, and those of the tragedy, which is regarded as silly and childish. The moments of the train – its speed, its acceleration, its catastrophe – are inseparable from the states of the mechanic, from Sisyphus in steam and Prometheus in fire to Oedipus in snow. The kinetic union of man and machine was to define a new Human Beast – quite different from the puppet brought to life, whose new dimensions Renoir, drawing on Gance's legacy, would also be able to explore.

From this was to emerge an abstract art, in which pure movement was sometimes extracted from deformed objects by progressive abstraction, sometimes from geometrical elements in periodic transformation, a transformative group affecting the whole [*ensemble*] of space. It was the search for a kinetics as properly visual art, which raised – even in the silent cinema – the problem of a relationship between the movement-image, colour and music. *Le Ballet mécanique* by the painter Fernand Léger was inspired more by simple machines, while Epstein's *Photogénies* and Grémillon's *La Photogénie mécanique* were inspired instead by industrial machines. As we will see, an even deeper impulse ran through French cinema: a general predilection for water, the sea or rivers (L'Herbier, Epstein, Vigo, Grémillon). This was in no sense a renunciation of the mechanical: on the contrary, it was the transition from a mechanics of solids to a mechanics of fluids which, from a concrete point of view, was to find in the liquid image a new extension of the quantity of movement as a whole [*dans son ensemble*]. It provided better conditions to pass from the concrete to the abstract, a greater possibility of communicating an irreversible duration to movements, independently of their figurative characters, a more certain power of extracting movement from the thing moved.[14] Water had a vivid presence in American and Soviet cinema, benevolent as well as devastating: but, for better or worse, it was confronted with, and related to, organic ends. It is the French school which emancipates water, gives it its own finalities and makes them the form of that which has no organic consistency.

When Delluc, Germaine Dulac and Epstein, speak of 'photogeny' [*photogénie*], it is obviously not a question of the quality of the photo, but, on the contrary, of defining the cinematographic image in its difference from the photo. Photogeny is the image as it is 'majored' [*majorée*] by movement.[15] The problem lies precisely in defining this 'majorer' [*majorante*]. It implies, firstly, the interval of time as variable present. In his very first film, *The Crazy Ray*, René Clair had impressed Vertov by separating out such intervals as points where movement stops, re-starts, reverses itself, accelerates or slows down: a sort of differential of movement.[16] But the interval in this sense is effected as a numerical unit which produces a maximum quantity of movement in the image *in relation to other determinable factors*, and which varies from one image to the next according to the variation of these factors themselves. These factors are of very different kinds: the nature and dimensions of the framed space, the distribution of moving and fixed objects, the angle of framing, the lens, the chronometric duration of the shot, the light and its degrees, its tonalities, and also figural and affective tonalities (not to mention the colour, the sound, the speech and the music). Between the interval or the numerical unit and these factors there is a set of *metrical relations* which constitute the 'numbers', the rhythm, and give the 'measure' of the greatest quantity of relative movement. Montage had undoubtedly always implied such calculations, on the one hand empirical and intuitive, but tending on the other to a certain scientificity.[17] But what seems to characterise the French school – in this sense Cartesian – is that it simultaneously raised the calculation beyond its empirical condition, to make it into a sort of 'algebra' – to use Gance's word – and made the result of this each time the maximum possible quantity of movement as a function of all the variables, or the form of that which goes beyond the organic. L'Herbier's monumental interiors in Léger's or Barsacq's sets (*The New Enchantment, L'Argent*) are the best examples of a space subject to metrical relationships, according to which the forces or factors which are at work in it determine the greatest quantity of movement.

Contrary to what happens in German Expressionism, everything is for movement, even light. To be sure, light is not merely a factor given value by the movement which it accompanies, undergoes, or even conditions. There is a French luminism created by some great cameramen (such as Périnal), where the light is valued by itself. But, in fact, by itself it is already movement – pure movement of extension which is realised in grey, in a 'cameo-image playing on all the nuances in the greys'.[18] It is a light which constantly circulates in a homogeneous space and creates luminous forms by its own mobility, even more than by its encounter with objects on the move. The French school's luminous grey is already like a movement-colour. It is not – in the manner of Eisenstein – the dialectical unity which divides up into black and white, or which derives from them as a new quality. But still less is it – in the manner of the Expressionists – the result of a violent struggle between light and darkness, or of an embrace of light and dark. Grey, or light as movement, is alternating movement. To have substituted alternation for dialectical opposition was undoubtedly something original to the French school. It reaches its high point in Grémillon: the regular alternation of light and shadow that the lighthouse itself sets in motion in *Gardiens de la phare*; also the alternation of the daytime and nocturnal town in *L'étrange Monsieur Victor*. There is alternation in extension, and not conflict, because from both aspects it is light – sunlight and moonlight, sunlit landscape and moonlit landscape – which communicate in grey and pass through all its nuances. Such a conception of light, in spite of appearances, owes much to Delaunay's colourism.

It is obvious that the greatest quantity of movement must, up to this point, be understood as a relative maximum, since it depends on the numerical unit chosen as interval, on the variable factors of which it is a function, and on the metrical relationships between the factors and the unit which gives movement a form. It is the 'best' quantity of movement, taking into account all the elements. The maximum is qualified each time, it is a quality itself: fandango, farandole, ballet, etc. Depending on the variations of the present or the contractions and dilations of the interval, one might say that a very slow movement realises the greatest possible quantity of movement, just as much as a very fast movement does in another case: if Gance's *La Roue* was a model of increasingly fast movement, with accelerated montage, then Epstein's *The Fall of the House of Usher* remains the masterpiece of a slow motion which nevertheless constitutes the maximum of movement in a form which is infinitely drawn out. At this point we must therefore pass on to the other aspect, that is, the absolute of the quantity of movement, the absolute maximum. Far from being contradictory, these aspects are strictly inseparable and implied each other, presupposed each other from the beginning. Already in Descartes there is an eminently relative quantification of movement in variable sets, but there is also an absolute quantity of movement in the whole of the universe. The cinema rediscovers this correlation, which is necessary for its most profound conditions. On the one hand, the shot is directed towards framed sets and introduces a maximum of relative movement between their elements: on the other, it is directed towards a changing whole whose change is expressed in an absolute maximum of movement. The difference is not simply between each image for itself (framing) and the relations between images (montage). The movement of the camera introduces many images into one, with re-framings, and also makes a single image capable of expressing the whole. This is particularly clear in Gance, who justifiably boasted that in *Napoleon* he had emancipated the camera, not just from its supports on the ground but also from its relationship with the man who carries it, so as to mount it on horseback, hurl it like a weapon, roll it along like a ball and send it spiralling down into the sea.[19] However, our previous observation – for which we are indebted to Burch – remains valid: movement of the camera, in the majority of the directors that we discuss in this chapter, is still reserved for remarkable moments, whilst ordinary, pure movement is in fact referred to a succession of fixed shots, so that montage is in both aspects of the shot: in the aspect of the framed set [*ensemble*], which is not content with a single image, but manifests relative movement in a sequence where the unit of measurement changes; and in the aspect of the whole of the film, which is not content with a succession of images, but expresses itself in an absolute movement, whose nature we must now discover.

Kant said that as long as the numerical unit of measurement is homogeneous, one can easily go on to infinity, but only abstractly. On the other hand, when the unit of measurement is variable, the imagination quickly runs up against a limit: beyond a short sequence it is no longer capable of *comprehending* the set of magnitudes or movements that it successively apprehends. Nevertheless, Thought, the Soul, by virtue of a demand proper to it, must understand the set of movements in Nature or the Universe *as a whole*. This latter is what Kant calls the mathematical sublime: the imagination devotes itself to apprehending relative movements, and in so doing quickly exhausts its forces in converting the units of measurement. But thought must attain that which surpasses all imagination, that is, the set of movements as whole, absolute maximum of movement, absolute movement which is in itself identical to the incommensurable or the measureless, the gigantic, the immense: canopy of the heavens or limitless sea.[20] This is the second aspect of time: it is no longer the interval as variable present, but the fundamentally open whole as the immensity of future and past. It is no longer time as succession of movements, and of their units, but time as simultaneism and simultaneity (for simultaneity, no less than succession, belongs to time; it is time as whole). It is this ideal of simultaneism which has constantly haunted French cinema, just as it inspired painting, music and even literature. Of course, one can believe that it is possible and easy to pass from the first to the second aspect: is succession not infinite by right, and does it not have as its limit – whether it accelerates increasingly, or whether it is infinitely drawn out – a simultaneity to which it draws close, at infinity? It is in this sense that Epstein speaks of 'rapid angular succession which tends towards the perfect circle of impossible simultaneism'.[21] Vertov, or indeed the Futurists, might have spoken in this way. In the French school, however, there is a dualism between the two aspects: relative movement belongs to content, and describes the sets which can be discerned in it or made to communicate through 'imagination'; whilst absolute movement belongs to spirit and expresses the psychic character of the whole which changes. So that one does not pass from one to the other by bringing into play units of measurement – however large or small – but only by attaining something measureless, Overmuch or Excess in relation to all measurement, which can only be conceived by a thinking soul. In L'Herbier's *L'Argent*, Noel Burch identifies a particularly interesting case of this construction of a necessarily measureless whole of time.[22] In any case, the acceleration or deceleration of relative movement, the essential relativity of the units of measurement, the dimensions of the set [*décor*], play an indispensable role: but they accompany or condition the other aspect rather than themselves bringing about the transition between the two. French dualism maintains the difference between the spiritual and the material, while showing the complementarity of the two: not only in Gance, but in L'Herbier and in Epstein himself. It has often been noted that the French school gave just as much importance to and developed the subjective image to the same extent as German Expressionism had, albeit in a different way. Indeed it neatly summarises the dualism and the complementarity of the two terms: on the one hand it multiplies the relative maximum of quantity of possible movement by joining the movement of a body which sees to the movement of the bodies seen; but on the other hand it constitutes under these conditions the absolute maximum of the quantity of movement in relation to an independent Soul which 'envelops' and 'precedes' the bodies.[23] As, for example, in the celebrated case of the soft focus in the dance of *El Dorado*.

This spiritualism and dualism were given to the French cinema by Gance. We can see it clearly in the two aspects of montage in his work. In the first of these, which he does not claim to have invented, but which controls the running of the film, relative movement finds its law in a 'successive vertical montage': a famous case is accelerated montage as it appears in *La Roue* and again in *Napoleon*. But absolute movement is defined by a quite different figure, which Gance calls 'simultaneous horizontal montage' and which finds its two principal forms in *Napoleon*: on the one hand the invention of the triple screen and polyvision; on the other hand the original use of superimpressions. By superimposing a very large number of superimpressions (sixteen at times), by introducing little temporal shifts between them, and by adding some and removing others, Gance is perfectly aware that the spectator will not see what is superimposed: the imagination is, as it were, surpassed, saturated, quickly reaching its limit. But Gance relies on an effect of all these superimpressions in the soul, on the constitution of a rhythm of added and subtracted values, which presents to the soul the idea of a whole as the feeling of measurelessness and immensity. By inventing the triple screen, Gance achieves the simultaneity of three aspects of a same scene, or of three different scenes, and constructs so-called 'non-retrogradable' rhythms, rhythms whose two extremes are the retrogradation of one by the other, with a central value common to both. By uniting the simultaneity of superimpression, and the simultaneity of counter-impression, Gance truly constitutes the image as the absolute movement of the whole which changes. It is no longer the relative domain of the variable interval, of kinetic acceleration or deceleration in the content, but the absolute domain of luminous simultaneity, of light in extension, of the whole which changes and is Spirit (a great spiritual helix, which is sometimes directly revealed in camera-movement in Gance and in L'Herbier). This would be the point of contact with Delaunay's simultaneism.[24]

In short, with Gance the French school invents a cinema of the sublime. The composition of movement-images always presents the image of time in its two aspects: time as interval and time as whole; time as variable present and time as immensity of past and future. For example, in Gance's *Napoleon*, the constant references to the man of the people, to the soldier of the Old Guard, and to the cook, introduce a naive, immediate witness's present chronicle into the epic immensity of a reflected future and past.[25] Conversely, in René Clair we constantly find, in a charming, magical form, this whole of time which runs up against the variations of the present. What appeared in this way with the French school was a new way of conceiving the two signs of time: the interval has become the variable and successive numerical unit, which enters into metrical relationships with the other factors, in each case defining the greatest relative quantity of movement in the content and for the imagination; the whole has become the simultaneous, the measureless, the immense, which reduces imagination to impotence and confronts it with its own limit, giving birth in the spirit to the pure thought of a quantity of absolute movement which expresses its whole history or change, its universe. This is exactly Kant's mathematical sublime. This montage, this conception of montage, was to be described as spiritual-mathematical, psychic-extensive or poetic-quantitative (Epstein spoke of 'lyrosophy').

The French school could be contrasted point by point with German Expressionism. The reply to 'more movement!' is 'more light!' Movement is unleashed, but to serve the light, to make it scintillate, to form or dismember stars, multiply reflections, leave brilliant trails, as in the great music-hall scene in Dupont's *Vaudeville*, or in the dream in Murnau's *The Last Laugh*. Of course light is movement, and the movement-image and the light-image are two facets of one and the same appearing. But light as an immense movement of extension, as before, is very different from the way it is presented in Expressionism – as a potent movement of intensity, intensive movement par excellence. There is indeed an abstract kinetic art (Richter, Ruttmann), but the extensive quantity, the shifting in space, are like the mercury which indirectly measures the intensive quantity, its rise or fall. Light and shadow no longer constitute an alternative movement in extension and enter into an intense struggle which has several stages.

Firstly the infinite force of light is opposed to darkness as an equally infinite force without which it would not be able to manifest itself. It opposes darkness in order to manifest itself. This is therefore not a dualism and neither is it a dialectic, since we are outside any organic unity or totality. It is an infinite opposition as it appeared in Goethe and the Romantics: light would be nothing, or at least nothing manifest, without the opaque to which it is opposed and which makes it visible.[26] The visual image is therefore divided in two along a diagonal or jagged line so that it makes the light 'presuppose a dreary half of shadow', as Valéry says. It is not just a division of the image or the shot, as is already found in Rippert's *Homunculus*, or as rediscovered by Lang and Pabst. It is also a matrix of montage in Pick's *New Year's Eve*, which opposes the opacity of the slum and the luminosity of the elegant hotel, or in Murnau's *Sunrise*, which opposes the luminous town and the opaque marshland. In the second place, the confrontation of two infinite forces determines a zero-point, in relation to which all light is a finite degree. Light's role, effectively, is to develop a relationship with black as negation $= 0$, as a function of which it is defined as intensity, as intensive quantity. Here the instant appeared (contrary to the extensive unit and part) as that which apprehends the luminous magnitude or degree in relation to black. That is why intensive movement is inseparable from a fall, even a virtual one, which only expresses this distance of the degree of light from zero. Only the idea of the fall measures the degree to which the intensive quantity *rises* and, even in its greatest glory, natural light falls and continues to fall. Therefore the idea of fall must also necessarily be actualised, and become a real or material fall in individual beings. Light only has one ideal fall, but daylight has a real fall: such is the adventure of the individual soul, caught up in a black hole, of which Expressionism was to give us some dizzy examples (Marguerite's fall in Murnau's *Faust*, that of the hero of *The Last Laugh*, devoured by the black hole of the washrooms in the grand hotel, or that of Pabst's *Lulu*).

We see here how light as degree (white) and the zero (black) enter into concrete relations of contrast or mixing. As we have seen, this is the whole contrasting series of white and black lines, rays of light and outlines of shadow: a striated, striped world which could already be seen in the painted canvases of Wiene's *The Cabinet of Dr Caligari*, but which took on its full range of luminous values with Lang in *Die Nibelungen* (for example the light in the undergrowth, or the clusters of lamps through the window). Or else it is the blended series of chiaroscuro, the continual transformation of all its degrees, forming a 'fluid range of gradations which constantly succeed one another', Wegener and, above all, Murnau, were the masters of this formula. In fact the great directors were able to advance on both fronts, and while Lang achieved the most subtle chiaroscuros (*Metropolis*) Murnau traced out the most contrasting rays: thus in *Sunrise* the scene of the search for the drowned woman starts with the luminous streaks of the lanterns on the black waters, giving way suddenly to the transformations of a chiaroscuro which graduates the tones along its whole track. However much he differs from Expressionism (particularly in his conception of time and the fall of souls), Stroheim takes over its treatment of light and appears as a luminist as profound as Lang and even Murnau: sometimes this is shown in a series of streaks as the luminous bars that the half-closed slatted shutters project on to the bed, the face and shoulders of the sleeping woman in *Foolish Wives*; sometimes in all the degrees of chiaroscuro, with back-lighting and the play of soft-focus, as in the dinner of *Queen Kelly*.[27]

In all this, Expressionism was breaking with the principle of organic composition introduced by Griffith and taken up by most of the Soviet dialecticians. But it made this rupture in a completely different way from the French school. It does not invoke the clear mechanics of the quantity of movement in the solid or the fluid but a dark, swampy life into which everything plunges, whether chopped up by shadows or plunged into mists. *The non-organic life of things*, a frightful life, which is oblivious to the wisdom and limits of the organism, is the first principle of Expressionism, valid for the whole of Nature, that is, for the unconscious spirit, lost in darkness, light which has become opaque, *lumen opacatum*. From this point of view natural substances and artificial creations, candelabras and trees, turbine and sun are no longer any different. A wall which is alive is dreadful; but utensils, furniture, houses and their roofs also lean, crowd around, lie in wait, or pounce. Shadows of houses pursue the man running along the street.[28] In all these cases, it is not the mechanical which is opposed to the organic: it is the vital as potent pre-organic germinality, common to the animate and the inanimate, to a matter which raises itself to the point of life, and to a life which spreads itself through all matter. The animal has lost the organic, as much as matter has gained life. Expressionism can claim kinship with a pure kinetics; it is a violent movement which respects neither the organic contour nor the mechanical determinations of the horizontal and the vertical; its course is that of a perpetually broken line, where each change of direction simultaneously marks the force of an obstacle and the power of a new impulse; in short, the subordination of the extensive to intensity. Worringer, its first theoretician, created the term 'Expressionism', and defined it as the opposition of vital force [*élan vital*] to organic representation, invoking the 'Gothic or Northern' decorative line, a broken line which forms no contour by which form and background might be distinguished, but passes in a zigzag between things, sometimes drawing them into a bottomlessness in which it loses itself, sometimes whirling them in a formlessness into which it veers in a 'disorderly convulsion'.[29] Thus automata, robots and puppets are no longer mechanisms which validate or 'major' [*majorent*] a quantity of movement, but somnambulists, zombies or golems who express the intensity of this non-organic life: not simply Wegener's *The Golem*, but also the Gothic horror film of around 1930, for example Whale's *Frankenstein* and *The Bride of Frankenstein* and Halpérin's *White Zombie*.

Geometry is not deprived of its rights, but it is a quite different geometry from that of the French school, because it is emancipated – at least directly – from the co-ordinates which condition the extensive quantity, and from the metrical relationships which regulated movement in homogeneous space. It is a 'Gothic' geometry which constructs space instead of describing it: it no longer proceeds by measuring out but by extension and accumulation. The lines are extended beyond all measure to their meeting-points, while their breaking-points produce accumulations. The accumulation may be of light or of shadow, just as the extensions may be of shadow or of light. Lang invents luminous false continuities, which express the intensive changes of the whole. It is a violent perspectivist geometry, which works through projections and expanses of shadow, with oblique perspectives. The diagonals and cross-diagonals tend to replace the horizontal and the vertical, the cone replaces the circle and the sphere, acute angles and sharp triangles replace curved or rectangular lines (Caligari's doors, the Golem's gables and hats). If we compare L'Herbier's monumental architecture with Lang's (*Die Nibelungen, Metropolis*), we see how Lang works by extending lines and points of accumulation which are now only indirectly translated into metrical relationships.[30] And, if the human body enters drectly into these 'geometrical groupings', if it is 'a basic factor in this architecture', it is not exactly because 'stylisation transforms the human into mechanical factor', a formula which would be better suited to the French school; it is because all difference between the mechanical and the human has dissolved, but this time to the advantage of the potent non-organic life of things.

In contrasts of black and white, or in the variations of chiaroscuro, one might say that white is darkened and black is toned down. It is as though two degrees were apprehended in an instant, points of accumulation which would correspond to the upsurge of colour in Goethe's theory: blue as lightened black, yellow as darkened white. And, despite Griffith's and Eisenstein's attempts in monochrome, and even in polychrome, it is undoubtedly Expressionism which was the precursor of real colourism in the cinema. Goethe explained precisely that the two fundamental colours – yellow and blue as degrees – were grasped in a *movement of intensification*, which was accompanied in both cases by a reddish reflection. The intensification of the degree is like the instant raised to the power two, which is expressed in this reflection. The reddish or glowing reflection will pass through all the stages of intensification: shimmering, glistening, scintillation, sparkling, a halo effect, fluorescence, phosphorescence. All these aspects punctuate the creation of the robot in *Metropolis*, like that of Frankenstein and his bride. From them, Stroheim creates extraordinary combinations to which he surrenders living creatures, evildoers or innocent victims alike. Thus, according to Lotte Eisner's analysis, in the supper of *Queen Kelly*, the ingenuous girl is caught between two sources of light, that of the candles on the table before her which *glisten* on her face, and that of the fire in the fireplace behind her which surrounds her with a luminous *halo* (she will therefore be too hot and allow her coat to be removed . . .). But

Murnau is the true master of all these stages and aspects which simultaneously announce the arrival of the Devil and the wrath of God.[31] In fact, Goethe clearly shows that the intensification of the two aspects (yellow and blue) did not stop at the reddish reflection which accompanies them as the growing effects of brilliance, but culminated in a vivid red, as third colour which has become independent, pure incandescence or blazing of a terrible light, which burned the world and its creatures. It is as if finite intensity now recovered, at the height of its own intensification, a burst of the infinite which had been the starting-point. The infinite had not ceased to work in the finite, which reinstates it in this still sensible form. Spirit had not left Nature, it animates all non-organic life, but it can only discover and rediscover itself as the spirit of evil which burns Nature in its entirety. It is the flaming circle of the invocation of the demon, in Wegener's *The Golem* or Murnau's *Faust*. It is Faust's funeral pyre. It is the 'phosphorescent demon's head with sad and empty eyes' in Wegener. It is the blazing head of Mabuse and of Mephisto. These are the moments of the sublime, the rediscovery of the infinite in the spirit of evil: in Murnau, in particular, *Nosferatu* does not merely pass through all the spects of chiaroscuro, of back-lighting and of the non-organic life of shadows, he does not merely produce all the moments of a reddish reflection, but he reaches a climax when a powerful light (a pure red) isolates him from his shadowy background, making him burst forth from an even more direct bottomlessness, giving him an aura of omnipotence which goes beyond his two-dimensional form.[32]

This new sublime is not the same as that of the French school. Kant distinguished two kinds of Sublime, mathematical and dynamic, the immense and the powerful, the measureless and the formless. Both had the property of decomposing organic composition, the first by going beyond it, the second by breaking it. In the mathematical sublime, the extensive unit of measurement changes so much that the imagination is no longer able to comprehend it, runs up against its own limit and is annihilated; but it gives way to a thinking faculty which forces us to conceive the immense or the measureless as whole. In the dynamic sublime, it is intensity which is raised to such a power that it dazzles or annihilates our organic being, strikes terror into it, but arouses a thinking faculty by which we feel superior to that which annihilates us, to discover in us a supra-organic spirit which dominates the whole inorganic life of things: then we lose our fear, knowing that our spiritual 'destination' is truly invincible.[33] Likewise, according to Goethe, blazing red is not merely the frightful colour in which we burn, but the noblest colour, which contains all the others, and engenders a superior harmony as the whole chromatic circle. And this is indeed what happens, or has a chance of happening, in the story which Expressionism tells us, from the aspect of the dynamic sublime: *the non-organic life of things* culminates in a fire, which burns us and which burns all of Nature, acting as the spirit of evil or of darkness. But this latter, by the ultimate sacrifice which it demands of us, unleashes in our soul *a non-psychological life of the spirit*, which no longer belongs either to nature or to our organic individuality, which is the divine part in us, the spiritual relationship in which we are alone with God as light. Thus the soul seems to *rise up again* towards the light; but it has rather rejoined the luminous part of itself, which only had an ideal fall, and which fell upn the world, rather than being engulfed in it. The blazing has become the supernatural and the supra-sensible; for example, Ellen's sacrifice in *Nosferatu*, or that of *Faust*, or even Indre's in *Sunrise*.

We can note, here, the considerable difference between Expressionism and Romanticism. For it is no longer the case, as in Romanticism, of a reconciliation between Nature and Spirit, of Spirit as it is alienated in Nature, and of Spirit as it reconquers itself in itself. This conception was implied as the dialectical development of a totality which was still organic. Whilst Expressionism only conceives in principle the whole of a spiritual Universe engendering its own abstract forms, its creatures of light, its continuities which seem false to the eye of the sensible. It keeps the chaos of man and Nature in the background.[34] Or rather it tells us that there is - and there will only be - chaos if we do not regain this spiritual universe which it often has occasion to doubt itself: often the fire of chaos has the upper hand, or is pronounced as triumphant for a long time to come. In short, Expressionism keeps on painting the world red on red; the one harking back to the frightful non-organic life of things, the other to the sublime, non-psychological life of the spirit. Expressionism attains the cry, Marguerite's cry, Lulu's cry, which marks the horror of non-organic life as much as the opening-up of a spiritual universe which may be illusory. Eisenstein also attained the cry, but in the manner of a dialectician, that is, as the qualitative leap which made the whole evolve. Now, on the contrary, the whole is on high, and is identical to the ideal summit of a pyramid which, in rising up, constantly pushes down its base. The whole has become the truly infinite intensification which is extracted from all the degrees, which has passed through the fire, but only to break its sensible attachments to the material, the organic, and the human, to detach itself from all the states of the past, and thus to discover the spiritual abstract Form of the future (Hans Richter's *Rhythms*).

We have thus seen four types of montage. The movement-images are the subject of very different compositions each time: the organic-active, empirical, or rather empiricist montage of American cinema; the dialectical montage of Soviet cinema, organic or material; the quantitative-psychic montage of the French school, in its break with the organic; the intensive-spiritual montage of the German school, which binds together a non-organic life and a non-psychological life. These are the great visions of film-makers, with their concrete practices. For example, we should not think that parallel montage is a given which is found everywhere, except in a very general sense, since Soviet cinema replaces it with a montage of opposition, Expressionist cinema with a montage of contrast, etc. What we have tried to show is the practical and theoretical variety of types of montage, according to the conceptions of the composition of movement-images, whether organic, dialectical, extensive, or intensive. This was the thought, or the philosophy of the cinema, no less than its technique. It would be obtuse to say that one of these theory-practices was better than another, or represents progress (technical progress was made in each of these directions, and presupposes rather than determines them). The only generality about montage is that it puts the cinematographic image into a relationship with the whole; that is, with time conceived as the Open. In this way it gives an indirect image of time, simultaneously in the individual movement-image and in the whole of the film. On the one hand, it is the variable present; on the other the immensity of future and past. It has seemed to us that the forms of montage determined these two aspects differently. The variable present could become interval, qualitative leap, numerical unit, intensive degree; and the whole could become organic whole, dialectical totalisation, measureless totality of the mathematical sublime, intensive totality of the dynamic sublime. It is only later that we can see the indirect image of time and the comparative probabilities of a direct time-image. At present, if it is true that the movement-image has two facets, one of which is oriented towards sets and their parts, the other towards the whole and its changes, it is this that we must examine – the movement-image for itself, in all its varieties and both its facets.

4 The movement-image and its three varieties
Second commentary on Bergson

1 The identity of the image and the movement

The historical crisis of psychology coincided with the moment at which it was no longer possible to hold a certain position. This position involved placing images in consciousness and movements in space. In consciousness there would only be images – these were qualitative and without extension. In space there would only be movements – these were extended and quantitative. But how is it possible to pass from one order to the other? How is it possible to explain that movements, all of a sudden, produce an image – as in perception – or that the image produces a movement – as in voluntary action? If we invoke the brain, we have to endow it with a miraculous power. And how can movement be prevented from already being at least a virtual image, and the image from already being at least possible movement? What appeared finally to be a dead end was the confrontation of materialism and idealism, the one wishing to reconstitute the order of consciousness with pure material movements, the other the order of the universe with pure images in consciousness.[1] It was necessary, at any cost, to overcome this duality of image and movement, of consciousness and thing. Two very different authors were to undertake this task at about the same time: Bergson and Husserl. Each had his own war cry: all consciousness is consciousness *of* something (Husserl), or more strongly, all consciousness *is* something (Bergson). Undoubtedly many factors external to philosophy explain why the old position had become impossible. These were social and scientific factors which placed more and more movement into conscious life, and more and more images into the material world. How therefore was it possible not to take account of the cinema, which was being developed at that very moment, and which would produce its own evidence of a *movement-image*?

It is true that Bergson, as we have seen, apparently found the cinema only a false ally. As for Husserl, as far as we know, he never mentions the cinema at all (it is noteworthy that Sartre too, much later, in making an inventory and analysis of all kinds of images in

The Imagination, does not cite the cinematographic image). It is Merleau-Ponty who attempts, only incidentally, a confrontation between cinema and phenomenology, but he also sees the cinema as an ambiguous ally. It is simply that the reasons given by phenomenology and those of Bergson are so different that their very opposition should guide us. What phenomenology sets up as a norm is 'natural perception' and its conditions. Now, these conditions are existential co-ordinates which define an 'anchoring' of the perceiving subject in the world, a being in the world, an opening to the world which will be expressed in the famous 'all consciousness is consciousness of something. . .'. Hence movement, perceived or made, must be understood not of course in the sense of an intelligible form (Idea) which would be actualised in a content, but as a sensible form (Gestalt) which organises the perceptive field as a function of a situated intentional consciousness. The cinema can, with impunity, bring us close to things or take us away from them and revolve around them, it suppresses both the anchoring of the subject and the horizon of the world. Hence it substitutes an implicit knowledge and a second intentionality for the conditions of natural perception.[2] It is not the same as the other arts, which aim rather at something unreal through the world, but makes the world itself something unreal or a tale [*récit*]. With the cinema, it is the world which becomes its own image, and not an image which becomes world. It will be noted that phenomenology, in certain respects, stops at pre-cinematographic conditions which explains its embarrassed attitude: it gives a privilege to natural perception which means that movement is still related to *poses* (simply existential instead of essential). As a result, cinematographic movement is both condemned as unfaithful to the conditions of perception and also exalted as the new story capable of 'drawing close to' the perceived and the perceiver, the world and perception.[3]

Bergson condemns the cinema as an ambiguous ally in a completely different way. For if the cinema misconceives movement, it does so in the same way as natural perception and for the same reasons: 'We take snapshots, as it were, of passing reality. . . . Perception, intellection, language so proceed in general.'[4] For Bergson, that is to say, the model cannot be natural perception, which does not possess any privilege. The model would be rather a state of things which would constantly change, a flowing-matter in which no point of anchorage nor centre of reference would be assignable. On the basis of this state of things it would be necessary to show how, at any point, centres can be formed which would impose fixed instantaneous views. It would therefore be a question of 'deducing' conscious, natural *or* cinematographic perception.[5] But the cinema perhaps has a great advantage: just because it lacks a centre of anchorage and of horizon, the sections which it makes would not prevent it from going back up the path that natural perception comes down. Instead of going from the acentred state of things to centred perception, it could go back up towards the acentred state of things, and get closer to it. Broadly speaking, this would be the opposite of what phenomenology put forward. Even in his critique of the cinema Bergson was in agreement with it, to a far greater degree than he thought. We see this in the brilliant first chapter of *Matter and Memory*.

We find ourselves in fact faced with the exposition of a world where IMAGE = MOVEMENT. Let us call the set of what appears 'Image'. We cannot even say that one image acts on another or reacts to another. There is no moving body [*mobile*] which is distinct from executed movement. There is nothing moved which is distinct from the received movement. Every thing, that is to say every image, is indistinguishable from its actions and reactions: this is universal variation. Every image is 'merely a road by which pass, in every direction, the modifications propagated throughout the immensity of the universe'. *Every image acts on others and reacts to others, on 'all their facets at once' and 'by all their elements'.*[6] 'The truth is that the movements of matter are very clear, regarded as images, and that there is no need to look in movement for anything more than what we see in it.'[7] An atom is an image which extends to the point to which its actions and reactions extend. My body is an image, hence a set of actions and reactions. My eye, my brain, are images, parts of my body. How could my brain contain images since it is one image among others? External images act on me, transmit movement to me, and I return movement: how could images be in my consciousness since I am myself image, that is, movement? And can I even, at this level, speak of 'ego', of eye, of brain and of body? Only for simple convenience; for nothing can yet be identified in this way. It is rather a gaseous state. Me, my body, are rather a set of molecules and atoms which are constantly renewed. Can I even speak of atoms? They are not distinct from worlds, from interatomic influences.[8] It is a state of matter too hot for one to be able to distinguish solid bodies in it. It is a world of universal variation, of universal undulation, universal rippling: there are neither axes, nor centre, nor left, nor right, nor high, nor low. . . .

This infinite set of all images constitutes a kind of plane [*plan*] of immanence. The image exists in itself, on this plane. This in-itself of the image is matter: not something hidden behind the image, but on the contrary the absolute identity of the image and movement. The identity of the image and movement leads us to conclude immediately that the movement-image and matter are identical. 'You may say that my body is matter or that it is an image.'[9] The *movement-image* and *flowing-matter* are strictly the same thing.[10] Is this material universe the universe of mechanism? No, for (as *Creative Evolution* shows) mechanism involves closed systems, actions of contact, immobile instantaneous sections. Now, of course, closed systems, finite sets, are cut from this universe or on this plane; it makes them possible by the exteriority of its parts. But it is not one itself. It is a set, but an infinite set. The plane of immanence is the movement (the facet of movement) which is established between the parts of each system and between one system and another, which crosses them all, stirs them all up together and subjects them all to the condition which prevents them from being absolutely closed. It is therefore a section; but, despite some terminological ambiguities in Bergson, it is not an immobile and instantaneous section, it is a mobile section, a temporal section or perspective. It is a bloc of space-time, since the time of the movement which is at work within it is part of it every time. There is even an infinite series of such blocs or mobile sections which will be, as it were, so many presentations of the plane, corresponding to the succession of movements in the universe.[11] And the plane is not distinct from this presentation of planes. This is not mechanism, it is machinism. The material universe, the plane of immanence, is the *machine assemblage*[12] *of movement-images*. Here Bergson is startlingly ahead of his time: it is the universe as cinema in itself, a metacinema. This implies a view of the cinema itself which is totally different from that which Bergson proposed in his explicit critique.

But how is it possible to speak of images in themselves which are not for anyone and are not addressed to anyone? How is it possible to speak of an Appearing [*Apparaître*], since there is not even an eye? It is possible for at least two reasons. The first is in order to distinguish them from things conceived of as bodies. Indeed, our perception and our language distinguish bodies (nouns), qualities (adjectives) and actions (verbs). But actions, in precisely this sense, have already replaced movement with the idea of a provisional place towards which it is directed or that of a result that it secures. Quality has replaced movement with the idea of a state which persists whilst waiting for another to replace it. Body has replaced movement with the idea of a subject which would carry it out or of an object which would submit to it, of a vehicle which would carry it.[13] We will see that such images *are* formed in the universe (action-images, affection-images, perception-images). But they depend on new conditions and certainly cannot appear for the moment. For the moment we only have movements, which are called images in order to distinguish them from everything that they have not yet become. However, this negative reason is not sufficient. The positive reason is that the plane of immanence is entirely made up of Light. The set of movements, of actions and reactions is light which diffuses, which is propagated 'without resistance and without loss'.[14] The identity of the image and movement stems from the identity of matter and light. The image is movement, just as matter is light. Later on Bergson will show, in *Durée et simultanéité*, the importance of the theory of Relativity's reversal of 'lines of light' and 'rigid lines', 'luminous figures' and 'solid or geometric figures': with Relativity 'it is the figure of light which imposes its conditions on the rigid figure'.[15] If we recall Bergson's profound desire to produce a philosophy which would be that of modern science (not in the sense of a reflection on that science, that is an epistemology, but on the contrary in the sense of an invention of autonomous concepts capable of corresponding with the new symbols of science), we can understand that Bergson's confrontation with Einstein was inevitable. Now, the first aspect of this confrontation is the affirmation of a diffusion or propagation of light on the whole plane of immanence. In the movement-image there are not yet bodies or rigid lines, but only lines or figures of light. Blocs of space-time are such figures. They are images in themselves. If they do not appear to anyone, that is to an eye, this is because light is not yet reflected or stopped, and passing 'on unopposed [is] never . . . revealed'.[16] In other words, the eye is in things, in luminous images in themselves. '*Photography, if there is photography, is already snapped, already shot, in the very interior of things and for all the points of space. . . .*'

This breaks with the whole philosophical tradition which placed light on the side of spirit and made consciousness a beam of light which drew things out of their native darkness. Phenomenology was still squarely within this ancient tradition: but, instead of making light an internal light, it simply opened it on to the exterior, rather as if the intentionality of consciousness was the ray of an electric lamp ('all consciousness is consciousness *of* something . . .'). For Bergson, it is completely the opposite. Things are luminous by themselves without anything illuminating them: all consciousness *is* something, it is indistinguishable from the thing, that is from the image of light. But here it is a consciousness by right [*en droit*], which is diffused everywhere and yet does not reveal its source [*ne se révèle pas*]: it is indeed a photo which has already been taken and shot in all things and for all points, but which is 'translucent'. If, subsequently, a *de facto* consciousness is constituted in the universe, at a particular place on the plane of immanence, it is because very special images will have stopped or reflected the light, and will have provided the 'black screen' which the plate lacked.[17] In short, it is not consciousness which is light, it is the set of images, or the light, which is consciousness, immanent to matter. As for *our* consciousness of fact, it will merely be the opacity without which light 'is always propagated without its source ever having been revealed'. The opposition between Bergson and phenomenology is, in this respect, a radical one.[18]

We may therefore say that the plane of immanence or the plane of matter is: a set of movement-images; a collection of lines or figures of light; a series of blocs of space-time.

2 From the movement-image to its varieties

What happens and what can happen in this acentred universe where everything reacts on everything else? We must not introduce a different factor, a factor of another nature. So what can happen is this: at any point whatever of the plane an *interval* appears – a gap between the action and the reaction. All Bergson asks for are movements and intervals between movements which serve as units – it is also exactly what Dziga Vertov asked for, in his materialist conception of the cinema.[19] Clearly, this phenomenon of the interval is only possible in so far as the plane of matter includes time. For Bergson, the gap, the interval, will be sufficient to define one type of image among others, but a very special type – living images or matters [*matières*]. Whereas the other images act and react on all their facets and in all their parts, here we have images which only receive actions on one facet or in certain parts and only execute reactions by and in other parts. These are, so to speak, 'quartered' [*écartelées*][20] images. And from the outset their specialised facet, which will later be called receptive or sensorial, has a curious effect on the influencing images or the received excitations. It is as if this specialised facet isolated certain images from all those which compete and act together in the universe. It is here that closed systems, 'tableaux', can be constituted. Living beings 'allow to pass through them, so to speak, those external influences which are indifferent to them; the others isolated, become "perceptions" by their very isolation'.[21] It is an operation which is exactly described as a *framing*: certain actions undergone are isolated by the frame and hence, as we will see, they are forestalled, anticipated. But, on the other hand, executed reactions are no longer immediately linked with the action which is undergone. By virtue of the interval, these are delayed reactions, which have the time to select their elements, to organise them or to integrate them into a new movement which is impossible to conclude by simply prolonging the received excitation. Such reactions which present something unpredictable or new will be called 'action' strictly speaking. Thus the living image will be 'an instrument of analysis in regard to the movement received, and an instrument of selection in regard to the movement executed'.[22] Because they only owe this privilege to the phenomenon of the gap, or interval between a received and an executed movement, living images will be 'centres of indetermination', which are formed in the acentred universe of movement-images.

If we consider the other aspect, the luminous aspect of the plane of matter, one can say this time that the images or living matter provide the black screen which the plate lacked, and which prevented the influencing image (the photo) from being developed. This time, instead of diffusing and propagating in all directions 'without resistance or dwindling', the line or image of light runs up against an obstacle, that is an opacity which will reflect it. The image reflected by a living image is precisely what will be called perception. And these two aspects are strictly complementary: the special image, the living image, is indissolubly the centre of indetermination or black screen. An essential consequence follows – *the existence of a double system, of a double régime of reference of images*. There is firstly a system in which each image varies for itself, and all the images act and react as a function of each other, on all their facets and in all their parts. But to this is added another system where all vary principally for a single one, which receives the action of the other images on one of its facets and reacts to them on another facet.[23]

We have not finished with the matter-movement-image. Bergson constantly says that we cannot understand anything unless we are first given the set of images. It is only on this plane that a simple interval of movements can be produced. And the brain is nothing but this – an interval, a gap between an action and a reaction. The brain is certainly not a centre of images from which one could begin, but itself constitutes one special image among the others. It constitutes a centre of indetermination in the acentred universe of images. But with the brain-image Bergson puts forward almost immediately, in *Matter and Memory*, a highly complex and organised state of life. This is because he is not considering life as a problem there (and indeed, in *Creative Evolution*, he will give serious consideration to life, but from another point of view). However, it is not difficult to fill in the gaps that Bergson has voluntarily left. Even at the level of the most elementary living beings one would have to imagine micro-intervals. Smaller and smaller intervals between more and more rapid movements. Moreover, biologists speak of 'primeval soup', which made living beings possible, and where forms of matter known as dextrogyres and levogyres play an essential role. It is here that outlines of axes appear in an acentred universe, a left and a right, a high and a low. One should therefore conceive of micro-intervals even in the primeval soup. Biologists say that these phenomena could not be produced when the earth was very hot. Therefore one should conceive of a cooling down of the plane of immanence, correlative to the first opacities, to the first screens obstructing the diffusion of light. It is here that the first outlines of solids or rigid and geometric bodies would be formed. Finally, as Bergson was to say, the same evolution which organises matter into solids will organise the image in more and more elaborate perception, which has solids as its objects.

The thing and the perception of the thing are one and the same thing, one and the same image, but related to one or other of two systems of reference. The thing is the image as it is in itself, as it is related to all the other images to whose action it completely submits and on which it reacts immediately. But the perception of the thing is the same image related to another special image which frames it, and which only retains a partial action from it, and only reacts to it mediately. In perception thus defined, there is never anything else or anything more than there is in the thing: on the contrary, there is 'less'.[24] We perceive the thing, minus that which does not interest us as a function of our needs. By need or interest we mean the lines and points that we retain from the thing as a function of our receptive facet, and the actions that we select as a function of the delayed reactions of which we are capable. Which is a way of defining the first material moment of subjectivity: it is subtractive. It subtracts from the thing whatever does not interest it. But, conversely, the thing itself *must* then be presented in itself as a complete, immediate, diffuse perception. The thing is image and, in this respect, is perceived itself and perceives all the other things inasmuch as it is subject to their action and reacts to them on all its facets and in all its parts. An atom, for example, perceives infinitely more than we do and, at the limit perceives the whole universe – from the point where the actions which are exercised on it begin, to the point where the actions which it emits go. In short, things and perceptions of things are *prehensions*, but things are total objective prehensions, and perceptions of things are incomplete and prejudiced, partial, subjective prehensions.

If the cinema does *not* have natural subjective perception as its model, it is because the mobility of its centres and the variability of its framings always lead it to restore vast acentred and deframed zones. It then tends to return to the first régime of the movement-image; universal variation, total, objective and diffuse perception. In fact, it travels the route in both directions. From the point of view which occupies us for the moment, we go from total, objective perception which is indistinguishable from the thing, to a subjective perception which is distinguished from it by simple elimination or subtraction. It is this unicentred subjective perception that is called perception strictly speaking. And it is the first avatar of the movement-image: when it is related to a centre of indetermination, it becomes *perception-image*.

However, we should not think that the whole operation consists only of a subtraction. There is something else as well. When the universe of movement-images is related to one of these special images which forms a centre in it, the universe is incurved and organised to surround it. We continue to go from the world to the centre, but the world has taken on a curvature, it has become a periphery, it forms a horizon.[25] We are still in the perception-image, but we are already entering the action-image as well. In fact, perception is only one side of the gap, and action is the other side. What is called action, strictly speaking, is the delayed reaction of the centre of indetermination. Now, this centre is only capable of acting – in the sense of organising an unexpected response – because it perceives and has received the excitation on a privileged facet, eliminating the remainder. All this amounts to recalling that all perception is primarily sensory-motor: perception 'is no more in the sensory centres than in the motor centres; it measures the complexity of their relations'.[26] If the world is incurved around the perceptive centre, this is already from the point of view of action, from which perception is inseparable. By incurving, perceived things tender their unstable facet towards me, at the same time as my delayed reaction, which has become action, learns to use them.

Distance is in fact a radius [*rayon*] which goes from the periphery to the centre: perceiving things here where they are, I grasp the 'virtual action' that they have on me, and simultaneously the 'possible action' that I have on them, in order to associate me with them or to avoid them, by diminishing or increasing the distance. It is thus the same phenomenon of the gap which is expressed in terms of time in my action and in terms of space in my perception. The more the reaction ceases to be immediate and becomes truly possible action, the more the perception becomes distant and anticipatory and extracts the virtual action of things. 'Perception is master of space in the exact measure in which action is master of time.'[27]

This is therefore the second avatar of the movement-image: it becomes *action-image*. One passes imperceptibly from perception to action. The operation under consideration is no longer elimination, selection or framing, but the incurving of the universe, which simultaneously causes the virtual action of things on us and our possible action on things. This is the second material aspect of subjectivity. And, just as perception relates movement to 'bodies' (nouns), that is to rigid objects which will serve as moving bodies or as things moved, action relates movement to 'acts' (verbs) which will be the design for an assumed end or result.[28]

But the interval is not merely defined by the specialisation of the two limit-facets, perceptive and active. There is an in-between. Affection is what occupies the interval, what occupies it without filling it in or filling it up. It surges in the centre of indetermination, that is to say in the subject, between a perception which is troubling in certain respects and a hesitant action. It is a coincidence of subject and object, or the way in which the subject perceives itself, or rather experiences itself or feels itself 'from the inside' (third material aspect of subjectivity).[29] It relates movement to a 'quality' as lived state (adjective). Indeed, it is not sufficient to think that perception – thanks to distance – retains or reflects what interests us by letting pass what is indifferent to us. There is inevitably a part of external movements that we 'absorb', that we refract, and which does not transform itself into either objects of perception or acts of the subject; rather they mark the coincidence of the subject and the object in a pure quality. This is the final avatar of the movement-image: *the affection-image*. It would be wrong to consider it a failure of the perception-action system. On the contrary, it is a third absolutely necessary given. For we, living matter or centres of indetermination, have specialised one of our facets or certain of our points into receptive organs at the price of condemning them to immobility, while delegating our activity to organs of reaction that we have consequently liberated. In these conditions, when our immobilised receptive facet absorbs a movement instead of reflecting it, our activity can only respond by a 'tendency', an 'effort' which replaces the action which has become momentarily or locally impossible. This is the origin of Bergson's wonderful definition of affection as 'a kind of motor tendency on a sensible nerve', that is, a motor effort on an immobilised receptive plate.[30]

There is therefore a relationship between affection and movement in general which might be expressed as follows: the movement of translation is not merely interrupted in its direct propagation by an interval which allocates on the one hand the received movement, and on the other the executed movement, and which might make them in a sense incommensurable. Between the two there is affection which re-establishes the relation. But, it is precisely in affection that the movement ceases to be that of translation in order to become movement of expression, that is to say quality, simple tendency stirring up an immobile element. It is not surprising that, in the image that we are, it is the face, with its relative immobility and its receptive organs, which brings to light these movements of expression while they remain most frequently buried in the rest of the body. All things considered, *movement-images divide into three sorts of images when they are related to a centre of indetermination as to a special image*: perception-images, action-images and affection-images. And each one of us, the special image or the contingent centre, is nothing but an assemblage [*agencement*] of three images, a consolidate [*consolidé*] of perception-images, action-images and affection-images.

3 *The reverse proof: how to extinguish the three varieties*

We might also retrace the lines of differentiation of these three types of images, and try to rediscover the matrix or the movement-image as it is in itself, in its acentred purity, in its primary régime of variation, in its heat and its light, while it is still untroubled by any centre of indetermination. How can we rid ourselves of ourselves, and demolish ourselves? This is the astonishing attempt made by Beckett in his cinematographic work entitled *Film*, with Buster Keaton. *Esse est percipi*, to be is to be perceived, declares Beckett, taking up the Irish Bishop Berkeley's formula of the image. But can one escape from 'the happinesses of the percipere and the percipi' – given that one perception at least will subsist as long as we live, the most awesome, that of self by self? Beckett elaborates a system of simple cinematographic conventions in order to pose the problem and carry out the operation. Nevertheless, in our view, the directions and the schemas that he gives himself, and the moments that he distinguishes in his film, only go half-way towards disclosing his intention.[31] For, in fact, the three moments are the following. In the first, the character O rushes forward and flees horizontally along a wall; then, along a vertical axis, tries to climb a staircase, always sticking to the edge of the wall. He 'acts', it is a perception of action, or an *action-image*, subject to the following convention: the camera OE only films him from the back, from an angle not exceeding forty-five degrees; if the camera which follows him happens to exceed this angle, the action will be blocked, extinguished, the character will stop, hiding the threatened part of his face. The second moment: the character has come into a room and, as he is no longer against a wall, the angle of immunity of the camera is doubled – forty-five degrees on each side, thus ninety degrees. O perceives (subjectively) the room, the things and the animals which are there, whilst OE perceives (objectively) O himself, the room, and its contents: this is the perception of perception, or the *perception-image*, considered under a double régime, in a double system of reference. The camera remains subject to the condition, that it does not exceed ninety degrees behind the character, but the convention which is added is that the character must expel the animals, and cover up all the objects which can act as mirrors or even frames, in such a way that the subjective perception is eliminated and only the objective perception OE remains. Then O can be installed in the rocking chair and rock gently with his eyes closed. But it is at this moment, the third and last, that the greatest danger is revealed: the extinction of subjective perception has freed the camera of the forty-five degree restriction. With great caution, it advances beyond, into the domain of the remaining two hundred and seventy degrees, but each time wakens the character who regains a scrap of subjective perception, hides, curls up and forces the camera to move back again. Finally, taking advantage of O's torpor, OE succeeds in coming round to face him, and comes closer and closer to him. The character O is thus now seen from the front, at the same time as the new and last convention is revealed: the camera OE is the double of O, the same face, a patch over one eye (monocular vision), with the single difference that O has an anguished expression and OE has an attentive expression: the impotent motor effort of the one, the sensitive surface of the other. We are in the domain of the perception of affection, the most terrifying, that which still survives when all the others have been destroyed: it is the perception of self by self, the *affection-image*. Will it die out and will everything stop, even the rocking of the rocking chair, when the double face slips into nothingness? This is what the end suggests – death, immobility, blackness.[32]

But, for Beckett, immobility, death, the loss of personal movement and of vertical stature, when one is lying in a rocking chair which does not even rock any more, are only a subjective finality. It is only a means in relation to a more profound end. It is a question of attaining once more the world before man, before our own dawn, the position where movement was, on the contrary, under the régime of universal variation, and where light, always propagating itself, had no need to be revealed. Proceeding in this way to the extinction of action-images, perception-images and affection-images, Beckett ascends once more towards the luminous plane of immanence, the plane of matter and its cosmic eddying of movement-images. He traces the three varieties of image back to the mother movement-image. We will see later that an important tendency of the so-called experimental cinema consists in recreating this acentred plane of pure movement-images in order to establish itself there: and there it often uses complex technical means. But here Beckett's originality is to be content to elaborate a symbolic system of simple conventions – according to which the three images are successively extinguished – as the condition which makes possible this general tendency of the experimental cinema.

For the moment we are taking the opposite path – from the movement-image to the varieties which it takes on. We already have, therefore, four kinds of images: firstly *movement-images*. Then, when they are related to a centre of indetermination, they divide into three varieties – *perception-images, action-images, affection-images*. There is every reason to believe that many other kinds of images can exist. Indeed, the plane of movement-images is a mobile section of a Whole which changes, that is, of a duration or of a 'universal becoming'. The plane of movement-images is a bloc of space-time, a temporal perspective, but, in this respect, it is a perspective on real Time which is not at all the same as the plane [*plan*] or the movement. We are therefore justified in thinking that there are time-images which are themselves capable of having all kinds of varieties. In particular, there are indirect images of time, in so far as they result from a comparison of movement-images between themselves, or from a combination of the three varieties – perceptions, actions, affections. But this point of view which makes the whole depend on 'montage', or the time of the confrontation of images of another kind, does not give us a time-image for itself. On the other hand the centre of indetermination, which can avail itself of a special situation on the plane of movement-images, can itself have a special relationship with the whole, duration or time. Perhaps here there is the possibility of a direct time-image: for example, what Bergson calls the 'memory-image', or other types of time-image, but which would be in any event very different from movement-images? Thus we have a great number of varieties of images of which we would have to make an inventory.

C. S. Peirce is the philosopher who went the furthest into a systematic classification of images. The founder of semiology, he necessarily associated with it a classification of signs which is the richest and the most numerous that has ever been established.[33] We do not yet know what relationship Peirce proposes between the sign and the image. It is clear that the image gives rise to signs. For our part, a sign appears to be a particular image which represents a type of image, sometimes from the point of view of its composition, sometimes from the point of view of its genesis or its formation (or even its extinction). Therefore there are several signs – two at least for each type of image. We will have to compare the classification of images and signs that we propose with Peirce's great classification: why do they not coincide, even at the level of distinct images? But, before this analysis – which can only be carried out later – we will constantly use the terms that Peirce created to designate particular signs, sometimes retaining their sense, sometimes modifying it or even changing it completely (for reasons that we will make clear each time).

We will begin here by setting out the three sorts of movement-images and the search for corresponding signs. It is easy, in the cinema, to recognise on a practical level these three kinds of images which pass across the screen, without even making use of explicit criteria. The scene from Lubitsch's *The Man I Killed* which was mentioned previously is an exemplary perception-image: the crowd seen from behind, at waist height, leaves a gap which corresponds to a cripple's missing leg; through this gap another cripple, who is legless, sees the parade which passes. Fritz Lang provides a famous example of the action-image in *Dr Mabuse the Gambler*: an organised action, segmented in space and in time, with the synchronised watches whose ticking punctuates the murder in the train, the car which carries off the stolen document, the telephone which warns Mabuse. The action-image will remain marked by this model, to the point of finding a privileged milieu in the *film noir* and the ideal of a detailed segmentarised action in the hold-up. In comparison, the Western presents not only action-images, but also an almost pure perception-image: it is a drama of the visible and of the invisible as much as an epic of action; the hero only acts because he is the first to see, and only triumphs because he imposes on action the interval or the second's delay which allows him to see everything (Anthony Mann's *Winchester '73*). As for the affection-image, we will find striking cases in the face of Dreyer's Joan of Arc, and in most of the close-ups of the face in general.

A film is never made up of a single kind of image: thus we call the combination of the three varieties, montage. Montage (in one of its aspects) is the assemblage [*agencement*] of movement-images, hence the inter-assemblage of perception-images, affection-images and action-images. Nevertheless a film, at least in its most simple characteristics, always has one type of image which is dominant: one can speak of an active, perceptive or affective montage, depending on the predominant type. It has often been said that Griffith invented montage precisely by creating the montage of action. But Dreyer invents a montage and even a framing of affection, with other laws, in so far as *The Passion of Joan of Arc* is the case of an almost exclusively affective film. Vertov is perhaps the inventor of properly perceptive montage, which was to be developed by the whole of the experimental cinema. These three kinds of spatially determined shots can be made to correspond to these three kinds of varieties: the long shot would be primarily a perception-image; the medium shot an action-image; the close-up an affection-image. But, at the same time, according to one of Eisenstein's instructions, each of these movement-images is a point of view on the whole of the film, a way of grasping this whole, which becomes affective in the close-up, active in the medium shot, perceptive in the long-shot – each of these shots ceasing to be spatial in order to become itself a 'reading' of the whole film.[34]

5 The perception-image

1 The two poles, objective and subjective

We have seen that perception was double, or rather had a double reference. It can be objective or subjective. But the difficulty lies in knowing how an objective perception-image and a subjective perception-image are presented in the cinema. What distinguishes them? It could be said that the subjective-image is the thing seen by someone 'qualified', or the set as it is seen by someone who forms part of that set. This reference of the image to the person who sees is marked by various factors. There is the sensory factor, in the famous example from Gance's *La Roue*, where the character whose eyes are damaged sees his pipe in soft focus. There is the active factor, when the dance or the festival are seen by someone taking part in it: as in a film by Epstein or L'Herbier. There is the affective factor, which makes the hero of Fellini's *The White Sheikh* be perceived by the woman who admires him as if he were swaying at the top of an enormous tree, while in fact he is see-sawing just above the ground. But, if it is easy to check the subjective character of the image, this is because we compare it with the modified, restored image, which is supposed to be objective: we will see the white sheikh come off his grotesque see-saw; we had seen the pipe and the injured man before we saw the pipe seen by the injured man. It is here that the difficulty begins.

We should be able to say, in fact, that the image is objective when the thing or the set are seen from the viewpoint of someone who remains external to that set. And this is a possible definition, but one which is purely nominal, negative, and provisional. For what is to tell us that what we initially think external to a set may not turn out to belong to it? Lewin's *Pandora and the Flying Dutchman* opens with the long shot of a beach where groups are running towards a point; the beach is seen from a distance and from a height, through a telescope on the promontory of a house. But very quickly we learn that the house is inhabited, and the telescope used, by people who are very much part of the set under consideration: the beach, the point which attracts the groups, the event taking place there, the people mixed up in it. . . . Has the image not become subjective, as in Lubitsch's example? And is it not the cinema's perpetual destiny to make us move from one of its poles to the other, that is, from an objective perception to a subjective perception, and vice versa? It is therefore our two initial definitions which are nominal, and merely nominal.

Jean Mitry noted the importance of one of the functions of the 'shot–reverse shot' complementarity: when it intersects with that other complementarity, 'observer-observed'. First of all we are shown someone watching, then what he sees. But we cannot even say that the first image is objective and the second subjective. For what is seen, in the first image, is already subjective, observing. And, in the second image, the observed may be shown for itself, no less than for the observing character. Furthermore, an extreme contraction of the shot-reverse shot may take place as in L'Herbier's *El Dorado*, where the distraught woman who sees in soft focus is herself seen in soft focus. Consequently, if the cinematographic perception-image constantly passes from the subjective to the objective, and vice versa, should we not ascribe to it a specific, diffuse, supple status, which may remain imperceptible, but which sometimes reveals itself in certain striking cases? Very early on, the mobile camera anticipated characters, recaptured them, let them go or picked them up again. Very early too, in Expressionism, it filmed or followed a character from behind (Murnau's *Tartuffe*, Dupont's *Vaudeville*). Finally, the liberated camera performed 'tracking shots in a closed circuit' (Murnau's *The Last Laugh*) in which it no longer confines itself to following characters, but moves amongst them. In response to these developments, Mitry put forward the notion of the generalised semi-subjective image, in order to designate this 'being-with' of the camera: it no longer mingles with the character, nor is it outside: it is with him.[1] It is a kind of truly cinematographic *Mitsein* – or what Dos Passos aptly called 'the eye of the camera', the anonymous viewpoint of someone unidentified amongst the characters.

Let us suppose the perception-image to be semi-subjective. But it is difficult to find a status for this semi-subjectivity, since it has no equivalent in natural perception. This is why Pasolini, for his part, used a linguistic analogy. It might be said that a subjective perception-image is a direct discourse and, in a more complex way, that the objective perception-image is like an indirect discourse (the spectator sees the character in such a way as to be able, sooner or later, to state what the latter is supposed to be seeing). Now Pasolini thought that the essential element of the cinematographic image corresponded neither to a direct discourse, nor to an indirect discourse, but to a *free indirect discourse*. This form, which is particularly prominent in Italian and Russian, raises many problems for grammarians and linguists: it consists of an enunciation [*énonciation*] taken within an utterance [*énoncé*], which itself depends on another enunciation. For example, in French 'Elle rassemble son énergie: *elle souffrira plutôt la torture que perdre sa virginité*' [She summons up her strength: *she will rather endure torture than lose her virginity*]. The linguist Bakhtin, from whom we borrow this example, states the problem clearly: there is not a simple combination of two fully-constituted subjects of enunciation, one of which would be reporter, the other reported. It is rather a case of an assemblage of enunciation, carrying out two inseparable acts of subjectivation simultaneously, one of which constitutes a character in the first person, but the other of which is present at his birth and brings him on to the scene. There is no mixture or average of two subjects, each belonging to a system, but a differentiation of two correlative subjects in a system which is itself heterogeneous. This view of Bakhtin's - which seems to be taken up by Pasolini - is very interesting; also very difficult.[2] It is no longer metaphor which is the fundamental act of language, inasmuch as it 'homogenises' the system; it is free indirect discourse, inasmuch as it testifies to a system which is always heterogeneous, far from equilibrium. Free indirect discourse, however, is not amenable to linguistic categories, because these are only concerned with homogeneous or homogenised systems. It is a matter of style, of stylistics, Pasolini says. And Pasolini adds a valuable comment: the richer a language is in dialects, the more it allows free indirect discourse to flourish, or rather instead of establishing itself on an 'average level' it is differentiated into 'low language and high language' (sociological condition). For his part, Pasolini calls this operation of the two systems of enunciation, or of the two languages in free indirect discourse, Mimesis. This word is perhaps unfortunate, since it is not a case of imitation, but of correlation between two asymmetrical proceedings, acting within language. It is like communicating vessels. However, Pasolini clung to the word 'Mimesis' to emphasise the sacred character of the operation.

Can we not find this dividing-in-two, or this differentiation of the subject in language, in thought and in art? It is the *Cogito*: an empirical subject cannot be born into the world without simultaneously being reflected in a transcendental subject which thinks it and in which it thinks itself. And the *Cogito* of art: there is no subject which acts without another which watches it act, and which grasps it as acted, itself assuming the freedom of which it deprives the former. 'Thus two different egos [*moi*] one of which, conscious of its freedom, sets itself up as independent spectator of a scene which the other would play in a mechanical fashion. But this dividing-in-two never goes to the limit. It is rather an oscillation of the person between two points of view on himself, a hither-and-thither of the spirit. . .', a being-with.[3]

What, in all this, relates to the cinema? Why does Pasolini think that the cinema is involved, to the extent that an equivalent of free indirect discourse, in the image, allows 'the cinema of poetry' to be defined? A character acts on the screen, and is assumed to see the world in a certain way. But simultaneously the camera sees him, and sees his world, from another point of view which thinks, reflects and transforms the viewpoint of the character. Pasolini says: the director 'has replaced wholesale the neurotic's vision of the world by his own delirious vision of aestheticism'. It is in fact a good thing that the character should be neurotic, to indicate more effectively the difficult birth of a subject into the world. But the camera does not simply give us the vision of the character and of his world; it imposes another vision in which the first is transformed and reflected. This subdivision is what Pasolini calls a 'free indirect subjective'. We will not say that the cinema is always like this – we can see images in the cinema which claim to be objective or subjective – but here something else is at stake: it is a case of going beyond the subjective and the objective towards a pure Form which sets itself up as an autonomous vision of the content. We are no longer faced with subjective *or* objective images; we are caught in a correlation between a perception-image and a camera-consciousness which transforms it (the question of knowing whether the image was objective or subjective is no longer raised). It is a very special kind of cinema which has acquired a taste for 'making the camera felt'. And Pasolini analyses a certain number of stylistic procedures which illustrate this reflecting consciousness or this properly cinematographic *Cogito*: 'insistent' or 'obsessive' framing, which makes the camera await the entry of a character into the frame, wait for him to do and say something and then exit, while it continues to frame the space which has once again become empty, once more leaving the scene to its pure and absolute signification as scene; 'the alternation of different lenses on a same image' and 'the excessive use of the zoom', which doubles the perception of an independent aesthetic consciousness. . . . In short, the perception-image finds its status, as free indirect subjective, from the moment that it reflects its content in a camera-consciousness which has become autonomous ('cinema of poetry').

It may be that the cinema had to go through a slow evolution before attaining self-consciousness. Pasolini cites as examples Antonioni and Godard. And, indeed, Antonioni is one of the masters of obsessive framing: in it the neurotic, or the man losing his identity, enters into a 'free indirect' relationship with the poetic vision of the director who affirms himself in him, through him, whilst at the same time distinguishing himself from him. The pre-existing frame produces a curious detachment in the character, who watches himself act. The images of the neurotic man or woman thus become the visions of the director, who advances and reflects *through* the phantasms of his hero. Is this the reason why modern cinema has such need for neurotic characters: to sustain the free indirect discourse, or the 'low language' of the present-day world? But if Antonioni's vision of poetic consciousness is essentially aesthetic, Godard's is rather 'technicist' (but no less poetic). As Pasolini aptly comments, Godard also uses characters who are undoubtedly ill, 'seriously affected', but who are not undergoing treatment, and who have lost nothing of their material degrees of freedom, who are full of life, and who rather represent the birth of a new anthropological type.[4]

Pasolini might have added himself and Rohmer to his list of examples. For what characterises Pasolini's cinema is a poetic consciousness, which is not strictly aestheticist or technicist, but rather mystical or 'sacred'. This allows Pasolini to bring the perception-image, or the neurosis of his characters, on to a level of vulgarity and bestiality in the lowest subject-matter, while reflecting them in a pure poetic consciousness, animated by the mythical or sacralising element. It is this permutation of the trivial and the noble, this communication between the excremental and the beautiful, this projection into myth, which Pasolini had already diagnosed in free indirect discourse as the essential form of literature. And he succeeds in making it into a cinematographic form, capable of grace as well as horror.[5] As for Rohmer, he is perhaps the most striking example of the construction of free indirect subjective images, this time through the intermediary of a truly ethical consciousness. It is very strange, because these two directors – Pasolini and Rohmer – do not seem to have known each other's work very well, but it was they who looked the hardest for a new status for the image, both in order to express the modern world, and in order to introduce an equivalence between the cinema and literature. In Rohmer, on the one hand, it is a case of making the camera a formal ethical consciousness capable of bearing the free indirect image of the modern, neurotic world (the series of *Moral Tales*); on the other, of reaching a point common to the cinema and literature, with which Rohmer, like Pasolini, can only make contact by inventing a type of optical and sound image which is the exact equivalent of an indirect discourse (this leads Rohmer to the creation of two seminal works: *The Marquise of O* and *Perceval*).[6] They transformed the problem of the relationship of the image with the word, the sentence or the text: this is the origin of the special role of the commentary and the insert in their films.

What interests us for the moment is not the relationship with language, which we will only be able to consider later. Of Pasolini's extremely important thesis we retain only this: that the perception-image might find a particular status in the free indirect subjective, which would be like a reflexion of the image in a camera-self-consciousness. Knowing whether the image is objective or subjective no longer matters: it is semi-subjective, if one wishes, but this semi-subjectivity does not indicate anything variable or uncertain. It no longer marks an oscillation between two poles, but an immobilisation according to a higher aesthetic form. The perception-image finds here the particular sign of its composition. We might call it – to borrow one of Peirce's terms – a dicisign (but for Peirce this is the proposition in general, while for us it is the special case of the free indirect proposition, or rather, of the corresponding image). The camera-consciousness then takes on an extremely formal determination.

2   *Towards another state of perception: liquid perception*

This solution, however, only relates to a nominal definition of 'subjective' and 'objective'. It implies that the cinema has reached an evolved state, having learned to mistrust the movement-image. But what happens if we take as our starting-point a real definition of the two poles, or of the double system? Bergsonianism suggested the following definition: *a subjective perception is one in which the images vary in relation to a central and privileged image; an objective perception is one where, as in things, all the images vary in relation to one another, on all their facets and in all their parts.* These definitions affirm not only the difference between two poles of perception, but also the possibility of passing from the subjective to the objective pole. For the more the privileged centre is itself put into movement, the more it will tend towards an acentred system where the images vary in relation to one another and tend to become like the reciprocal actions and vibrations of a pure matter. What can be more subjective than a delirium, a dream, a hallucination? But what can be closer to a materiality made up of luminous wave and molecular interaction? The French school and German Expressionism discovered the subjective image, but at the same time they took it to the limits of the universe. By putting the centre of reference itself into movement, the movement of the parts was raised to the set [*ensemble*]; that of the relative to the absolute; that of succession to simultaneism. In Dupont's *Vaudeville* it was the music-hall scene where the swaying trapeze-artiste sees the crowd and the ceiling, one in the other, as a shower of sparks and a whirlpool of floating spots.[7] And in Epstein's *Coeur fidèle*, it was the travelling fair, where everything tends towards the simultaneity of the movement of the one who sees and the movement seen, in the dizzy disappearance of fixed points. Here the perception-image had already undoubtedly been transformed by an aesthetic consciousness (cf. the French school's famous 'photogeny'). But this aesthetic consciousness was not yet formal and reflected consciousness which went beyond movement – it was a naive, or rather non-thetic consciousness, as the phenomenologists would say, a consciousness in act [*en acte*], which amplified movement and introduced it into matter, with all the delight of discovering the activity of montage and of the camera. It was something different, neither better nor worse.

Jean Renoir's predilection for running water has often been discussed. But this predilection was common to all the members of the French school (although Renoir gave it a very special dimension). In the French school, it is sometimes the river and its course, sometimes the canal, its locks and its barges, sometimes the sea, its frontier with the land, the port, the lighthouse as luminous quality. If the idea of a passive camera had occurred to them, they would have set it up beside running water. L'Herbier had started off with a plan, *Le Torrent*, in which water was to be the main character. And *L'Homme du large* treated the sea not merely as an object of particular perception, but as a perceptive system distinct from earthly perceptions, a 'language' different from earthly language.[8] A considerable part of Epstein's and Grémillon's work forms a sort of Breton school, which realises the cinematographic dream of a drama without characters, or at least which would move from Nature to man. Why does water seem to correspond to all the requirements of this French school: abstract aesthetic requirement, social documentary requirement, narrative dramatic requirement? It is firstly because water is the most perfect environment in which movement can be extracted from the thing moved, or mobility from movement itself. This is the origin of the visual and auditory importance of water in research on rhythm. The liquid element was to prolong, transmit and diffuse in all directions what Gance had started with iron, with the railway. Jean Mitry, in his experimental attempts, began with the railway, and then moved on to water as the image which could give us the real as vibration in its deepest sense: from *Pacific 231* to *Images pour Debussy*.[9] And Grémillon's documentary work passes through this movement, from the mechanics of solids to a mechanics of fluids, from industry to its marine background.

The liquid abstract is also the concrete environment of a type of men, of a race of men who do not live in quite the same way as those of the earth, do not perceive and feel like them: Ouessant and then Sein gave Epstein the perfect documentary, where the inhabitants alone can play their own role (*Finis Terrae*, *The Sea of Ravens*). Finally, the limit of the earth and the waters becomes the scene of a drama where there is a confrontation between, on one hand, the land moorings and, on the other, the mooring – ropes, the two-ropes and free floating cords. Epstein's *La belle Nivernaise* already opposed – in relation to the barge – the solidity of the earth to the fluidity of the sky and the water, Grémillon's *Maldone* opposed the organisation of roots, land and household to the assemblage of the canal: 'man–ship–horse'. The drama was that it was necessary to break the links with the earth, of father with son, husband with wife and mistress, woman with lover, children with parents; to retreat into solitude to achieve human solidarity, class solidarity. And although a final reconciliation is not ruled out, the lighthouse or the dam were the scene of a deadly confrontation between the madness of the earth and the superior justice of the water; the lunacy of the furious son in *Gardiens de la phare*; the great fall of the lord in fancy dress in *Lumière d'été*. Of course not every occupation is related to the sea: but Grémillon's idea is that the proletarian or the worker reconstitutes everywhere – even on land and in the aerial element of *The Woman Who Dared* – the conditions of a floating population, of a sea people, capable of revealing and transforming the nature of the economic and commercial interests at play in a society, on the condition that, following the Marxist formula, it 'cuts the umbilical cord which attaches it to the earth'.[10] It is in this sense that occupations connected with the sea are not a relic or an insular type of folklore: they are the horizon of all occupations, even that of the woman doctor in *L'Amour d'une femme*. They extract the relationship with the Element and with Man, which is present in any occupation; and even mechanics, industry, proletarianisation find their truth in an empire of the seas (or of the air). Grémillon vigorously opposed the family and peasant [*terrien*] ideal of Vichy. Few directors have filmed man's work so well, even discovering in it the equivalent of a sea: even the avalanches of stones like waves.

These are the two opposed systems: the perceptions, affections and actions of men on land, and the perceptions, affections and actions of men of the sea. This comes across clearly in Grémillon's *Stormy Waters*, where the captain on land is drawn back to fixed centres, images of the wife or lover, image of the villa facing the sea, which are all so many points of egoistical subjectivation, whilst the sea presents him with an objectivity as universal variation, solidarity of all the parts, justice beyond men, where the fixed point of the tow-ropes, always called into question, no longer has validity except between two movements. But it is Vigo's *L'Atalante* which was to bring this opposition to its peak. As J. P. Bamberger shows, on land there is not the same régime of movement, not the same 'grace' as on the sea, in the sea: terrestrial movement is in perpetual disequilibrium because the motive force is always outside the centre of gravity (the newsvendor's bicycle); while aquatic movement is like the displacement of the centre of gravity, according to a simple objective law, straight or elliptical. (This accounts for the apparent clumsiness of this movement when it takes place on land or even on the barge – a crab-like walk, snaking or twirling – but this is like an other-worldly grace.) And on land, movement always takes place from one point to another, always between two points, while on water the point is always between two movements: it thus marks the conversion or the inversion of movement, as in the hydraulic relationship of a dive and counter-dive, which is found in the movement of the camera itself (the final fall of the entwined bodies of the two lovers has no end, but is converted into an ascending movement). Nor is it the same régime of passion, of affection: in one case dominated by commodities, the fetish, the article of clothing, the partial object and the memory-object: in the other case, attaining what has been called the 'objectivity' of bodies, which may reveal hideousness under clothing, but also grace under a coarse appearance. If there is any reconciliation between land and sea, this takes place in father Jules, but only because he knows how to impose spontaneously on the land the same law as the sea: his cabin contains the most extraordinary fetishes, partial objects, souvenirs and scrap; however, he does not make them a memory, but a pure mosaic of present states, down to the old record which works again.[11] Finally, a clairvoyant function is developed in water, in opposition to earthly vision: it is in the water that the loved one who has disappeared is revealed, as if perception enjoyed a scope and interaction, a truth which it did not have on land. Even in Nice, it was the very presence of water which allowed the bourgeoisie to be described as a monstrous organic body.[12] It is the water which revealed the hideousness of bourgeois bodies beneath their clothes, just as it now reveals the softness and strength of the loved one's body. The bourgeoisie is reduced to the objectivity of a fetish-body, a scrap-body, to which childhood, love, navigation oppose their integral bodies. 'Objectivity', equilibrium, justice are not of the earth: they are the preserve of water.

Finally, what the French school found in water was the promise or implication of another state of perception: a more than human perception, a perception not tailored to solids, which no longer had the solid as object, as condition, as milieu. A more delicate and vaster perception, a molecular perception, peculiar to a 'cine-eye'. This was the result of starting from a real definition of the two poles of perception: the perception-image was not to be reflected in a formal consciousness, but was to be split into two states, one molecular and the other molar, one liquid and the other solid, one drawing along and effacing the other. The sign of perception would not therefore be a 'dicisign', but a *reume*.[13] While the dicisign set up a frame which isolated and solidified the image, the *reume* referred to an image in the process of becoming liquid, which passed through or under the frame. The camera-consciousness became a *reume* since it was actualised in a flowing perception and thus arrived at a material determination, at a flowing-matter. The French school, however, pointed towards this other state, this other perception, this clairvoyant function, rather than assuming full responsibility for it. Other than in its abstract attempts (among which Vigo's *Taris, roi de l'eau* features), it created from it not the new image, but the limit or ultimate point of convergence of the movement-images, of the average-images in the context of a story that retained its solidity. This story was so deeply imbued with rhythm that this was certainly no defect.

3   *Towards a gaseous perception*

In the 'cine-eye', Vertov was aiming to attain or regain the system of universal variation, in itself. All the images vary as a function of each other, on all their facets and in all their parts. Vertov himself defined the cine-eye: it is that which 'couples together any point whatsoever of the universe in any temporal order whatsoever'.[14] Everything is at the service of variation and interaction: slow or high speed shots, superimposition, fragmentation, deceleration [*démultiplication*], micro-shooting [*micro-prise de vue*]. This is not a human eye – even an improved one. For, although the human eye can surmount some of its limitations with the help of contraptions and instruments, there is one which it cannot surmount, since it is its own condition of possibility. Its relative immobility as a receptive organ means that all images vary for a single one, in relation to a privileged image. And, if the camera is considered as apparatus for shooting film, it is subject to the same conditioning limitation. But the cinema is not simply the camera: it is montage. And if from the point of view of the human eye, montage is undoubtedly a construction, from the point of view of another eye, it ceases to be one; it is the pure vision of a non-human eye, of an eye which would be in things. Universal variation, universal interaction (*modulation*) is what Cézanne had already called the world before man, 'dawn of ourselves', 'iridescent chaos', 'virginity of the world'. It is not surprising that we have to construct it since it is given only to the eye which we do not have. It says a lot for Mitry's partisanship that he could condemn in Vertov a contradiction for which he would not dare to reproach a painter: a pseudo-contradiction between creativity (montage) and integrity (the real).[15] What montage does, according to Vertov, is to carry perception into things, to put perception into matter, so that any point whatsoever in space itself perceives all the points on which it acts, or which act on it, however far these actions and reactions extend. This is the definition of objectivity, 'to see without boundaries or distances'. Thus in this respect all procedures are legitimate, they are no longer trick shots.[16] The materialist Vertov realises the materialist programme of the first chapter of *Matter and Memory* through the cinema, the in-itself of the image. Vertov's non-human eye, the cine-eye, is not the eye of a fly or of an eagle, the eye of another animal. Neither is it – in an Epsteinian way – the eye of the spirit endowed with a temporal perspective, which might apprehend the spiritual whole. On the contrary, it is the eye of matter, the eye in matter, not subject to time, which has 'conquered' time, which reaches the 'negative of time', and which knows no other whole than the material universe and its extension (here Vertov and Epstein are contrasted as two different levels of the same montage-camera set).

This is Vertov's first assemblage. It is, first, a machine assemblage of movement-images. We have seen that the gap, the interval between two movements sketches out an empty place which prefigures the human subject in so far as he appropriates perception to himself. But, for Vertov, the most important thing was to restore the intervals to matter. This is the meaning of montage, and of the 'theory of intervals', which is more profound than that of movement. The interval is no longer that which separates a reaction from the action experienced, which measures the incommensurability and unforeseeability of the reaction but, on the contrary, that which – an action being given in a point of the universe – will find the appropriate reaction in some other point [*point quelconque*], however distant it is ('to find in life the response to the treated subject, the resultant among the millions of facts which bear a relation to this subject'). The originality of the Vertovian theory of the interval is that it no longer marks a gap which is carved out, a distancing between two consecutive images but, on the contrary, a correlation of two images which are distant (and incommensurable from the viewpoint of our human perception). And, on the other hand, the cinema could not run in this way from one end of the universe to the other without having at its disposal an agent which was capable of making all the parts converge: what Vertov took from the spirit – that is, the power of a whole which is constantly becoming – now passes into the correlate of matter, of its variations and interactions. In fact the machine assemblage of things, of images in themselves, has as its correlate a collective assemblage of enunciation. Already in the silent film, Vertov used the intertitle in an original way, so the word formed a bloc with the image, a sort of ideogram.[17] These are the two fundamental aspects of the assemblage: the image-machine is inseparable from a type of utterances, from a properly cinematographic enunciation. In Vertov this is clearly a case of Soviet revolutionary consciousness, of the 'communist deciphering of reality'. It is that which unites the man of tomorrow with the world before man, communist man with the material universe of interactions defined as 'community' (reciprocal action between the agent and the patient).[18] *A Sixth of the World* shows the interaction at a distance, within the USSR, between the most varied peoples, herds of animals, industries, cultures, exchanges of all kinds in the process of conquering time.

Annette Michelson is right to say that *Man with a Movie-Camera* represents an evolution on Vertov's part, as though he had discovered a more complete conception of the assemblage. For the previous conception went no further than the movement-image, that is, an image composed of photogrammes, an intermediate-image endowed with movement. It was therefore still an image corresponding to human perception, whatever the treatment to which it was subjected by montage. But what happens if montage is introduced into the very constituent of the image? We go back from an image of a peasant woman to a series of its photogrammes, or else we move from a series of photogrammes of children to images of these children in movement. By extending this procedure, we contrast the image of a cyclist cycling, and the same image, re-filmed, reflected, presented as though projected on a screen. René Clair's *The Crazy Ray* had a great influence on Vertov: for it reconciled a human world with the absence of man. For the ray of the mad scientist (the film-maker) froze movement, blocked the action, in order to release it in a sort of 'electrical discharge'. The town-desert, the town absent from itself, will always haunt the cinema, as though possessing a secret. The secret is yet another meaning of the notion of interval: it now designates the point at which movement stops and, in stopping, gains the power to go into reverse, accelerate, slow down. . . . No longer is it enough to reverse movement, as Vertov did in the name of interaction when he moved from the dead meat to the live flesh. The point which makes the reversal or modification necessary must be reached.[19] For, in Vertov's view, the frame is not simply a return to the photo: if it belongs to the cinema, this is because it is the genetic element of the image, or the differential element of the movement. It does not 'terminate' the movement without also being the principle of its acceleration, its deceleration and its variation. It is the vibration, the elementary solicitation of which movement is made up at each instant, the *clinamen* of Epicurean materialism. Thus the photogramme is inseparable from the series which makes it vibrate in relation to the movement which derives from it. And, if the cinema goes beyond perception, it is in the sense that it reaches to the *genetic element* of all possible perception, that is, the point which changes, and which makes perception change, the differential of perception itself. Vertov thus puts the three inseparable aspects of a single going beyond into effect: from the camera to montage, from movement to the interval, from the image to the photogramme.

As a Soviet film-maker, Vertov develops a scientific conception of montage. But dialectical montage seems to be a place of confrontation, of opposition rather than an intermediary. When Eisenstein condemns Vertov's 'Formalist fooling about', this must surely be because the two directors have neither the same conception, nor the same practice of the dialectic. For Eisenstein, there is only a dialectic of man *and* of Nature, man in Nature, and Nature in man; 'non-indifferent' Nature and non-separated Man. For Vertov, the dialectic is in matter and of matter, and can only reconcile a non-human perception with the overman of the future, material community and formal communism. This helps us to reach a conclusion about the differences between Vertov, on the one hand, and the French school on the other. If we consider the identical procedures used by both – quantitative montage, high speed and slow motion, superimposition, or even immobilisation – we see that with the French these show primarily a spiritual power of the cinema, a spiritual aspect of the 'shot'. It is through the spirit that man goes beyond the limits of perception, and, as Gance says, superimpositions are the images of feelings and thoughts by which the soul 'envelops' bodies and 'precedes' them. Vertov's use of these procedures is quite different: for him superimposition was to express the interaction of distant material points, and high speed and slow motion the differential of physical movement. But perhaps even from this point of view we do not grasp the radical difference. It emerges as soon as we return to the reasons which made the French give such prominence to the liquid image: for it was there that human perception went beyond its own limits, and movement discovered the spiritual totality which it expressed, whilst for Vertov the liquid image is still inadequate, failing to reach the particle of matter. Movement must go beyond itself, but to its material, energic element. The cinematographic image does not therefore have the '*reume*' as sign, but the 'gramme', the 'engramme', the 'photogramme'. It is its sign of genesis. In the final analysis, we would have to speak of a perception which was no longer liquid but gaseous. For, if we start out from a solid state, where molecules are not free to move about (molar or human perception), we move next to a liquid state, where the molecules move about and merge into one another, but we finally reach a gaseous state, defined by the free movement of each molecule. According to Vertov, it is perhaps necessary to move beyond flowing to that stage: the particle of matter or gaseous perception.

In any case, the American experimental cinema was to go as far as that and, breaking with the French school's aquatic lyricism, was to recognise Vertov's influence. A whole aspect of that cinema is concerned with attaining a pure perception, as it is in things or in matter, to the point to which molecular interactions extend. Brakhage explores a Cézannian world before man, a dawn of ourselves, by filming all the shades of green seen by a baby in the prairie.[20] Michael Snow deprives the camera of any centre and films the universal interaction of images which vary in relation to one another, on all their facets and in all their parts (*The Central Region*).[21] Belson and Jacobs trace coloured forms and movements back to molecular or atomic forces (*Phenomena, Momentum*). Now, if there is any constant factor in this cinema, it is the construction by various means of gaseous states of perception. Flickering montage: extraction of the photogramme beyond the intermediate image, and of vibration beyond movement, (whence the notion of the 'photogramme-shot', as defined by the loop procedure, in which a series of photogrammes are repeated with the contingent intervals allowed by the superimposition). Hyper-rapid montage: extraction of a point of inversion or transformation (for the correlation of the immobilisation of the image is the extreme mobility of the support, and the photogramme acts as the differential element, producing refulgence and great haste). Refilming or re-recording: extraction of a particle of matter (the refilming producing a flattening of space, which takes on a 'pointilliste' texture in the manner of Seurat, allowing the interaction of two points at a distance to be apprehended).[22] In all these respects, the photogramme is not a reversion to photography but rather, following Bergson's formula, the creative apprehension of this photo 'snapped and taken in the interior of things and for all the points of space'. And we are increasingly witnessing, from the photogramme to the video, the formation of an image defined by molecular parameters.

All these procedures act together and vary to form the cinema as machine assemblage of matter-images. The question of the corresponding assemblage of enunciation remains open, since Vertov's answer (Communist society) has lost its meaning. Might the answer be: drugs as the American community? If drugs have this effect, however, it is only because of the perceptive experimentation which they induce, which may be brought about by quite different means. In reality, we will only be able to raise the problem of enunciation when we are in a position to analyse the sound image for itself. To follow Castaneda's programme of initiation: drugs are supposed to *stop the world*, to release the perception of 'doing', that is, to substitute pure auditory and optical perceptions for motor-sensory perceptions; *to make one see the molecular intervals*, the holes in sounds, in forms, and even in water; but also, in this stopped world, *to make lines of speed pass through* these holes in the world.[23] This is the programme of the third state of the image, the gaseous image, beyond the solid and the liquid: to reach 'another' perception, which is also the genetic element of all perception. Camera-consciousness raises itself to a determination which is no longer formal or material, but genetic and differential. We have moved from a real to a genetic definition of perception.

Landow's film, *Bardo Follies*, sums up in this respect the whole of the process, and the transition from the liquid state to the gaseous state:

*

The film opens with an image, on a film loop, of a woman floating with a lifebouy, who waves to us at each return of the loop. After about ten minutes (there is also an abridged version), the same loop appears twice inside two circles on a black ground. Then, for a moment, three circles appear. The image of the film in the circles starts to burn, inducing the spread of a seething mould of a predominantly orange colour. The whole screen is filled by the photogramme on fire, which disintegrates in slow motion into a very granular soft focus. Another photogramme burns; the whole screen throbs with melting celluloid. This effect was probably obtained by several series of re-filmings on screen, the result being that the screen itself seems to throb and be consumed. The tension of the desynchronised loop is kept up throughout the whole of this fragment, in which the film itself seems to die. After a long pause, the screen divides up into bubbles of air in water, filmed through a microscope with coloured filters, a different colour for each side of the screen. By means of changes in focal distance, the bubbles lose their form and dissolve into each other, and the four coloured filters are mingled. At the end – some forty minutes after the first loop – the screen turns blank.[24]

6 The affection-image
Face and close-up

1 The two poles of the face: power and quality

The affection-image is the close-up, and the close-up is the face....
Eisenstein suggested that the close-up was not merely one type of
image among others, but gave an affective reading of the whole film.
This is true of the affection-image: it is both a type of image and a
component of all images. But that is not all there is to it. In what sense
is the close-up identical to the whole affection-image? And why
would the face be identical to the close-up, since the latter merely seems
to carry out a magnification *of the* face, and also of many other things?
And how can we extract poles which can guide us in the analysis of
the affection-image from the magnified face?

Let us start from an example which is *not* a face: a clock which is
presented to us in close-up several times. Such an image does indeed
have two poles. On the one hand it has hands moved by micro-
movements, at least virtual ones, even if we are only shown it once, or
several times at long intervals: the hands necessarily form part of an
intensive series which marks an ascent towards . . . or tends towards a
critical instant, prepares a paroxysm. On the other hand it has a face as
receptive immobile surface, receptive plate of inscription, impassive
suspense: it is a *reflecting and reflected unity*.

The Bergsonian definition of the affect rested on these two very
characteristics: a motor tendency on a sensitive nerve. In other
words, a series of micro-movements on an immobilised plate of
nerve. When a part of the body has had to sacrifice most of its
motoricity in order to become the support for organs of reception,
the principal feature of these will now only be tendencies to
movement or micro-movements which are capable of entering into
intensive series, for a single organ or from one organ to the other.
The moving body has lost its movement of extension, and movement
has become movement of expression. It is this combination of a
reflecting, immobile unity and of intensive expressive movements
which constitutes the affect. But is this not the same as a Face itself?
The face is this organ-carrying plate of nerves which has sacrificed
most of its global mobility and which gathers or expresses in a free
way all kinds of tiny local movements which the rest of the body

usually keeps hidden. Each time we discover these two poles in something – reflecting surface and intensive micro-movements – we can say that this thing has been treated as a face [*visage*]: it has been 'envisaged' or rather 'faceified' [*visagéifiée*], and in turn it stares at us [*dévisage*], it looks at us . . . even if it does not resemble a face. Hence the close-up of the clock. As for the face itself, we will not say that the close-up deals with [*traite*] it or subjects it to some kind of treatment: there is no close-up *of* the face, the face is in itself close-up, the close-up is by itself face and both are affect, affection-image.

In painting, the techniques of the portrait have accustomed us to these two poles of the face. Sometimes painting grasps the face as an outline, by an encircling line which traces the nose, the mouth, the edge of the eyelids, and even the beard and the cap: it is a surface of faceification [*visagéification*]. Sometimes, however, it works through dispersed features taken globally; fragmentary and broken lines which indicate here the quivering of the lips, there the brilliance of a look, and which involve a content which to a greater or lesser extent rebels against the outline: these are the traits of faceicity [*visagéité*].[1] And it is no accident that the affect appeared from these two points of view in the great conceptions of the Passions which run through both philosophy and painting: what Descartes and Le Brun call *admiration*, which marks a minimum of movement for a maximum of unity, reflecting and reflected on the face; and what is called *desire*, inseparable from the little solicitations or impulsions which make up an intensive series expressed by the face. It matters little that some consider admiration to be the origin of the passions precisely because it is the degree zero of movement, whilst others put desire first, or restlessness, because immobility itself presupposes the reciprocal neutralisation of the corresponding micro-movements. Rather than an exclusive origin, it is a matter of two poles, sometimes one prevailing over the other and appearing almost pure, sometimes the two being mixed in one direction or the other.

There are two sorts of questions which we can put to a face, depending on the circumstances: what are you thinking about? Or, what is bothering you, what is the matter, what do you sense or feel? Sometimes the face thinks about something, is fixed on to an object, and this is the sense of admiration or astonishment that the English word *wonder* has preserved. In so far as it thinks about something, the face has value above all through its surrounding outline, its reflecting unity which raises all the parts to itself. Sometimes, on the contrary, it experiences or feels something, and has value through the intensive series that its parts successively traverse as far as paroxysm, each part taking on a kind of momentary independence. We can already recognise in this the two types of close-up, one of which was the hallmark of Griffith, and the other of Eisenstein. There are famous Griffith close-ups in which everything is organised for the pure and soft outline of a feminine face (notably the iris procedure): a young woman thinks about her husband in *Enoch Arden*. But, in Eisenstein's *The General Line*, the handsome face of the priest is dissolved, giving way to a cheating look which links up with the narrow back of the head and the fleshy earlobe: it is as if the traits of faceity were escaping the outline, and testifying to the priest's *ressentiment*.

It should not be thought that the first pole is reserved for the tender emotions and the second for dark passions. It will be recalled, for example, how Descartes considers contempt to be a special case of 'admiration'.[2] On the one hand there are reflecting acts of spitefulness, reflected terrors and despairs, even, and above all, in Griffith's or Stroheim's young women. On the other hand there are the intensive series of love or tenderness. Moreover, each aspect brings together very different states of the face. The aspect of *wonder* can affect an impassive face which is pursuing an impenetrable or criminal thought: but it can equally take possession of a juvenile or curious face, so animated by little movements that these dissolve and are neutralised (thus in Sternberg, *The Scarlet Empress* - a girl again - looks in all directions and is surprised by everything when the Russian envoys take her away). And the other aspect has no less variety depending on the series considered.

Where, therefore, is the criterion of distinction? In fact, we find ourselves before an intensive face each time that the traits break free from the outline, begin to work on their own account, and form an autonomous series which tends toward a limit or crosses a threshold: ascending series of anger, or, as Eisenstein says, 'the rising line of annoyance' (*Battleship Potemkin*). This is why this serial aspect is best embodied by several simultaneous or successive faces, although a single face can suffice if it puts its different organs or features into series. Here the intensive series discloses its function, which is to pass from one quality to another, to emerge on to a new quality. To produce a new quality, to carry out a qualitative leap, this is what Eisenstein claims for the close-up: from the priest-man of God to the priest-exploiter of peasants; from the anger of the sailors to the revolutionary explosion; from the stone to the scream, as in the three postures of the marble lions ('and the stones have roared').

On the other hand, we are before a reflexive or reflecting face as long as the features remain grouped under the domination of a thought which is fixed or terrible, but immutable and without becoming, in a way eternal. In Griffith's *Broken Blossoms*, the martyred girl nevertheless retains a petrified face, which, even in death still seems to reflect and ask why, whilst the Chinese lover, for his part, preserves on his face the stupor of opium and the reflection of Buddha. Admittedly, this case of the reflecting face seems less well determined than the other, for this relationship between a face and what it is thinking about is often arbitrary. We can only know that Griffith's young woman is thinking about her husband because we see the image of the husband immediately afterwards: we had to wait and the link seems to be merely associative. So it can be safer to reverse the order, and to begin with a close-up of the object which will inform us of the imminent thought of the face: in Pabst's *Lulu* the close-up of the knife prepares us for the terrible thought of Jack the Ripper (or in Clouzot's *The Murderer Lives at Number 21* the whirling groups of three objects make us understand that the heroine is thinking of the figure 3 as key to the mystery). However, we have not yet reached the most profound aspect of the reflection-face. Mental reflection is undoubtedly the process by which one thinks of something. But it is cinematographically accompanied by a more radical reflection expressing a pure quality, which is common to several different things (the object which carries it, the body which submits to it, the idea which represents it, the face which has this idea. . .). The reflecting faces of young women in Griffith can express white, but it is also the white of a snowflake caught on an eye-lash, the spiritual white of an internal innocence, the dissolved white of a moral degradation, the hostile and searing white of the iceberg where the heroine will wander (*Orphans of the Storm*). In *Women in Love* Ken Russell was able to play with the quality common to a hardened face, an internal frigidity, a funereal glacier. In short, the reflecting face is not content to think about something. Just as the intensive face expresses a pure Power – that is to say, is defined by a series which carries us from one quality to another – the reflexive face expresses a pure Quality, that is to say a 'something' common to several objects of different kinds. We can therefore draw up a table of the two poles:

Sensible nerve	Motor tendency
Immobile receptive plate	Micro-movements of expression
Faceifying outline	Characteristics of faceicity
Reflecting unity	Intensive series
Wonder	Desire

(admiration, surprise)	(love-hate)
Quality	Power
Expression of a quality common to several different things	Expression of a power which passes from one quality to another

2 Griffith and Eisenstein

Pabst's *Lulu* shows the extent to which one goes from one pole to the other in a relatively short sequence: first the two faces, of Jack and of Lulu, are relaxed, smiling, dreamy, *wondering;*[3] then Jack's face, above Lulu's shoulder, sees the knife and goes into an ascending series of terror (*'the fear becomes a paroxysm . . . his pupils grow wider and wider . . . the man gasps in terror . . .'*); finally Jack's face relaxes, Jack accepts his destiny and now reflects death as a quality common to his killer's mask, the availability of the victim and the irresistible call of the instrument: *'the knife blade gleams. . .'.*[4]

It is certainly true that in a given director one of the poles will prevail but it is always in a more complex way than one would at first think. Eisenstein writes in a famous text: 'It is the kettle which began. . . .' (You will recognize here, he says, a phrase from Dickens, but also one of Griffith's close-ups, the kettle looks at us.)[5] In this text, he analyses the difference between himself and Griffith from the point of view of the close-up or the affection-image. He says that Griffith's close-up is merely subjective, that is to say it is concerned with the spectator's conditions of vision, that it remains separated, and only has an associative or anticipatory role. Whilst his own, Eisenstein's, close-ups are faded, objective and dialectical, for they produce a new quality, they carry out a qualitative leap. We recognise immediately the duality of the reflexive face and the intensive face, and it is true that Griffith gave precedence to one, Eisenstein to the other. Nevertheless, Eisenstein's analysis is too hasty, or rather partial. For in his work there are also outline-faces, strong in thought: the Tsarina Anastasia, when she has a foreboding of death; Alexander Nevsky, the pensive hero *par excellence*. And most importantly, there are already intensive series in Griffith: sometimes on a single face, when, starting from amazement or from global bewilderment, annoyance or fear arise and assume different features (*Hearts of the World, Broken Blossoms*); sometimes even on several faces, when the close-ups of the combatants punctuate the whole of the battle (*Birth of a Nation*).

It is true that these different faces in Griffith do not follow one another immediately, but their close-ups alternate with long shots, according to a binary structure which he favours (public–private, collective–individual).[6] In this sense, Eisenstein's innovation was not to have invented the intensive face, nor even to have constituted the intensive series with several faces, several close-ups; it was to have produced compact and continous intensive series, which go beyond all binary structures and exceed the duality of the collective and the individual. Rather, they attain a new reality which could be called Dividual, directly uniting an immense collective reflection with the particular emotions of each individual; in short expressing the unity of power and quality.

It appears that a director always gives pre-eminence to one of the two poles – reflecting face or intensive face – but also gives himself the means to get back to the other pole. We would like to consider under this head another pair, that of Expressionism and lyrical abstraction. Of course, Expressionism can be just as abstract as lyricism. But the route is not at all the same. Expressionism is essentially the intensive play of light with the opaque, with darkness [*ténèbres*]. Their mixture is like the power which makes people fall into the black hole or ascend towards the light. This mixture constitutes a series, sometimes in an alternating form of streaks or lines, sometimes in the compact, ascending and descending form of all the degrees of shadow which have value as colours. The Expressionist face concentrates the intensive series, in both forms which disturb its outline and deprive it of its features. In this way the face participates in the non-organic life of things as the primary pole of Expressionism. A striated, striped face, caught in a more or less fine net, catching the effects of a Venetian blind, of a fire, of foliage, of sun through trees. A vaporous, cloudy, smokey face, enveloped by a more or less dense veil. Attila's dark and furrowed head in Lang's *Die Nibelungen*. But at the maximum point of concentration or at the extreme limit of the series, we might say that the face is surrendered to the indivisible light or to the white quality, as to Kriemhilde's unshakeable reflection. It regains its firm outline and passes to the other pole; life of the mind or spiritual non-psychological life. The reddish reflections which accompanied the whole series of degrees of shadow are reunited, they form a halo around the face which has become phosphorescent, scintillating, brilliant, a being of light. Brilliance emerges out of the shadows, we pass from intensification to reflection. This operation may still be that of the devil, in the infinitely melancholy form of a demon who reflects the gloom, in a circle of flames where the non-organic life of things burns (the demon of Wegener's *Golem* or of Murnau's *Faust*). But it can be a divine operation when mind is reflected in itself, in the form of a Gretchen saved by a supreme sacrifice, ectoplasm or photogramme which would eternally consume itself in reaching the luminous internal life (in Murnau again, Ellen of *Nosferatu* or even Indre of *Sunrise*).

Lyrical abstraction in Sternberg proceeds completely differently. Sternberg is no less Goethean than the Expressionists, but he reflects another aspect of Goethe. This is the other aspect of the theory of colours: light no longer has to do with darkness, but with the transparent, the translucent or the white. The book translated into French as *Memoirs of a Shadow Showman* [*Souvenirs d'un montreur d'ombres*] is really entitled *Fun in a Chinese Laundry* [*Drôleries dans une blanchisserie chinoise*]. Everything happens between the light and the white. It is Sternberg's genius to have brought to realisation Goethe's splendid formula: 'between transparency and white opacity there exists an infinite number of degrees of cloudiness [*trouble*]. . . . One could call white the fortuitously opaque flash of pure transparency.'[7] This is because the white, for Sternberg, is primarily that which circumscribes a space corresponding to the luminous. And into this space is inserted a close-up face which reflects the light. Thus Sternberg begins from the reflexive or qualitative face. In *The Scarlet Empress*, we first of all see the white *wonder*[8] face of the young girl which inserts its outline in the narrow space delimited by a white wall and the white door which she closes again. But later, at the birth of her son, the face of the young woman is caught between the white of a voile curtain and the white of the pillow and the sheets where she is resting, until we see the astonishing image, which seems to have come from video, where the face is now only a geometric incrustation of the voile. The white space itself is in turn circumscribed, redoubled by a veil or a net which is superimposed, and gives it a volume, or rather what one calls in oceanography (but also in painting) a shallow depth. Sternberg has a great practical knowledge of linens, tulles, muslins and laces: he draws from them all the resources of a white on white within which the face reflects the light. Claude Ollier has analysed, in relation to *The Saga of Anatahan*, this reduction of space by abstraction, this compression of the location by artificiality which defines a field of operation and leads us by elimination of the whole universe, to a pure woman's face.[9] Between the white of the veil and the white of the background, the face holds itself up like a fish, and can lose its outline in giving way to a soft focus, a blurred shot ['*bougé*'], without losing anything of its reflecting power. One reaches aquarium atmospheres, as in Borzage, another adherent of this lyrical abstraction. The nets and the voile curtains of Sternberg are therefore quite distinct from the expressionist veils and nets – as his soft focuses are from their chiaroscuro.

It is no longer the struggle of light with darkness, but light's adventure with white: this is Sternberg's anti-Expressionism. We should not conclude that Sternberg confines himself to pure quality, and to its reflecting aspect, and that he is unaware of powers or intensities. Ollier impressively demonstrates that the more white space is closed and exiguous, the more precarious and open to the virtualities of the outside it is. As is said in *Shanghai Gesture*, 'anything can happen at any moment'. Everything is possible. . . . A knife cuts the net, a red-hot iron makes a hole in the veil, a dagger pierces the paper partition. The closed world will pass through the intensive series, depending on the rays, the people and the objects which penetrate it. The affect is made up of these two elements: the firm qualification of a white space, but also the intense potentialisation of that which is going to happen there.

We can certainly not say that Sternberg is ignorant of shadows and the series of their degrees up to darkness. He simply begins from the other pole, or from pure reflection. As early as in *The Docks of New York* the smoke fumes are white opacities, whose shadows are only consequences. Thus very early on Sternberg has the idea of what he wants. Later, even in *Macao* where the veils, the nets and also the Chinese have passed into shadow, space remains determined and distributed by the white suits of the two protagonists. The point is that for Sternberg, darkness does not exist by itself: it merely marks the place where the light stops. And shadow is not a mixture, but merely a result, a consequence – a consequence that cannot be separated from its premises. What are these premises? It is transparent, translucent or white space that has just been defined. Such a space retains the power to reflect light, but it also gains another power which is that of refracting, by diverting the rays which cross it. The face which remains in this space thus reflects a part of the light, but refracts another part of it. From being reflexive, it becomes intensive. Here there is something unique in the history of the close-up. The classical close-up ensures a partial reflection in so far as the face looks in a direction different from that of the camera, and thus forces the spectator to rebound on the surface of the screen. We are also familiar with very fine 'camera-looks', as in Bergman's *Summer with Monika*, which establish a total reflection and give the close-up a distance which is proper to it. But Sternberg seems to have been alone in doubling the partial reflection of a refraction, thanks to the translucent or white milieu that he was able to construct. Proust spoke of white veils 'whose super-imposition only refracts more richly the central captive ray which crosses them'. At the same time as the luminous rays manifest a deviation in space, the face – that is, the affection-image – is displaced, raised in the shallow depth, darkened at the edges, and enters an intensive series depending on whether the figure slides towards the dark edge, or the edge slides towards the light figure. The close-ups of *Shanghai Express* form an extraordinary series of variations at the edges. From the point of view of a prehistory of colour it is the opposite of Expressionism. Instead of a light which emerges from degrees of shadow by accumulation of red and extraction of brilliance, we have a light which creates degrees of blue shadow and puts brilliance into shadow (in *Shanghai Gesture*, the shadows affect the zone of the eyes in the face).[10] Sternberg is able to obtain effects analogous to those of Expressionism, as in *The Blue Angel*; but this is by simulation, with completely different means, inasmuch as refraction is much closer to a form of Impressionism where shadow is always a consequence. This is not just a parody of Expressionism, but more often a form of rivalry, that is to say a production of the same effects by opposite principles.

3 The affect as entity

We have seen the two poles of the affect – power and quality – and how the face necessarily passes from one to the other depending on the particular case. What compromises the integrity of the close-up in this respect is the idea that it presents to us a partial object, detached from a set or torn away from a set of which it would form part. Psychoanalysis and linguistics both get something out of this view, the one because it believes that it has discovered in it a structure of the unconscious (castration) in the image, the other that it has discovered in it a constitutive procedure of language (synecdoche, *pars pro toto*). When critics accept the idea of the partial object, they see in the close-up the mark of a fragmentation or a cut, some saying that it has to be reconciled with the continuity of the film, others that it shows, on the contrary, an essential filmic discontinuity. But in fact, the close-up, the close-up of the face, has nothing to do with a partial object (except in one case that we will see later). As Balázs has already accurately demonstrated, the close-up does *not* tear away its object from a set of which it would form part, of which it would be a part, but on the contrary *it abstracts it from all spatio-temporal co-ordinates*, that is to say it raises it to the state of Entity. The close-up is not an enlargement and, if it implies a change of dimension, this is an absolute change: a mutation of movement which ceases to be translation in order to become expression.

The expression of an isolated face is a whole which is intelligible by itself. We have nothing to add to it by thought, nor have we anything to add to that which is of space or time. When a face that we have just seen in the middle of a crowd is detached from its surroundings, put into relief, it is as if we were suddenly face to face with it. Or furthermore if we have seen it before in a large room, we will no longer think of this when we scrutinise the face in close-up. For the expression of a face and the signification of this expression have no relation or connection with space. Faced with an isolated face, we do not perceive space. Our sensation of space is abolished. A dimension of another order is opened to us.[11]

This is what Epstein was suggesting when he said: this face of a fleeing coward, as soon as we see it in close-up, we see cowardice in person, the 'feeling-thing', the entity.[12] If it is true that the cinematic image is always deterritorialised, there is therefore a very special deterritorialisation which is specific to the affection-image. And when Eisenstein criticised the others – Griffith or Dovzhenko – he reproached them for having sometimes failed in their close-ups because they allowed them to have a connotation of the spatio-temporal co-ordinates of a place, of a moment, without attaining what he himself called the 'pathetic' which element is apprehended in the ecstasy or the affect. [13]

What is curious is that Balázs denies to other close-ups what he has just accepted for the face: a hand, a part of the body or an object would remain irremediably in space, and would therefore become close-ups only as partial objects. This is to fail to recognise both the constancy of the close-up through its varieties and the strength of any object from the point of view of expression. Firstly, there is a great variety of close-ups of faces: sometimes outline, sometimes feature; sometimes a single face and sometimes several; sometimes successively, sometimes simultaneously. They can include a background, notably in the case of depth of field. But, in all these cases, the close-up retains the same power to tear the image away from spatio-temporal co-ordinates in order to call forth the pure affect as the expressed. Even the place, which is still present in the background, loses its co-ordinates and becomes 'any space whatever' [*espace quelconque*] (which restricts Eisenstein's objection). A feature of faceicity [*visagéité*] is no less a complete close-up than a whole face. It is merely another pole of the face, and there is as much intensity expressed by a feature as there is quality by the whole face. So there are no grounds for distinguishing close-ups and big close-ups or 'inserts', which would only show a part of the face. In many cases there is no more distinction between close-medium shots, two-shots, and close-ups. And why would a part of the body, chin, stomach or chest be more partial, more spatio-temporal and less expressive than an intensive feature of faceicity or a reflexive whole face? For example, the series of fat kulaks in Eisenstein's *The General Line*. And why is expression not available to things? There are affects of things. the 'edge', the 'blade', or rather the 'point' of Jack the Ripper's knife, is no less an affect than the fear which overcomes his features and the resignation which finally seizes hold of the whole of his face. The Stoics showed that things themselves were bearers of ideal events which did not exactly coincide with their properties, their actions and reactions: the edge of a knife. . . .

The affect is the entity, that is Power or Quality. It is something expressed: the affect does not exist independently of something which expresses it, although it is completely distinct from it. What expresses it is a face, or a facial equivalent (a faceified object) or, as we will see later, even a proposition. We call the set of the expressed and its expression, of the affect and the face, 'icon'. There are therefore icons of feature and icons of outline, or rather every icon has these two poles: it is the sign of the bipolar composition of the affection-image. The affection-image is power or quality considered for themselves, as expresseds. It is clear that powers and qualities can also exist in a completely different way: as actualised, embodied in states of things. A state of things includes a determinate space-time, spatio-temporal co-ordinates, objects and people, real connections between all these givens. In a state of things which actualises them the quality becomes the 'quale' of an object, power becomes action or passion, affect becomes sensation, sentiment, emotion or even impulse [*pulsion*] in a person, the face becomes the character or mask of the person (it is only from this point of view that there can be mendacious expressions). But now we are no longer in the domain of the affection-image, we have entered the domain of the action-image. The affection-image, for its part, is abstracted from the spatio-temporal co-ordinates which would relate it to a state of things, and abstracts the face from the person to which it belongs in the state of things.

C. S. Peirce, whose great importance for the classification of images
and signs we have already noted, distinguished between two sorts of
images which he called 'Firstness' and 'Secondness'.[14] Secondness
was wherever there were two by themselves: what is what it is in
relation to a second. Everything which only exists by being opposed,
by and in a duel, therefore belongs to secondness: exertion–resistance,
action–reaction, excitation–response, situation–behaviour, individual–
milieu. . . . It is the category of the Real, of the actual, of the existing,
of the individuated. And the first figure of secondness is that in which
power-qualities become 'forces', that is to say are actualised in
particular states of things, determinate space-times, geographical and
historical milieux, collective agents or individual people. It is here
that the action-image is born and developed. But however close these
concrete mixtures may be, firstness is an entirely different category,
which refers to another type of image with other signs. Peirce does
not conceal the fact that firstness is difficult to define, because it is felt,
rather than conceived: it concerns what is new in experience, what is
fresh, fleeting and nevertheless eternal. Peirce gives, as we shall see,
some very strange examples, but they all come down to this: these are
qualities or powers considered for themselves, without reference to
anything else, independently of any question of their actualisation. It
is that which is as it is for itself and in itself. It is, for example, a 'red',
as present in the proposition 'this *is not* red' as in 'this is red'. If you
like, it is an immediate and instantaneous consciousness, such as is
implied by every real consciousness which is itself never immediate
nor instantaneous. It is not a sensation, a feeling, an idea, but the
quality of a possible sensation, feeling or idea. Firstness is thus the
category of the Possible: it gives a proper consistency to the possible,
it expresses the possible without actualising it, whilst making it a
complete mode. Now, this is exactly what the affection-image is: it is
quality or power, it is potentiality considered for itself as expressed.
The corresponding sign is therefore expression, not actualisation.
Maine de Biran had already spoken of pure affections, unplaceable
because they have no relation to a determinate space, present in the
sole form of a 'there is . . .', because they have no relations to an ego
[*moi*] (the pains of a hemiplegic, the floating images of falling asleep,
the visions of madness).[15] The affect is impersonal and is distinct
from every individuated state of things: it is none the less *singular*, and
can enter into singular combinations or conjunctions with other
affects. The affect is indivisible and without parts; but the singular
combinations that it forms with other affects form in turn an
indivisible quality, which will only be divided by changing

qualitatively (the 'dividual'). The affect is independent of all determinate space-time; but it is none the less created in a history which produces it as the expressed and the expression of a space or a time, of an epoch or a milieu (this is why the affect is the 'new' and new affects are ceaselessly created, notably by the work of art).[16]

In short, affects, quality-powers, can be grasped in two ways: either as actualised in a state of things, or as expressed by a face, a face-equivalent or a 'proposition'. This is Peirce's secondness and firstness. Every set of images is made up of firstnesses, secondnesses and many other things besides. But affection-images, in the strict sense, only refer to firstness.

This is a phantasmal conception of the affect which has its risks: 'and when he was at the other side of the bridge the phantoms came to meet him. . .'. Ordinarily, three roles of the face are recognisable: it is individuating (it distinguishes or characterises each person); it is socialising (it manifest a social role); it is relational or communicating (it ensures not only communication between two people, but also, in a single person, the internal agreement between his character and his role). Now the face, which effectively presents these aspects in the cinema as elsewhere, loses all three in the case of close-up. Bergman is undoubtedly the director who has been most insistent on the fundamental link which unites the cinema, the face and the close-up: 'Our work begins with the human face. . . . The possibility of drawing near to the human face is the primary originality and the distinctive quality of the cinema.'[17] A character has abandoned his profession, renounced his social role; he is no longer able to, or no longer wants to communicate, is struck by an almost absolute muteness; he even loses his individuation, to the point where he takes on a strange resemblance to the other, a resemblance by default or by absence. Indeed, these functions of the face presuppose the reality of a state of things where people act and perceive. The affection-image makes them dissolve, disappear. We recognise one of Bergman's scripts.

There is no close-up of the face. The close-up is the face, but the face precisely in so far as it has destroyed its triple function – a nudity of the face much greater than that of the body, an inhumanity much greater than that of animals. The kiss already testifies to the integral unity of the face, and inspires in it the micro-movements that the rest of the body hides. But, more importantly, the close-up turns the face into a phantom, and the book of phantoms. The face is the vampire, and the letters are his bats, his means of expression. In *The Communicants*, 'while the pastor reads the letter, the woman in the foreground speaks the sentences without writing them', and, in *Autumn Sonata*, 'the text of the letter is divided between the woman who writes it, her husband who gets to know about it, and the addressee who has not yet received it'.[18] The faces converge, borrow their memories from each other and tend to become mixed up. It is fruitless to wonder, in *Persona*, if these are two people who resembled each other before, or who begin to resemble each other, or on the contrary a single person who splits in two. It is something else. The close-up has merely pushed the face to those regions where the principle of individuation ceases to hold sway. They are not identical because they resemble each other, but because they have lost individuation no less than socialisation and communication. This is the operation of the close-up. The close-up does not divide one individual, any more than it reunites two: it suspends individuation. Then the single and ravaged face unites a part of one to a part of the other. At this point it no longer reflects nor feels anything, but merely experiences a mute fear. It absorbs two beings, and absorbs them in the void. And in the void it is itself the photogramme which burns, with Fear as its only affect. The facial close-up is both the face and its effacement. Bergman has pushed the nihilism of the face the furthest, that is its relationship in fear to the void or the absence, the fear of the face confronted with its nothingness. In a whole section of his work Bergman reaches the extreme limit of the affection-image, he burns the icon, he consumes and extinguishes the face as certainly as Beckett.

Is this the inevitable route upon which the close-up as entity has set us? The phantoms threaten us all the more as they do not come from the past. Kafka distinguished two equally modern technological pedigrees: on the one hand the means of communication-translation, which ensure our insertion and our conquests in space and time (boat, car, train, aeroplane. . .); on the other hand the means of communication-expression which summon up phantoms on our route and turn us off course towards affects which are unco-ordinated, outside co-ordinates (letters the telephone, the radio, all the imaginable 'gramophones' and cinematographs. . .). This was not a theory, but Kafka's daily experience: each time one writes a letter, a phantom consumes its kisses before it arrives, perhaps before it leaves, so that it is already necessary to write another one.[19] But what can be done to stop the two correlative series leading to the worst, the one given up to movement which is increasingly military and policing, which drags puppet-characters into rigid social roles, into congealed characters, whilst the void ascends in the other series, affecting the surviving faces with a single and identical fear? This is already the case in Bergman's work even in its political aspects (*The Shame*, *The Serpent's Egg*) but also in the German school which extends and renews the project of such a cinema of fear. From this perspective Wenders attempts a transplantation and reconciliation of the two pedigrees: 'I'm afraid of being afraid.' In his work there is often an active series where the movements of translation are converted and interchanged – train, car, metro, aeroplane, boat – and constantly interfering, constantly intermingled, an affective series where one looks for and meets expressive phantoms, or one summons them up with printing, photography and cinema. The voyage of initiation *Kings of the Road* goes through the phantom machines of the old printing works and of the travelling cinema. The journey of *Alice in the Cities* is punctuated by polaroids, to the point where the images of the film are extinguished at the same rhythm, until the moment when the little girl says: 'Aren't you taking photos any more?' even if it means that the phantoms then take on another form.

Kafka suggested making mixtures, putting phantom machines on the apparatuses of translation: this was very new for the time, a telephone in a train, post-boxes on a boat, cinema in an aeroplane.[20] Is this not also the whole history of the cinema: the camera on rails, on a bicycle, aerial, etc.? And this is what Wenders wants when he makes the two series interpenetrate in his first films. The affection-image and the action-image will be saved somehow or other, the one by the other. . . . But is there not yet another way in which the affection-image might save itself and push back its own limit (a way sketched in Wenders' *American Friend*)? The affects would need to form singular, ambiguous combinations which were always recreated, in such a way that the related faces are turned away from each other just enough not to be dissolved and effaced. And movement in its turn would need to go beyond the states of things, to trace lines of flight, just enough to open up in space a dimension of another order favourable to these compositions of affects. This is the affection-image: it has as its limit the simple affect of fear and the effacement of faces in nothingness. But as its substance it has the compound affect of desire and of astonishment – which gives it life – and the turning aside of faces in the open, in the flesh.[21]

7 The affection-image
Qualities, powers, any-space-whatevers

1 The complex entity or the expressed

There are Lulu, the lamp, the bread-knife, Jack the Ripper: people who are assumed to be real with individual characters and social roles, objects with uses, real connections between these objects and these people – in short, a whole actual state of things. But there are also the brightness of the light on the knife, the blade of the knife under the light, Jack's terror and resignation, Lulu's compassionate look. These are pure singular qualities or potentialities – as it were, pure 'possibles'. Of course, power-qualities do relate to people and to objects, to the state of things, which are, as it were, their causes. But these are very special effects: taken all together they only refer back to themselves, and constitute the 'expressed' of the state of things, whilst the causes, for their part, only refer back to themselves in constituting the state of things. As Balázs says, however much the precipice may be the cause of vertigo, it does not explain the expression it produces on a face. Or, if you like, it explains it, but it does not make it comprehensible: 'The precipice above which someone leans perhaps explains his expression of fright, but it does not create it. For the expression exists even without justification, it does not become expression because a situation is associated with it in thought.'[1] And of course, power-qualities have an anticipatory role, since they prepare for the event which will be actualised in the state of things and will modify it (the slash of the knife, the fall over the precipice). But in themselves, or as expresseds, they are already the event in its eternal aspect, in what Blanchot calls 'the aspect of the event that its accomplishment cannot realise'.[2]

Whatever their mutual involvements, we can therefore distinguish two states of power-qualities, that is, of affects: as they are actualised in an individuated state of things and in the corresponding *real connections* (with a particular space-time, *hic et nunc*, particular characters, particular roles, particular objects) and as they are expressed for themselves, outside spatio-temporal co-ordinates, with their own ideal singularities and their *virtual conjunction*. The first dimension is essential to the action-image and to medium-shots; but the other dimension constitutes the affection-image or the close-up. The pure affect, the pure expressed of the state of things in fact relates to a face which expresses it (or to several faces, or to equivalents, or to propositions). It is the face – or the equivalent – which gathers and expresses the affect as a complex entity, and secures the virtual conjunctions between singular points of this entity (the brightness, the blade, the terror, the compassionate look. . .).

Affects are not individuated like people and things, but nevertheless they do not blend into the indifference of the world. They have singularities which enter into virtual conjunction and each time constitute a complex entity. It is like points of melting, of boiling, of condensation, of coagulation, etc. This is why faces which express various affects, or the various points of the same affect, do not merge into a single fear which would obliterate them (obliterating fear is merely a limit-case). The close-up does indeed suspend individuation and Roger Leenhardt, who hates the close-up, is right to say that it makes all faces look alike: all non-made-up faces look like Falconetti, all made-up ones like Garbo.[3] One only need recall that the actor himself does not recognise himself in the close-up (according to Bergman, 'we were setting out to do the cutting and editing and Liv said: look at Bibi, she's awful! and Bibi said in turn: no, it's not me, it's you. . .'.) This is simply to say that the close-up of the face acts not through the individuality of a role or of a character, or even through the personality of the actor – at least not directly. But nevertheless they do not all have the same value. If a face is of a kind which expresses some singularities rather than others this is through the differentiation of its own material parts and its capacity to make their relations vary: parts which are hard and tender, shadowy and illuminated, dull and shiny, smooth and grainy, jagged and curved, etc. One imagines therefore that a face is suited to one particular type of affect or entity rather than others. The close-up makes the face the pure building material of the affect, its 'hylé'.[4] Hence these strange cinematographic nuptials in which the actress provides her face and the material capacity of her parts, whilst the director invents the affect or the form of the expressible which borrows and puts them to work.

There is thus an internal composition of the close-up, that is a genuinely affective framing, cutting [*découpage*] and montage. The relationship of the close-up to other shots and to other types of images might be called external composition. But internal composition is the relationship of the close-up, either to other close-ups, or to itself, its elements and dimensions. There is, moreover, no great

difference between the two: there can be a succession of close-ups –
compact or at intervals – but also a single close-up can successively
develop particular features or parts of the face and allow us to witness
their changing relationships. And a single close-up can simultaneously
join several faces, or parts of different faces (and not only for a kiss).
Finally, it can include a space-time, in depth or on the surface, as if it
had torn it away from the co-ordinates from which it was abstracted:
it carries off with it a fragment of the sky, of countryside or of an
apartment, a scrap of vision with which the face is formed in power or
quality. It is like a short-circuit of the near and the far. An Eisenstein
close-up: Ivan's immense profile, whilst the sinuous line of the
miniaturised crowd of supplicants is horizontally opposed to the
sharp angles of the nose, the beard and the skull. An Oliveira close-
up: the two faces of the man, whilst, in depth this time, the horse
which has mounted the stairs prefigures the affects of the seduction
and the musical ride. In fact we have seen that as soon as the close-up
is defined, not by its relative dimensions but by its absolute
dimension or its function – in other words, when the affect is
expressed as entity – it is hardly possible to distinguish the big close-
up [*très gros plan*], the close-up, the close shot *]plan rapproché*] or even
the two-shot [*plan américain*]. What we call the internal composition
of the close-up will therefore rest on the following elements: the
expressed complex entity, with the singularities that it includes; the
face or faces which express it, with particular differentiated material
parts and particular variable relationships between the parts (a face
hardens or becomes tender); the space of the virtual conjunction
between the singularities, which tends to coincide with the face, or
which, on the contrary, goes beyond it; the turning away [*détournement*]
of face or faces, which opens and describes this space. . . .

All these aspects are linked. Firstly, turning away [*détournement*] is
not the opposite of, 'turning towards' [*se tourner*]. Both are
inseparable; the one would be rather the motor movement of desire,
and the other the reflecting movement of admiration. As Courthial
shows, they both belong to the face, but they are not opposed to each
other, they are both opposed to the idea of an indifferent, dead and
fixed face which would obliterate all faces and would lead them to
nothingness. As long as there are faces, they turn like planets around
a fixed star and, in turning, they are constantly turning away. A very
small change of direction of the face varies the relationship of its hard
and tender parts, and so modifies the affect. Even a single face has a
coefficient of turning away and turning towards. It is by turning
towards-turning away [*tournement-détournement*] that the face expresses

the affect, its increase and decrease, whilst obliteration goes beyond the threshold of decrease, plunges the affect into the void and makes the face lose its features. In Pabst's *Lulu* Jack's face turns away from that of the woman, modifies its affect and makes it increase in another direction, up to its brutal decrease into nothingness. Bergman's cinema finds its culmination in the obliteration of faces: it will have let them live, given them the time to accomplish their strange, even shameful or hateful, revolution. The old woman with bulging eyes is like the black sun around which the heroine of *Face to Face* turns, but whilst turning away. The servant girl in *Cries and Whispers* holds out her broad, soft, mute face, but the two sisters only survive by turning around her and turning away from each other: and it is the mutual turning away which also constitutes the survival of the sisters of *Silence*, and the vacillating life of the two protagonists of *Persona*.[5] Up to the glorious moment when the turned-away faces regain their full force, beyond nothingness and, in turning around the mummy, enter a virtual conjunction which forms an affect as powerful as a weapon crossing space, setting fire to the unjust state of things instead of burning the things themselves, and restoring life to primary life, in the form of a hermaphrodite's face and a child's face (*Fanny and Alexander*).

The expressed entity is what the Middle Ages called the 'signifiable complex' of a proposition, distinct from the state of things. The expressed – that is, the affect – is complex because it is made up of all sorts of singularities that it sometimes connects and into which it sometimes divides. This is why it constantly varies and changes qualitatively according to the connections that it carries out or the divisions that it undergoes. This is the Dividual, that which neither increases nor decreases without changing qualitatively. What produces the unity of the affect at each instant is the virtual conjunction assured by the expression, face or proposition. Brilliance, terror, decisiveness and compassion are very different qualities and powers which are sometimes connected and sometimes separated. The first is a power or quality 'of' sensation, the next of feeling, the next of action and the last of state. We say 'quality *of* sensation', etc. because the sensation or the feeling, etc. is precisely that in which the power-quality is actualised. Nevertheless, the power-quality must not be confused with the state of things which it actualises in this way: brightness is not the same as a particular sensation, nor decisiveness the same as a particular action. They are pure possibilities, pure virtualities, which will be accomplished in particular conditions by the sensation that gives us the knife under the light, or by the action of the knife in our hand. As Peirce would have said, a colour like red, a value like brightness, a power like decisiveness, a quality like hardness or tenderness, are primarily positive possibilities which refer only to themselves.[6] Therefore, just as they can be separated from each other, they can be connected and can refer to one another, in a virtual conjunction which, in turn, is not to be confused with the real connection between the lamp, the knife and the people – although this conjunction is actualised here and now in this connection. We must always distinguish power-qualities in themselves, as expressed by a face, faces or their equivalents (affection-image of firstness) and these same power-qualities as actualised in a state of things, in a determinate space-time (action-image of secondness).

In the affective film *par excellence*, Dreyer's *Passion of Joan of Arc*, there is a whole historical state of things, social roles and individual or collective characters, real connections between them – Joan, the bishop, the Englishman, the judges, the kingdom, the people: in short, the trial. But there is something else, which is not exactly eternal or suprahistorical: it is what Péguy called 'internal'. It is like two presents which ceaselessly intersect, one of which is endlessly arriving and the other is already established. Péguy also said that one goes the whole length of the historical event, but that one ascends inside the other event: the first has long been embodied, but the second continues to express itself and is even still looking for an expression. It is the same event but one part of it is profoundly realised in a state of things, whilst the other is all the more irreducible to all realisation. This mystery of the present in Péguy or Blanchot – but also in Dreyer and Bresson – is the difference between the trial and the Passion, which are nevertheless inseparable. Active causes are determined in the state of things: but the event itself, the affective, the effect, goes beyond its own causes, and only refers to other effects, whilst the causes for their part fall aside. It is the anger *of* the bishop and the martyrdom *of* Joan; but, all that will be preserved from the roles and situations will be what is needed for the affect to be extracted and to carry out its conjunctions – this 'power' of anger or of ruse, this 'quality' of victim or of martyrdom. To extract the Passion from the trial, to extract from the event this inexhaustible and brilliant part which goes beyond its own actualisation, 'the completion which is never completed'. The affect is like the expressed of the state of things, but this expressed does not refer to the state of things, it only refers to the faces which express it and, coming together or separating, give it its proper moving context. Made up of short close-ups, the film took upon itself that part of the event which does not allow itself to be actualised in a determinate milieu.

The perfect fit between the technical means and this end is also important. Affective framing proceeds by *cutting close-ups [gros plans coupants]*. Sometimes howling lips or toothless sneers are cut into the mass of the face. Sometimes the frame cuts a face horizontally, vertically or aslant, obliquely. And movements are cut in their course, the continuity shots systematically false, as if it was necessary to break over-real or over-logical connections. Also, Joan's face is often pushed back to the lower part of the image, so that the close-up carries with it a fragment of white décor, an empty zone, a space of sky from which she draws an inspiration. It is an extraordinary document on the turning toward and turning away of faces. These cutting frames respond to the notion of 'unframing', proposed by Bonitzer to designate unusual angles which are not completely justified by the requirements of action or perception. Dreyer avoids the shot-reverse shot *[champ-contrechamp]* procedure which would maintain a real relation between each face and the other, and would still be part of an action-image. He prefers to isolate each face in a close-up which is only partly filled, so that the position to the right or to the left directly induces a virtual conjunction which no longer needs to pass through the real connection between the people.

Affective cutting in turn proceeds by what Dreyer himself called 'flowing close-ups'. This is, undoubtedly, a continuous movement by which the camera passes from the close-up to the medium or full shot, but it is primarily a way of treating the medium shot and the full shot *as* close-ups – by the absence of depth or the suppression of perspective. Now it is not the close shot *[plan rapproché]*, which can take on the status of the close-up, but any kind of shot: the distinctions inherited from space tend to fade. By suppressing 'atmospheric' perspective Dreyer produces the triumph of a properly temporal or even spiritual perspective. Flattening the third dimension, he puts two-dimensional space into immediate relation with the affect, with a fourth and fifth dimension, Time and Spirit. Of course the close-up can, in principle; subordinate or join in with the backgrounds *[arrière-fonds]* by depth of field. But this is not the case with Dreyer, in whose work depth, when it is introduced, indicates the obliteration of a character. In his work, on the contrary, the negation of depth and of perspective, the ideal plane-ness of the image, allow the assimilation of the medium or full shot to the close-up, the making equivalent of a space or a white background with the close-up – not only in a film like *Joan of Arc*, where the close-ups dominate, but even more so in the films where they no longer dominate, no longer need to dominate, having 'flowed' so well that they permeate all the other shots in advance. Everything is then ready for affective montage, that is, for the relations between cuttings and flowings, which will make all shots particular instances of close-ups, and inscribe them or combine them on the plane-ness of a single shot-sequence which is by right unlimited (the tendency of *Ordet* and *Gertrud*).[7]

2 The spiritual affect and space in Bresson

Although the close-up extracts the face (or its equivalent) from all spatio-temporal co-ordinates, it can carry with it its own space-time – a scrap of vision, sky, countryside or background. Sometimes it is depth of field which gives the close-up a behind. Sometimes, on the contrary, it is the negation of perspective and of depth which assimilates the medium shot to a close-up. But, if the affect obtains a space for itself in this way, why could it not do so even without the face, and independently of the close-up, independently of all reference to the close-up?

Take, for example, Bresson's *The Trial of Joan of Arc*. Jean Sémolué and Michel Estève have clearly indicated its differences with, and similarities to, Dreyer's Passion. The major similarity is that it concerns the affect as complex spiritual entity: the white space of conjunctions, meetings and divisions; the part of the event which is not reducible to the state of things, the mystery of this begun-again present. However, the film is primarily made up of medium shots, shots and reverse-shots; and Joan is perceived at her trial rather than in her Passion, as a prisoner who resists rather than as victim and martyr.[8] Whilst it is certainly true that this expressed trial is not to be confused with the historical trial, it is itself Passion – in Bresson as much as in Dreyer – and enters into a virtual conjunction with that of Christ. But, in Dreyer, the Passion appeared in the 'ecstatic' mode and passed through the face, its exhaustion, its turning away, its encounter with the limit. Whilst, in Bresson it is in itself 'trial' [*procès*] that is *halt* [*station*], step and advance (*Diary of a Country Priest* highlights this aspect of stations on a pathway to the Cross). It is the construction of a space, fragment by fragment, a space of tactile value, where the hand ends up by assuming the directing function which returns to it in *Pickpocket*, dethroning the face. The law of this space is 'fragmentation'.[9] Tables and doors are not given whole. Joan's room and the courtroom, the death cell, are not presented to us in long shots but successively apprehended from continuity shots which make them a reality which is closed each time, but to infinity. Hence the special role of deframings. The external world itself therefore seems to be a cell, like the aquarium-forest of *Lancelot du Lac*. It is as if the mind collides with each part as if it were a closed angle, but enjoying a manual freedom in the linking of the parts. Indeed, the linking of neighbouring areas can be done in many different ways and depends on new conditions of speed and of movement, on rhythmic values which are opposed to all prior determination – 'A new dependence. . . .' Longchamp and the Gare de Lyon in *Pickpocket* are vast fragmented spaces, transformed through rhythmic continuity shots which correspond to the affects of the thief. Ruin and salvation are played on an amorphous table whose successive parts await the connection which they lack from our gestures, or rather from the mind. Space itself has left behind its own co-ordinates and its metric relations. It is a tactile space. In this way Bresson can achieve a result which in Dreyer was only indirect. The spiritual affect is no longer expressed by a face and space no longer needs to be subjected or assimilated to a close-up, treated as a close-up. The affect is now directly presented in medium shot, in a space which is capable of corresponding to it. And the famous treatment of voices by Bresson, white voices, not only marks an upsurge of free indirect discourse in every expression, but also a potentialisation of what happens and is expressed – an equivalence of space and the affect expressed as pure potentiality.

Space is no longer a particular determined space, it has become *any-space-whatever* [*espace quelconque*], to use Pascal Augé's term. Certainly, Bresson does not invent any-space-whatevers (although he constructs them on his own account and in his own way). Augé would prefer to look for their source in the experimental cinema. But it could equally be said that they are as old as the cinema itself. Any-space-whatever is not an abstract universal, in all times, in all places. It is a perfectly singular space, which has merely lost its homogeneity, that is, the principle of its metric relations or the connection of its own parts, so that the linkages can be made in an infinite number of ways. It is a space of virtual conjunction, grasped as pure locus of the possible. What in fact manifests the instability, the heterogeneity, the absence of link of such a space, is a richness in potentials or singularities which are, as it were, prior conditions of all actualisation, all determination. This is why, when we define the action-image by quality or power as actualised in a determined space (state of things), it is not sufficient to oppose to it an affection-image which relates qualities and powers to the preactual state that they assume on a face. We now say that there are two kinds of signs of the affection-image, or two figures of firstness: *on the one hand the power-quality expressed by a face or an equivalent; but on the other hand the power-quality presented in any-space-whatever* [*un espace quelconque*]. And perhaps the second is more subtle than the first, more suitable for extracting the birth, the advance and the spread of the affect. The point is that the face remains a large unit whose movements, as Descartes remarked, express compound and mixed affections. The famous Koulechov affect is explained less by the association of the face with a variable object than by an ambiguity of its expressions which always suit different affects. On the contrary, as soon as we leave the face and the close-up, as soon as we consider complex shots which go beyond the simplistic distinction between close-up, medium shot and long shot, we seem to enter a 'system of emotions' which is much more subtle and differentiated, less easy to identify, capable of inducing non-human affects.[10] So that the affection-image would be like the perception-image: it would also have two signs, one of which would be merely a sign of bipolar composition, and the other a genetic or differential sign. The any-space-whatever would be the genetic element of the affection-image.

The young schizophrenic experiences his 'first feelings of unreality' before two images: that of a comrade who draws near and whose face enlarges exaggeratedly (one might say like a lion); that of a field of corn which becomes boundless, 'dazzling yellow immensity'.[11] To use Peirce's terms, these two signs of the affection-image would be designated as follows: *Icon*, for the expression of a power-quality by a face, *Qualisign* (or *Potisign*) for its presentation in any-space-whatever. Some of Jorge Iven's films give us an idea of what a qualisign is:

> *Rain* is not a determined, concrete rain which has fallen somewhere. These visual impressions are not unified by spatial or temporal representations. What is perceived here with the most delicate sensibility, is not what rain really is, but the way in which it appears when, silent and continuous, it drips from leaf to leaf, when the mirror of the pool has goose-pimples, when the solitary drop hesitatingly seeks its pathway on the window-pane, when the life of a city is reflected on the wet asphalt. . . . And even when it's a matter of a unique object, like the *Bridge* of Rotterdam, this metallic construction is dissolved in immaterial images, framed in a thousand different ways. The fact that this bridge can be seen in a

multiplicity of ways renders it, as it were, unreal. It does not appear to us as the creation of engineers aiming at a determinate end, but like a curious series of optical effects. These are visual variations on which it would be difficult for a goods train to travel.[12]

This is not a concept of bridge, but neither is it the individuated state of things defined by its form, its metallic matter, its uses and functions. It is a potentiality. The rapid montage of seven hundred shots means that different views can be fitted together in an infinite number of ways and, because they are not oriented in relation to each other, constitute the set of singularities which are combined in the any-space-whatever in which this bridge appeared as pure quality, this metal as pure power, Rotterdam itself as affect. And neither is the rain the concept of rain nor the state of a rainy time and place. It is a set of singularities which presents the rain as it is in itself, pure power or quality which combines without abstraction all possible rains and makes up the corresponding any-space-whatever. It is rain as affect, and nothing is more opposed to an abstract or general idea, although it is not actualised in an individual state of things.

3 The construction of any-space-whatevers

How can any-space-whatever be constructed (in the studio or on location)? How can any-space-whatever be extracted from a given state of things, from a determinate space? The first way was shadow, shadows: a space full of shadows, or covered with shadows, becomes any-space-whatever. We have seen how Expressionism operates with darkness and light, the opaque black background and the luminous principle: the two powers couple together gripping like wrestlers, giving space a great depth, a prominent and distorted perspective, which will be filled with shadows, sometimes in the form of all the degrees of chiaroscuro, sometimes in the form of alternating and contrasted streaks. A 'Gothic' world, which drowns and breaks the contours, which endows things with a non-organic life in which they lose their individuality, and which potentialises space, whilst making it something unlimited. Depth is the location of the struggle, which sometimes draws space into the bottomlessness of a black hole, and sometimes draws it towards the light. And of course, a character may also become strangely and terribly flat, against the background of a luminous circle, or his shadow may lose all its thickness, by backlighting [*contre-jour*], on a white

background; but it is by an 'inversion of the values of light
and dark', by an inversion of perspective which puts depth to the
forefront.[13] Shadow then exercises all its anticipatory function,
and presents the affect of Menace in its purest state, like the shadow of
Tartuffe, that of *Nosferatu*; or that of the priest on the sleeping lovers,
in *Tabu*. The shadow extends to infinity. In this way it determines
the virtual conjunctions which do not coincide with the state of
things or the position of characters which produce it: in Arthur
Robison's *Warning Shadows*, two hands only intertwine by the
extension of their shadows, a woman is only caressed by the shadow
of the hands of her admirers on the shadow of her body. This film
freely develops the virtual conjunctions, by showing what would
happen if roles, characters and the state of things did not finally melt
away at the actualisation of the jealousy-affect: it makes the affect all
the more independent of the state of things. In the neo-Gothic space
of horror films, Terence Fisher takes this autonomy of the affection-
image a long way when he makes Dracula perish nailed to the
ground, but in virtual conjunction with the sails of a burning
windmill which project the shadow of a cross at the exact place of the
torture (*The Brides of Dracula*).

Lyrical abstraction is a different method. We have seen that it is
defined by the relationship of light with white, but that shadow
retains an important role – albeit very different from its role in
Expressionism. The point is that Expressionism develops a principle
of opposition, of conflict or of struggle: struggle of the spirit with
darkness. While for the adherents of lyrical abstraction, the act of the
spirit is not a struggle but an alternative, a fundamental 'Either . . .
or'. Shadow is therefore no longer an extension to infinity, or a
reversal to the limit. It no longer extends a state of things to infinity, it
will, rather, express an alternative between the state of things itself
and the possibility, the virtuality, which goes beyond it. Thus
Jacques Tourneur breaks with the Gothic tradition of the horror
film; his pale and luminous spaces, his nights against a light
background, make him a representative of lyrical abstraction. In the
swimming pool of *Cat People*, the attack is only seen on the shadows
of the white wall: is it the woman who has become a leopard (virtual
conjunction) *or* merely the leopard which has escaped (real connection)?
And in *I Walked with a Zombie* is it a Zombie in the service of the
priestess, or a poor girl under the influence of the missionary?[14] It is
not surprising that we are led to quote very diverse representatives of
this 'lyrical abstraction': they are no more diverse than are the
Expressionists among themselves and diversity of adherents has

never prevented a concept from being consistent. What in fact seems to us essential in lyrical abstraction is that the spirit is not caught in a combat but is prey to an alternative. This alternative can be presented in an aesthetic or passional (Sternberg), ethical (Dreyer) or religious (Bresson) form, or can even play between these different forms. For example, in Sternberg, although the choice that the heroine must make between a white or scintillating frozen androgyne and an amorous or even domesticated woman, can only explicitly appear on certain occasions (*Morocco, Blonde Venus, Shanghai Express*), it is none the less present throughout his work. *The Scarlet Empress* contains a single close-up divided by shadow, and it is just here that the princess renounces love and chooses the cold conquest of power, whilst the heroine of *Blonde Venus*, on the other hand, gives up the white tuxedo in order to rediscover domestic and maternal love. And, although essentially sensual, Sternberg's alternatives are no less spiritual than the apparently supra-sensual ones of Dreyer or Bresson.[15] In any case, it is not only a matter of passion or of affect, in so far as, in Kierkegaard's phrase, faith is still a matter of passion, of affect and nothing else.

From its essential relation with the white, lyrical abstraction draws two consequences which accentuate its difference from Expressionism: an alternation of terms instead of an opposition; an alternative, a spiritual choice instead of a struggle or a fight. On the one hand it is the white–black alternation: the white which captures the light, the black at the point where the light stops and sometimes the half-tone, the grey as indiscernability which forms a third term. The alternations are established between one image and the next, or in the same image. In Bresson, these are rhythmic alternations as in *Diary of a Country Priest* or even, in *Lancelot du Lac*, between day and night. In Dreyer, the alternations reach a high geometric composition, like a 'tonal construction' and a mosaic of space (*Day of Wrath, Ordet*). On the other hand, the spiritual alternative seems to correspond to the alternation of terms, good, evil and uncertainty or indifference, but in a very mysterious way. It is indeed doubtful whether one 'must' choose the white. In Dreyer and Bresson, cell-like and clinical white has a terrifying, monstrous character no less than the frozen white of Sternberg. The white that *The Scarlet Empress* chooses implies a cruel renunciation of the values of intimacy, that the blonde Venus rediscovers, however, by renouncing the white. These are the same values of intimacy that the heroine of *Day of Wrath* finds for a moment in impenetrable shadow, instead of the Presbyterian white. The white which imprisons the light is worth no more than the black, which remains foreign to it. Finally, the spiritual alternative never bears directly on the alternation of terms, although the latter serves as its basis.[16] A fascinating idea was developed from Pascal to Kierkegaard: the alternative is not between terms but between the modes of existence of the one who chooses. There are choices that can only be made on condition that one persuades oneself that one has no choice, sometimes by virtue of a moral necessity (good, right), sometimes by virtue of a physical necessity (the state of things, the situation), sometimes by virtue of a psychological necessity (the desire that one has for something). The spiritual choice is made between the mode of existence of him who chooses on the condition of not knowing it, and the mode of existence of him who knows that it is a matter of choosing. It is as if there was a choice of choice *or* non-choice. If I am conscious of choice, there are therefore already choices that I can no longer make, and modes of existence that I can no longer follow – all those I followed on the condition of persuading myself that 'there was no choice'. This is all that Pascal's wager says: the alternation of terms is indeed the affirmation of the existence of God, its negation, and its suspension (doubt, uncertainty); but the spiritual alternative is elsewhere, it is between the mode of existence of him who 'wagers' that God exists and the mode of existence of him who wagers for non-existence or who does not want to wager. According to Pascal, only the first is conscious that it is a matter of choosing; the others are only able to make their choice on the condition of not knowing what it relates to. In short, choice as spiritual determination has no other object than itself: I choose to choose, and by that I exclude all choice made on the mode of not having the choice. This was also to be the essential point of what Kierkegaard calls 'alternative', and Sartre 'choice', in the atheist version which he puts forward.

A whole line of inspiration can be traced from Pascal to Bresson, from Kierkegaard to Dreyer. In the directors of lyrical abstraction, there is a rich series of characters who *are* so many modes of concrete existence. There are the white men of God, of Good and of Virtue, Pascal's 'devotees', tyrannical, hypocritical perhaps, guardians of order in the name of a moral or religious necessity. There are the grey men of uncertainty (like the hero of Dreyer's *Vampyr* or Bresson's Lancelot, or even the hero of *Pickpocket*, a possible title of which was in fact 'Uncertainty'). There are the creatures of evil, numerous in Bresson (Helen's revenge in *Ladies of the Park*, Gérard's wickedness in *Balthazar*, the thefts of *Pickpocket*, Yvon's crimes in *L'Argent*). And, in his extreme Jansenism, Bresson shows the same infamy from the perspective of works, that is to say, from the perspective of evil and good: in *L'Argent*, the devout Lucien will only practise charity in terms of the false testimony and the theft which he has set himself as conditions, whilst Yvon only launches into the crime on the condition of the other. One would think that the man of good necessarily begins from the place where the man of evil ends up. But why should there not be, rather than a choice of evil which would still be desire, a choice 'for' evil in full knowledge of the facts? Bresson's answer is the same as that of Goethe's Mephistopheles: we other devils or vampires are free for the first act, but have already become slaves for the second. This is what good sense says (less well), like the commissioner in *Pickpocket*: 'you don't stop', you have chosen a situation which already no longer allows you to choose. It is in this sense that the three preceding types of character are part of a false choice, of that choice which is only made on condition of denying that there is choice (or that there is still choice). We understand at last, from the point of view of lyrical abstraction, what the choice is, the consciousness of choice as steadfast spiritual determination. It is not the choice of Good, any more than of evil. It is a choice which is not defined by what it chooses, but by the power that it possesses to be able to start afresh at every instant, of starting afresh itself, and in this way confirming itself by itself, by putting the whole stake back into play each time. And even if this choice implies the sacrifice of the person, this is a sacrifice that he only makes on condition of knowing that he will start it afresh each time, and that he does it for all times (here again, this is a very different conception from that of Expressionism, for which the sacrifice is once and for all). In Sternberg himself, the true choice lies not with the *Scarlet Empress*, nor with the one who has chosen revenge in *The Shanghai Gesture*, but with the one who has made the choice of self-sacrifice in *Shanghai Express*. He has chosen on a single condition: not justifying himself, that of not having to justify himself, to give accounts. The character of true choice is discovered in sacrifice or rediscovered beyond the sacrifice which constantly begins over again in Bresson; it is Joan of Arc, it is the person condemned to death, the parish priest. In Dreyer, it is Joan of Arc again, but it is also the great trilogy, Anne of *Day of Wrath*, Inger of *Ordet*, finally *Gertrud*. A fourth type must therefore be added to the three preceding ones: the character who makes an authentic choice, or has the consciousness of choice. It is definitely a question of the affect; for, if the others maintain the affect as actuality in an established order or disorder, the character who makes true choice raises the affect to its pure power or potentiality, as in Lancelot's courtly love, but also embodies it and carries it into effect all the more as it liberates in him the part of that which does not let itself be actualised, of that which goes beyond all execution (the eternal rebirth). And Bresson adds yet a fifth type, a fifth character – the beast or the ass in *Balthazar* possessing the innocence of him who does not have to choose. The ass only knows the effect of the non-choices or choices of man, that is, the facet of events which is accomplished in bodies and wounds them, without being able to reach (but without being able to betray either) that which goes beyond execution, or spiritual determination. Thus the ass is the preferred object of men's wickedness, but also the preferential union of Christ or of the man of choice.

This extreme moralism which is opposed to morality, this faith which is opposed to religion, is a strange way of thinking. It has nothing to do with Nietzsche, but has much in common with Pascal and Kierkegaard, with Jansenism and Reformism (even in the case of Sartre). It weaves a whole set of relations of great value between philosophy and the cinema.[17] In Rohmer as well, a whole story [*histoire*] of modes of existence, of choices, of false choices and of the consciousness of choice, dominates the series of *Moral Tales* (notably *My Night at Maud's*; and more recently *Le beau Mariage* presents us with a girl who chooses to get married, and broadcasts it, for the very reason that she has chosen it in the same way that she would have been able to choose, in another epoch, *not* to marry, with the same Pascalian consciousness or the same claim to the eternal, to the infinite). Why have these themes so much philosophical and cinematographic importance? Why do all these points have to be emphasised? It is because, in philosophy as in the cinema, in Pascal as in Bresson, in Kierkegaard as in Dreyer, the true choice, that which consists in choosing choice, is supposed to restore everything to us. It will enable us to rediscover everything, in the spirit of sacrifice, at the moment of the sacrifice or even before the sacrifice is performed. Kierkegaard said that true choice means that by abandoning the bride, she is restored to us by that very act; and that by sacrificing his son, Abraham rediscovers him through that very act. Agamemnon sacrifices his daughter, Iphigenia, but out of duty, duty alone, and in choosing not to have the choice. Abraham, on the contrary, sacrifices his son, whom he loves more than himself, through choice alone, and through consciousness of the choice which unites him with God, beyond good and evil: thus his son is restored to him. This is the history [*histoire*] of lyrical abstraction.

We began from a determined space of states of things, made up of an alternation white–black–grey, white–black–grey. . . . And we

said the white marks our duty, or our power, the black our
impotence, or our thirst for evil, and the grey our uncertainty, our
seeking or our indifference. And then we raised ourselves to the
spiritual alternative, we had to choose between modes of existence.
Some, white, black or grey, implied that we did not have the choice
(or that we no longer had the choice), but only one other implied that
we chose to choose, or that we had consciousness of choice – pure,
immanent or spiritual light, beyond white, black and grey. As soon
as this light is reached it restores everything to us. It restores the
white to us, but a white which no longer confines the light. It finally
restores the black to us, the black which is no longer the cessation of
light. It even restores to us the grey, which is no longer uncertainty
or indifference. We have reached a spiritual space where what we
choose is no longer distinguishable from the choice itself. Lyrical
abstraction is defined by the adventure of light and white. But it is the
episodes of this adventure which mean that, firstly, the white which
confines the light alternates with the black where it stops; and then,
the light is liberated in an alternative, which restores to us the white
and the black. We have passed, on the spot, from one space to the
other, from physical space to spiritual space which restores a physics
(or a metaphysics) to us. The first space is cell-like and closed, but the
second is not different, it is the same in so far as it has merely
discovered the spiritual opening which overcomes all its formal
obligations and material constraints by a theoretical or practical
evasion. This is what Bresson suggested in his principle of
'fragmentation': we pass from a closed set that is fragmented to an
open spiritual whole that is created or recreated. Or take for example
Dreyer, where the Possible has opened up space as a dimension of the
spirit (fourth or fifth dimension). *Space is no longer determined, it has*
become the any-space-whatever which is identical to the power of the
spirit, to the perpetually renewed spiritual decision: it is this decision
which constitutes the affect, or the 'auto-affection', and which takes
upon itself the linking of parts.

Darkness and the struggle of the spirit, white and the alternative of
the spirit are the first two procedures by which space becomes any-
space-whatever and is raised to the spiritual power of the luminous.
Now we must consider yet a third procedure, colour. This is no
longer the space of Expressionism, nor the white space of lyrical
abstraction, but the colour-space of colourism. As in painting,
colourism is distinct from monochromy or polychromy which,
already in Griffith or in Eisenstein, merely produced a coloured
image and preceded the colour-image.

In certain respects, Expressionist darkness and lyrical white played the role of colours. But the true colour-image constitutes a third mode of the any-space-whatever. The principal forms of this image – the surface-colour of the great uniform tints [*grands aplats*], the atmospheric colour which pervades all the others, movement-colour which passes from one tone to another – perhaps originate in the musical comedy and its capacity for extracting an unlimited virtual world from a conventional state of things. Of these three forms it is only movement-colour which seems to belong to the cinema, the others already being entirely part of the powers of painting. Nevertheless, in our view, the colour-image of the cinema seems to be defined by another characteristic, one which it shares with painting, but gives a different range and function. This is the *absorbent* characteristic. Godard's formula, 'it's not blood, it's red' is *the* formula of colourism. In opposition to a simply coloured image, the colour-image does not refer to a particular object, but absorbs all that it can: it is the power which seizes all that happens within its range, or the quality common to completely different objects. There *is* a symbolism of colours, but it does not consist in a correspondence between a colour and an affect (green and hope . . .). Colour is on the contrary the affect itself, that is, the virtual conjunction of all the objects which it picks up. Thus Ollier is led to say that Agnès Varda's films, notably *Le Bonheur*, 'absorb', and absorb not only the spectator, but the characters themselves, and the situations, in complex movements affected by the complementary colours.[18] This was already true of *La Pointe courte* where the white and the black were treated as complementary, and where the white took hold of the feminine aspect – white work, white love and death – whilst the black took the male aspect, and the two protagonists of the 'abstract couple' traced out in their speech the space of the alternative or of complementarity. It is this composition which reaches a colourist perfection in *Le Bonheur* with the complementarity of violet, purple and oranged gold, and the successive absorption of the characters in the mysterious space which corresponds to the colours. Now, if we continue to refer to very different directors in order to explore the possible validity of a concept more clearly, it must be said that, from the beginning of a total cinema of colour, Minnelli had made absorption the properly cinematographic power of this new dimension of the image. This is the source of the role of the dream in his work: the dream is only the absorbent form of colour. His work in musical comedy, but also in all other genres, follows the obsessive theme of characters literally absorbed by their own dream, and above all by the dream of others and the past of others (*Yolanda and the Thief*, *The Pirate*, *Gigi*, *Melinda*) by the dream of power of an Other (*Les Ensorcelés*). And Minnelli reaches the highest level with *The Four Horsemen of the Apocalypse*, when the beings are caught up in the nightmare of war. Throughout his work the dream becomes space, but like a spider's web, made less for the dreamer himself than for the living prey that he attracts. If states of things become movement of the world, and if characters become the figure of a dance, this is inseparable from the splendour of colours, and from their almost carnivorous, devouring, destructive, absorbent function (like the bright yellow caravan of *The Long, Long Trailer*). It is appropriate that Minnelli should have tackled a subject which is ideal for expressing this adventure without return: the hesitation, the fear and the respect with which Van Gogh approaches colour, his discovery and the splendour of his creation, and his own absorption in what he creates, the absorption of his being and of his reason in yellow (*Lust for Life*).[19]

Antonioni, another of the cinema's greatest colourists, makes use of cold colours pushed to the limit of their plenitude or intensification in order to go beyond the absorbent function, which still maintained the transformed characters and situations in the space of a dream or a nightmare. In Antonioni, colour carries space as far as the void, it effaces what it has absorbed. Bonitzer says:

Since *L'Avventura*, Antonioni's great project has been the empty shot, the de-peopled [*deshabité*] shot. At the end of *Eclipse* all the shots through which the couple have passed are surveyed and corrected by the void, as the title of the film indicates. . . . Antonioni looks for the desert: *Red Desert*, *Zabriskie Point*, *The Passenger* . . . [which] is completed by a forward travelling shot on the empty field, in an interlacing of insignificant tracks, at the limit of the non-figurative. . . . The object of Antonioni's cinema is to reach the non-figurative through an adventure whose end is the eclipse of the face, the obliteration of characters.[20]

It is certainly true that the cinema had succeeded long before in obtaining great effects of resonance by juxtaposing a single space, at one time populated and at another empty (notably Sternberg, in *The Blue Angel*, for example, with Lola's theatre box, or with the class-room). But, in Antonioni, the idea takes on a previously unknown range, and it is colour which controls the juxtaposition. Colour elevates space to the power of the void, when that which can be realised in the event is accomplished. Space does not emerge from it depotentialised, but on the contrary, all the more charged with potential. Here there is both a similarity to and a difference from Bergman: Bergman went beyond the action-image towards the affective instance of the close-up or of the face that he confronted with the void. But, in Antonioni, the face disappeared at the same time as the character and the action, and the affective instance is that of the any-space-whatever, which Antonioni in turn pushes as far as the void.

Moreover, it seems that the any-space-whatever takes on a new nature here. It is no longer, as before, a space which is defined by parts whose linking up and orientation are not determined in advance, and can be done in an infinite number of ways. It is now an amorphous set which has eliminated that which happened and acted in it. It is an extinction or a disappearing, but one which is not opposed to the genetic element. It is clear that the two aspects are complementary, and reciprocally presuppose each other: the amorphous set in fact is a collection of locations or positions which coexist independently of the temporal order which moves from one part to the other, independently of the connections and orientations which the vanished characters and situations gave to them. There are therefore two states of the any-space-whatever, or two kinds of 'qualisigns', qualisigns of deconnection and of emptiness. These two states are always implied in each other, and we can only say that the one is 'before' and the other 'after'. The any-space-whatever retains one and the same nature: it no longer has co-ordinates, it is a pure potential, it shows only pure Powers and Qualities, independently of the states of things or milieux which actualise them (have actualised them or will actualise them, or neither the one nor the other – it hardly matters).

It is therefore shadows, whites and colours which are capable of producing and constituting any-space-whatevers, *deconnected or emptied spaces*. But, with all these means and with others as well, after the war, a proliferation of such spaces could be seen both in film sets [*décors*] and in exteriors, under various influences. The first, independent of the cinema, was the post-war situation with its towns demolished or being reconstructed, its waste grounds, its shanty towns, and even in places where the war had not penetrated, its undifferentiated urban tissue, its vast unused places, docks, warehouses, heaps of girders and scrap iron. Another, more specific to the cinema, as we shall see, arose from a crisis of the action-image: the characters were found less and less in sensory-motor 'motivating' situations, but rather in a state of strolling, of sauntering or of rambling which defined *pure optical and sound situations*. The action-image then tended to shatter, whilst the determinate locations were blurred, letting any-spaces-whatever rise up where the modern affects of fear, detachment, but also freshness, extreme speed and interminable waiting were developing.

In the first place, if Italian neo-realism was opposed to realism, this is because it broke with spatial co-ordinates, with the old realism of places, and mixed up the references which gave the film movement (as in the marshes or the fortress in Rossellini's *Païsa*), or constituted visual 'abstracts' (the factory of *Europa '51*) in the indefinite lunar spaces.[21] The French New Wave also broke shots open, obliterated their distinct spatial determination in favour of a non-totalisable space: for example Godard's unfinished apartments permitted discordances and variations, like all the ways of passing through a door with a missing panel, which takes on an almost musical value and serves as accompaniment to the affect (*Le Mépris*). Straub constructs astonishing amorphous shots, deserted, ambiguous or deepened geological spaces, theatres emptied of the operations which took place there.[22] The German school of fear – notably Fassbinder and Daniel Schmid – worked out its exteriors as city-deserts, its interiors divided in two by mirrors, with a minimum of reference points and a multiplication of points of view with no connection (Schmid's *Violanta*). The New York school imposed a horizontal view of the city, at ground level, where events are born on the pavement and now only have an undifferentiated space as their location, as in Lumet. Cassavetes provides an even better example. He began with films dominated by the face and the close-up (*Shadows*, *Faces*) constructed deconnected spaces, with a strong affective tenor (*The Killing of a Chinese Bookie*, *Too Late Blues*). He thus passed from one type of the affection-image to the other. This is because it was a matter of undoing space, no less as a function of a face which is abstracted from spatio-temporal co-ordinates than of an event which exceeds its actualisation in all ways, sometimes because it procrastinates and dissolves, sometimes on the contrary because it comes into view too quickly.[23] In *Gloria*, the heroine has long periods of waiting, but also has not got the time to look back, her pursuers are already there, as if they had been settled there the whole time, or rather as if the location itself had abruptly changed co-ordinates, was no longer the same location and yet at the same place as the any-space-whatever. This time, it is the empty space which is all of a sudden filled. . . .

We will have occasion to return to certain of these points. But this proliferation of any-space-whatevers perhaps has one of its points of origin, as Pascal Augé says, in the experimental cinema which breaks with the narration of actions and the perception of determinate places. If the experimental cinema tends towards a perception as it was before men (or after), it also tends towards the correlate of this, that is, towards an any-space-whatever released from its human co-ordinates. Michael Snow's *The Central Region* does not raise perception to the universal variation of a raw and savage matter without also extracting from it a space without reference points where the ground and the sky, the horizontal and the vertical, interchange. Nothingness itself is diverted towards that which comes out of it or falls back on it, the genetic element, the fresh or vanishing perception, which potentialises a space by retaining only the shadow or the account of human events. In *Wavelength* Snow uses a forty-five minute zoom in order to explore a room lengthwise from one end to the other, as far as the wall on which a photograph of the sea is stuck: from this room he extracts a potential space, whose power and quality he progressively exhausts.[24] Some girls come to listen to the radio, they hear a man climb the stairs and collapse to the floor, but the zoom has already passed him, giving way to one of the girls who is describing the event on the telephone. A phantom of the girl, in negative superimposition, redoubles the scene, whilst the zoom continues as far as the final image of the sea on the wall which it has now reached again. The space re-enters the empty sea. All the preceding elements of the any-space-whatever, the shadows, the whites, the colours, the inexorable progression, the inexorable reduction, elevation plane [*épure*], the disconnected parts, the empty set: all come into play here in what, according to Sitney, defines the 'structural film'.

Marguerite Duras' *Agatha et ses lectures illimitées* follows a similar structure by giving it the necessity of an account or rather of a reading (read the image and not only see it). It is as if the camera began from the bottom of a large, empty, unused room where the two characters will only be their own phantom, their shadow. At the opposite end, there is the empty beach, on to which the windows look. The time that the camera takes to go from the end of the room to the windows and to the beach, with pauses and returns, is the time of the account. And the account itself, the sound-image, unites a time of after and a time of before, moves from the former to the latter: a time of after men, since the account reports the history of a primordial couple which is already finished, and a time of before men, where no presence troubled the beach. From the former to the latter, a slow celebration of the affect, here the incest of brother and sister.

8 From affect to action
The impulse-image

1 Naturalism

When qualities and powers are apprehended as actualised in states of things, in milieux which are geographically and historically determinable, we enter into the realm of the action-image. The realism of the action-image is opposed to the idealism of the affection-image. However, between the two, between firstness and secondness, there is something which is like the 'degenerate' affect, or the 'embryonic' action. It is no longer the affection-image, but is not yet the action-image. As we have seen, the former is developed in the Any-Space-Whatevers/Affects pair. The second will be developed in the Determined Milieux/Modes of Behaviour pair. But, between the two, we come across a strange pair: Originary Worlds/Elementary Impulses. An originary world is not an any-space-whatever (although it may resemble one), because it only appears in the depths of determined milieux; but neither is it a determined milieu, which only derives from the originary world. An impulse is not an affect, because it is an impression in the strongest sense and not an expression. But neither is it like the feelings or emotions which regulate and deregulate behaviour. Now we must recognise that this new set is not a mere intermediary, a place of transition, but possesses a perfect consistency and autonomy, with the result that the action-image remains powerless to represent it, and the affection-image powerless to make it felt.

Take a house, a country or a region. These are real milieux of geographical and social actualisation. But it looks as if, in whole or in part, they communicate from within with originary worlds. The originary world may be marked by the artificiality of the set (a comic opera kingdom, a studio forest, or marsh) as much as by the authenticity of a preserved zone (a genuine desert, a virgin forest). It is recognisable by its formless character. It is a pure background, or rather a without-background, composed of unformed matter, sketches or fragments, crossed by non-formal functions, acts, or energy dynamisms which do not even refer to the constituted subjects. Here the characters are like animals: the fashionable gentleman a bird of prey, the lover a goat, the poor man a hyena. This is not because they have their form or behaviour, but because their acts are prior to all differentiation between the human and the animal. These are human animals. And this indeed is the impulse: the energy which seizes fragments in the originary world. Strictly speaking, impulses and fragments are correlates. Of course, impulses are not lacking in intelligence: they even have a diabolical intelligence which leads each to choose its part, await its moment, defer its gesture, and borrow the outlines of form which will best enable it to perform its act. Neither does the originary world lack a law to give it consistency. It is, first of all, Empedocles' world, made up of outlines and fragments, heads without necks, eyes without faces, arms without shoulders, gestures without form. But it is also the set which unites everything, not in an organisation, but making all the parts converge in an immense rubbish-dump or swamp, and all the impulses in a great death-impulse. The originary world is therefore both radical beginning and absolute end; and finally it links the one to the other, it puts the one into the other, according to a law which is that of *the steepest slope*. It is thus a world of a very special kind of violence (in certain respects, it is the radical evil); but it has the merit of causing an originary image of time to rise, with the beginning, the end, and the slope, all the cruelty of Chronos.

This is naturalism. It is not opposed to realism, but on the contrary accentuates its features by extending them in an idiosyncratic surrealism. Naturalism in literature is essentially Zola: he had the idea of making real milieux run in parallel with originary worlds. In each of his books, he describes a precise milieu, but he also *exhausts* it, and restores it to the originary world; it is from this higher source that the force of realist description derives. The real, actual milieu is the medium of a world which is defined by a radical beginning, an absolute end, a line of the steepest slope.

This is the essential point; the two will not let themselves be separated and do not take on distinct form. The originary world has no existence independent of the geographical and historical milieu which serves as its medium. It is the milieu which receives a beginning, an end and above all, a slope. This is why impulses are *extracted* from the real modes of behaviour current in a determinate milieu, from the passions, feelings and emotions which real men experience in this milieu. And the fragments are *torn from* objects which have effectively been formed in the milieu. It might be said that the originary world only appears when the invisible lines which divide up the real, which dislocate modes of behaviour and objects, are supercharged, filled out and extended. Actions go beyond themselves towards primordial acts which are not their components, objects towards fragments which would not reconstitute them, people towards energies which do not 'organise' them. The originary world only exists and operates in the depths of a real milieu, and is only valid through its immanence in this milieu, whose violence and cruelty it reveals. But at the same time the milieu only presents itself as real in its immanence in the originary world, it has the status of a 'derived' milieu, which receives a temporality as destiny from the originary world. Actions or modes of behaviour, people and objects, have to occupy the derived milieu, and are developed there, while impulses and fragments people the originary world which carries the whole along with it. For this reason, naturalist authors deserve the Nietzschean name 'physicians of civilisation'. They diagnose civilisation. The naturalist image, the impulse-image, has in fact two signs: symptoms, and idols or fetishes. Symptoms are the presence of impulses in the derived world, and idols and fetishes, the representation of the fragments. This is the world of Cain, the signs of Cain. In short, naturalism refers simultaneously to four co-ordinates: originary world/derived milieu; impulses/modes of behaviour. Let us imagine a work in which the derived milieu and the originary world are really distinct and well-separated. Although they may have all kinds of correspondences, it would not be a naturalist work.[1]

There were two great masters of naturalism in the cinema: Stroheim and Buñuel. In their works the invention of originary worlds can appear in localised forms which are very varied, artificial or natural. In Stroheim there is the mountain peak in *Blind Husbands*, the witch's hut in *Foolish Wives*, the palace of *Queen Kelly*, the swamp in the African episode of the same film, the desert at the end of *Greed*. In Buñuel there is the studio jungle in *Death in the Garden*, the drawing-room in *The Exterminating Angel*, the desert of columns in *Simon of the Desert*, the rock garden of *The Golden Age*. Even though it is localised, the originary world is still the overflowing location where the whole film happens, that is, the world which is revealed at the basis of the social milieux which are so powerfully described. For Stroheim and Buñuel are realists: never has the milieu been described with so much violence or cruelty, with its dual social division 'poor–rich', 'good men–evildoers'. But what gives their description such force is, indeed, their way of relating the features to an originary world, which rumbles in the depths of all the milieux and runs along beneath them. This world does not exist independently of the determinate milieux, but conversely makes them exist with characteristics and features which come from above, or rather, from a still more terrible depth. The originary world is a beginning of the world, but also an end of the world, and the irresistible slope from one to the other; it carries the milieu along and also makes it into a closed world, absolutely closed off, or else opens it up on to an uncertain hope. The rubbish tip where the corpse will be thrown is the image common to *Foolish Wives* and *The Young and the Damned*. Milieux constantly emerge from the originary world and retreat into it: they only barely emerge from it, like sketches which are already doomed, already scribbled over, to return to it even more definitively if they do not attain the salvation which itself can only come from this return to the origin. Such is the swamp in the African episode of *Queen Kelly*, and above all the cine-novel *Poto-Poto*, where the suspended lovers, bound face to face, await the ascent of the crocodiles. 'Here [. . .] the latitude is zero [. . .]. Here [. . .] no tradition, no precedent [. . .]. Here [. . .] each acts according to the impulse of the moment [. . .] and does what Poto-Poto impels him to do [. . .]. Poto-Poto is our only law.[. . .] And he is also our executioner [. . .]. We are all condemned to death.'[2] Zero latitude is also the primordial location of *The Exterminating Angel*. This was originally embodied in the mysteriously closed bourgeois drawing-room; then, when the drawing-room had scarcely been re-opened, it was re-established in the cathedral, where the survivors are once again united. It is the primordial location of *Discreet Charm of the Bourgeoisie*, which is reconstituted in all the successive derived locations, to prevent the event which is expected there. This had already been the matrix of *The Golden Age*, which punctuated all humanity's developments and re-absorbed them when they had barely emerged.

With naturalism, time makes a very prominent appearance in the cinematographic image. Mitry was right to say that *Greed* is the first film which testifies to a 'psychological duration' as evolution or ontogenesis of characters. And time is no less present in Buñuel, but as phylogenesis, periodisation of the ages of man (not only prominently, as in *The Golden Age*, but in *The Milky Way*, which borrows elements from all periods, playing havoc with their order).[3] However, in the first place, naturalist time seems to be under an inseparable curse. We might say of Stroheim what Thibaudet said of Flaubert: for him, duration is less that which forms itself [*se fait*] than that which undoes itself [*se défait*], and accelerates in undoing itself. It is therefore inseparable from an entropy, a degradation. And it is indeed in this way that Stroheim settles his acount with Expressionism. As we have seen, what he shares with Expressionism is a treatment of light and shade which puts him on a par with Lang or Murnau. But, in these latter, time only existed in relation to light and shade so that the degradation of a character only expressed a fall into darkness, into a black hole (hence Murnau's *The Last Laugh*, but also Pabst's *Lulu*, and even Sternberg's *The Blue Angel*, in his exercise in imitation of the Expressionists). While in Stroheim it is the reverse: he continually modelled light and shade on the stages of a degradation which fascinated him, he subordinates light to a time conceived as entropy.

In Buñuel, the phenomenon of degradation does not assume less autonomy – perhaps even more – since it is a degradation which extends explicitly to the human species. *The Exterminating Angel* shows a regression at least equal to that of the characters in *Greed*. However the difference between Stroheim and Buñuel is that in Buñuel the degradation is conceived less as accelerated entropy than as a precipitating repetition, eternal return. The originary world thus imposes upon the successive milieux not exactly a slope, but a curvature or cycle. It is true that a cycle –unlike a descent – cannot be entirely 'bad'; as in Empedocles, it alternates Good and Evil, Love and Hate and indeed the lover, the good man and even the saintly man take on an importance in Buñuel which they lack in Stroheim. But, in some respects, this remains secondary, for the male or female lover, the holy man himself are – according to Buñuel – no less harmful than the pervert or the degenerate (*Nazarin*). Whether it is time of entropy, or time of eternal return, in both cases time finds its source in the originary world, which confers upon it the role of a destiny which cannot be expiated. Curled up in the originary world which is like the beginning and the end of time, time unravels in derived milieux. This is almost a neo-Platonism of time. And it is undoubtedly one of the naturalist cinema's great achievements to have come so close to a time-image. However, what prevented it from reaching time as pure form was its obligation to keep time subordinate to naturalistic co-ordinates, to make it dependent on impulse. Consequently, naturalism could only grasp the negative effects of time; attrition, degradation, wastage, destruction, loss, or simply oblivion.[4] (We will see that when the cinema confronts the form of time directly, it can only construct its image by breaking with the naturalistic concern for the originary world and its impulses.)

In fact naturalism's most important element is the impulse-image. This embraces time, but only as the destiny of the impulse and the becoming of its object. A first aspect concerns the nature of impulses. For, if they are 'elementary' or 'raw', in the sense that they refer to originary worlds, they can assume configurations which are very complex, bizarre and unusual in relation to the derived milieux in which they appear. Certainly, they are often relatively simple – like the impulse of hunger, impulses to nourishment, sexual impulses, or even the impulse for gold in *Greed*. But already they are inseparable from the perverse modes of behaviour which they produce and animate: cannibalistic, sado-masochistic, necrophiliac, etc. . . . Buñuel was to expand the inventory by taking into account still more complex, properly spiritual impulses and perversions. And there are no limits in these biopsychic pathways. Marco Ferreri is without doubt one of the few recent directors to have inherited an authentic naturalistic inspiration and the art of evoking an originary world at the heart of realistic milieux (thus King Kong's enormous corpse on the site of the great modern development or the theatre-museum of *Rêve de singe*). There he implants strange impulses, like the maternal impulse of the male in *Rêve de singe*, or even the irresistible impulse to whistle in a balloon in *Break Up*.

The second aspect is the object of the impulse, that is, the fragment which simultaneously belongs to the originary world and is torn from the real object of the derived milieu. The object of the impulse is always the 'partial object', or the fetish; a haunch of meat, a raw morsel, a scrap, a woman's briefs, a shoe. The shoe as sexual fetish gives rise to confrontation between Stroheim and Buñuel, particularly in the former's *The Merry Widow*, and the latter's *Diary of a Chambermaid*. So that the impulse-image is undoubtedly the only case in which the close-up effectively becomes partial object; but this is *not* because the close-up 'is' partial object, it is because the partial object being that of the impulse then exceptionally becomes close-up. The impulse is an act which tears away, ruptures, dislocates. Perversion is therefore not its deviation, but its derivation, that is, its normal expression in the derived milieu. It is a constant predator-prey relationship. The invalid is the prey *par excellence*, since we no longer know what is fragment in him – the part which is lacking, or the rest of his body. But he is also predator and the non-satisfaction of the impulse, the hunger of the poor, is no less fragmenting than the satiety of the rich. The queen in *Queen Kelly* rummages in a box of chocolates like a beggar in a dustbin. The invalid and the monster gain such presence in naturalism because they are both the deformed object of which the act of the impulse takes possession and the ill-formed sketch, which serves as the subject of this act.

In the third place, the law or the destiny of the impulse is to take possession through guile, but violently, of everything that it *can* in a given milieu, and, if it can, to pass from one milieu to another. This exploration, this exhaustion of milieux, is constant. Each time, the impulse selects its fragment in a given milieu and yet it does not select it, it takes indiscriminately from what the milieu offers it, even if it then means going on further. A scene in Terence Fisher's *The Brides of Dracula* shows the vampire seeking the victim which he has chosen, but making do with another when he fails to find her: for his impulse for blood must be satisfied. This is an important scene, for it shows an evolution in the horror film from the Gothic to the neo-Gothic, from Expressionism to naturalism. We are no longer in the element of the affect, we have passed into the milieu of impulses (impulses, in another way, also animate the excellent work of Mario Bava). In Stroheim's *Foolish Wives*, the seducer hero moves from the maidservant to the society lady, to finish up with the sickly invalid, driven by the elemental force of a predatory impulse, which leads him to explore all milieux and to tear away what each one offers. Buñuel's *Susana* also achieves the complete exhaustion of a milieu: mother, servant, son and father.[5] The impulse must be exhaustive. It is not even sufficient to say that the impulse contents itself with what a milieu gives it or leaves to it. This contentment is not resignation, but a great joy in which the impulse rediscovers its power of choice, since it is, at the deepest level, the desire to change milieu, to seek a new milieu to explore, to dislocate, enjoying all the more what this milieu offers, however low, repulsive or disgusting it may be. The joys of the impulse cannot be measured against the affect, that is, against the intrinsic qualities of the possible object.

The originary world always contains a coexistence and a succession of distinct real milieux, as can be clearly seen in Stroheim and even more in Buñuel. And here, we must distinguish between the situation of the rich and that of the poor, of the masters and of the servants. It is more difficult for a poor servant to explore and exhaust a rich milieu than for a rich person – whether genuine or false – to penetrate a low milieu, to seize his prey from among the poor. Nevertheless, we must treat the evidence with caution. Stroheim primarily keeps to the evolution of the rich man in his own milieu and his descent into the lower depths. Buñuel (like Losey later) considers the reverse phenomenon, which is perhaps more terrifying because more subtle, more insinuating, closer to the hyena or the vulture which know how to wait – the invasion of the poor man or the servant, his investment of the rich milieu and the special way in which he exhausts it: not just *Susana*, but also the beggars and the servant woman of *Viridiana*. In the poor or the rich, impulses have the same goal and the same destiny: to smash into fragments, to tear off fragments, gather up the scraps, form the great rubbish dump and bring everything together in a single and identical death impulse. Death, the death impulse – naturalism is saturated with it. Here it attains its extreme of baseness, although this is not its last word. And, before the last word – which is not as desperate as might be expected – Buñuel also adds this: it is not only the poor and rich who participate in the same work of degradation, but so do good and holy men. For they also breed on scraps and remain stuck to the fragments which they carry away. This is why Buñuel's cycles form as much of a generalised degradation as does Stroheim's entropy. Beast of prey or parasite – everyone is both simultaneously. A diabolical voice can tell the holy man Nazarin, whose good works constantly hasten the degradation of the world: 'you are as useless as me', you are nothing but a parasite. The rich, beautiful, good Viridiana only evolves through the consciousness that she gains of her own uselessness and parasitism, which are inherent in the impulses of the Good. *There is an identical parasitic impulse everywhere*. This is the diagnosis. Hence the two poles of the fetish, fetishes of Good and fetishes of Evil, holy fetishes and fetishes of crime and sexuality also meet and interchange, like Buñuel's whole series of grotesque Christs, or the dagger-crucifix of *Viridiana*. The former might be called relics, and the latter, in the vocabulary of sorcery, 'vults' or voodoo objects. They are the two aspects of the same symptom. Even the two lovers of *The Golden Age* follow the upward course of the world less than its downward slope, attaching themselves to fetishes whose possession they dispute, each foreseeing time's attrition on the other, or the future accident and already separated. As Drouzy says, it is strange that the surrealists thought it was an example of mad love.[6] It is true that, from the start, Buñuel's relation to surrealism was almost as ambiguous as Stroheim's to Expressionism: he makes use of it, but for quite different ends which are those of an omnipotent naturalism.

2 *A characteristic of Buñuel's work: power of repetition in the image*

There are nevertheless great differences between Stroheim's naturalism and that of Buñuel. In literature, there is perhaps something analogous in the relationship between Zola and Huysmans. Huysmans said that Zola only imagined impulses of the body in stereotyped social milieux, where man was only reunited with the originary world of animals. For his part, he wanted a naturalism of the soul, which would better recognise the artificial constructions of perversion, but also perhaps the supernatural universe of faith. Similarly, in Buñuel, the discovery of impulses proper to the soul – as strong as hunger and sexuality and made up of them – was to give perversion a spiritual role which it lacked in Stroheim. And, above all, the radical critique of religion would gain nourishment from the sources of a possible faith, the violent critique of Christianity as institution would give a chance to Christ as person. Those who have seen an internal debate with a Christian impulse in Buñuel's work are not wrong: the perverse and, above all, Christ, sketch out a beyond rather than a within and give resonance to a question which is expressed as that of salvation, even if Buñuel has strong doubts about each of the means of this salvation; revolution, love, faith.

We can scarcely prejudge how Stroheim's work might have evolved.[7] But in the works which exist, the fundamental movement is that which the originary world imposes on milieux, that is, a degradation, a descent or an entropy. Consequently, the question of salvation can only be posed in the form of a local increase of entropy, which would indicate a capacity of the originary world to open up a milieu, instead of closing it. Thus the famous scene of the purest love among the apple trees in bloom in *The Wedding March*, and the second part, *The Honeymoon*, which was perhaps to have evoked the birth of a spiritual life. But, in Buñuel, as we have seen, entropy was replaced by the cycle or the eternal return. Now, the eternal return failed to be as catastrophic as entropy, just as the cycle failed to be as degrading in all its parts, but none the less they extract a spiritual power of repetition, which poses in a new way the question of a possible salvation. The good man, the saintly man, are imprisoned in the cycle, no less than the thug and the evildoer. But is not repetition capable of breaking out of its own cycle and of 'leaping' beyond good and evil? It is repetition which ruins and degrades us, but it is repetition which can save us and allow us to escape from the other repetition. Kierkegaard had already opposed a fettering, degrading repetition of the past to a repetition of faith, directed towards the future, which restored everything to us in a power which was not that of the Good but of the absurd. To the eternal return as reproduction of something always already-accomplished, is opposed the eternal return as resurrection, a new gift of the new, of the possible. Closer to Buñuel, Raymond Roussel, an author dear to the surrealists, developed 'scenes' or repetitions told twice over: in *Locus solus*, eight corpses in a glass cage reproduce the event of their life; and

Lucius Egroizard, artist and scholar of genius, who has gone mad after the murder of his daughter, repeats indefinitely the circumstances of the murder until he invents a machine to record the voice of a singer, deforms it, and restores so accurately the voice of his dead child that he regains everything: daughter, happiness. It moves from an indefinite repetition to repetition as decisive instant, from a closed repetition to an open repetition, from a repetition which not only fails, but induces failure, to a repetition which not only succeeds, but recreates the model or the originary.[8] We could mistake it for one of Buñuel's scripts. In fact the bad repetition does not occur simply because the event fails. It is that which makes the event fail, as in *The Discreet Charm of the Bourgeoisie*, where the repetition of lunch pursues its work of degradation through all the milieux which it closes on to themselves (Church, army, diplomacy . . .). And, in *The Exterminating Angel*, the law of bad repetition keeps the guests in the room whose boundaries cannot be crossed, while good repetition seems to abolish the limits and open them on to the world.

In Buñuel, as in Roussel, bad repetition appears in the form of inexactitude or imperfection: the introduction of the same two guests in *The Exterminating Angel* is on one occasion warm, and on the other frigid; or take the host's toast, which is made once in an atmosphere of indifference, the other time in one of general attention. However, repetition which saves appears to be exact, and the only one which is exact: it is when the virgin has offered herself to the God-host that the guests rediscover exactly their first position and at last find themselves free. But exactitude is a false criterion, standing in for something else. The repetition of the past is possible materially, but spiritually impossible, in the name of Time: on the contrary, the repetition of faith, directed towards the future, seems to be materially impossible, but spiritually possible, because it consists in beginning everything again, in ascending the path which is imprisoned by the cycle, by virtue of a creative instant of time. Are there thus two repetitions which confront each other, like a death impulse and a life impulse? Buñuel leaves us in a state of the greatest uncertainty, beginning with the distinction or the confusion of the two repetitions. The Angel's guests want to commemorate, that is, to repeat the repetition which has saved them; but in this way they fall back into a repetition which ruins them. Gathered together in the church for a *Te Deum*, they find themselves prisoners again in a deeper and greater way, as the revolution rumbles. In *The Milky Way* Christ as person has long maintained the chance of an opening-up of the world, through the varied milieux through which the pilgrims pass: but at the end, it indeed seems that all closes up again and that Christ is himself an enclosure instead of a horizon.⁹ To reach a repetition which saves, or which changes life, beyond good and evil, would it not be necessary to break with the order of impulses, to undo the cycles of time, reach an element which would be like a true 'desire', or like a choice capable of constantly beginning again (we have already seen this in respect of lyrical abstraction)?

Buñuel nevertheless gained something by making repetition, rather than entropy, the law of the world. *He injects the power of repetition into the cinematographic image.* In this way he is already going beyond the world of impulses, to knock on the doors of time and free it from the slope or the cycles which still subjugated it to a content. Buñuel does not cling to symptoms and to fetishes, he elaborates another type of sign which might be called 'scene' and which perhaps gives us a direct time-image. This is an aspect of his work which we will come across later, since it goes beyond naturalism. But it is from inside that Buñuel goes beyond naturalism, without ever renouncing it.

3 The difficulty of being naturalist

For the moment what interests us is not the way to get outside the limits of naturalism, but rather the manner in which some great directors have failed to come within them despite repeated attempts. This is because, while they were obsessed by the originary world of impulses, their particular genius none the less directed them towards other problems. Visconti, for example, from his first film to his last (*Obsession* and *The Innocent*) tries to reach raw and primordial impulses. But, too 'aristocratic', he does not succeed, because his true theme is elsewhere, and is immediately concerned with time. Renoir's case is different but analogous. Renoir is often led towards perverse and brutal impulses (notably in *Nana*, *The Diary of a Chambermaid* and *The Human Beast*), but he remains infinitely closer to Maupassant than to naturalism. Indeed, already in Maupassant, naturalism is nothing but a façade: things are seen as if through a window-pane or on the stage of a theatre, preventing duration from forming a coarse substance in the process of degradation; and when the pane thaws, it gives way to running water, which cannot be further reconciled with originary worlds, their impulses, their fragments and their outlines. Thus, everything which inspires Renoir turns him away from the naturalism which, none the less, continued to torment him.

Finally, the American directors. Some of them – notably Fuller – are deeply obsessed by naturalism and the world of Cain.[10] But they fail to achieve this because they are caught up in realism, that is, in the construction of a pure action-image which must be directly apprehended in the exclusive relationship between milieux and modes of behaviour (a type of violence completely different from naturalist violence). The action-image represses the impulse-image, which is too indecent because of its brutality, its very restraint, and its lack of realism. If there are naturalist pressures in the American cinema, they are perhaps to be found in certain female roles and through the intermediary of certain actresses. Indeed, the idea of an originary woman is easier to assimilate than all the other elements of naturalism, and in particular for the Americans. Zola introduced Nana as 'the principal flesh', 'the ferment', 'the golden fly', a basically good girl, but one who corrupts all that she touches, drawing it into an irresistible degradation which will rebound against her. Another type of originary woman, imperial and athletic, is often portrayed by Ava Gardner: three times impulse draws her irresistibly to marry the dead or impotent man (Lewin's *Pandora*, Mankiewicz's *The Barefoot Contessa*, Henry King's *The Sun Also Rises*). But the only American director who knew how to develop around a heroine a whole originary world seething with violent impulses was King Vidor, in the very post-war period when he distanced himself from Hollywood and from realism. In *Ruby Gentry*, the girl of the swamps (Jennifer Jones) pursues her revenge and manages to destroy the already exhausted milieu of the city and of men, making swamp return to swamp: one of the best studio swamps ever constructed. This is also the case in *Duel in the Sun*, a naturalist Western, and *Beyond the Forest*, where the characters seem to obey 'a secret, not yet identifiable force'.[11]

What makes the impulse-image so difficult to reach and even to define or identify, is that it is somehow 'stuck' between the affection-image and the action-image. Nicholas Ray's evolution would be a good example of this. It is true that his inspiration has often been described as 'lyrical': he belongs to lyrical abstraction. His colourism, which gives colours a maximum of absorbing power – as much as in Minnelli – does not cancel out white and black, but treats them as genuine colours. And, from this perspective, darkness is not a principle, but a consequence which flows from the relationship of light with colours and with white. Even the shadow of Christ, in the luminous exteriors of *King of Kings*, spreads out in chasing away the darkness: and in *The Savage Innocents* the immobile shots pick up a luminous whiteness, which refers back to the darkness of the Whites' civilisation (the Italian version is called *White Shadow*). It is as if violence is gone beyond: in this, Nicholas Ray's last period, the characters have mastered the level of abstraction and serenity, the spiritual determination which allows them to choose, and necessarily to choose the side which allows them to renew, to recreate the same choice constantly, whilst at the same time accepting the world. What was sought by the couple in *Johnny Guitar* or the one in *Run for Cover* and which they had begun to obtain, is fully achieved by the couple in *Party Girl*: that recreation of a chosen link which would otherwise fall into darkness. In all these senses, lyrical abstraction appears as the pure element which Ray constantly wanted to reach. Even in his early films where night features so prominently, the nocturnal life of the heroes is only a consequence of this, and the young man only takes refuge in the shade as a reaction. The house in *On Dangerous Ground* that shelters the blind girl and the irresponsible murderer, is like the reverse of the white snowscape that will be darkened by the shadowy lynch mob.

Ray nevertheless had to go through a slow evolution to master this element of lyrical abstraction.[12] He made his first films on the American model of the action-image, which brought him close to Kazan: the young man's violence is an active violence, a violence of reaction against the milieu, against society, against the father, against poverty and injustice, against solitude. The young man violently wants to become a man, but it is this very violence which gives him as his only choice either dying or remaining a child. The more violent he is, the more of a child he becomes (this remains the theme of *Rebel Without a Cause*; although the hero seems to succeed in his wager to 'become a man in a day', he does so too quickly to be pacified by it). A second period, many of whose elements had been embryonic in the first, was to modify the image of violence and of speed profoundly. They cease to be a reaction linked to a situation: they become internal and natural to the character, innate. It might be said that the rebel has chosen, not exactly evil, but 'for' evil, and that he attains a sort of beauty through and in a permanent upheaval. This is no longer an acted, but a compressed violence, from which only abrupt, effective and exact, often terrible acts which show a raw impulse, derive. In *Party Girl*, it is expressed in the life and death of the gangster friend, but also in the furious love of the couple, in the intensity of the woman's dances. And it is, above all, the new violence of *Wind Across the Everglades*, which makes this film a masterpiece of naturalism: the originary world, the swamp of the Everglades, its luminous greenery, its great white birds, the Man of impulses who wants to 'shoot God right in the face', his band of 'brothers of Cain', bird-killers. And their drunkenness responds to the hurricane and the thunderstorm. But already these images must be gone beyond: already the wager relates to the way out of the swamp, even at the price of death, revealing the possibility of an acceptance, a reconciliation. Finally, the surmounted violence and established serenity will constitute the ultimate form of a choice which chooses itself and ceaselessly begins itself again, bringing together in a final period all the elements of the lyrical abstraction which the realism of the first and the naturalism of the second had slowly elaborated.

It is difficult to reach the purity of the impulse-image and particularly to stay there, to find in it sufficient opening and creativity. The great directors we call naturalists are the ones who did. Losey (American, but so slightly . . .) is in fact the third, the equal of Stroheim and Buñuel. His whole work is situated within naturalist co-ordinates, while he renews them in his own way, as did his two predecessors. In Losey, what appears first is a very special violence which permeates or engulfs the characters, and precedes any action (an actor like Stanley Baker seems gifted with this violence which singles him out for Losey). It is the opposite of the realist violence of action. It is a violence in act [*en acte*], before coming into action. It is no more linked to an image of action than it is to the representation of a scene. It is a violence which is not merely internal or innate, but *static*, whose only equivalent is that of Bacon in painting, when he summons up an 'emanation' which arises from an immobile character, or that of Jean Genêt in literature, when he describes the extraordinary violence which can be contained in a motionless hand at rest.[13] *Time without Pity* shows a young defendant whom, we are told, is not merely innocent, but gentle and affectionate; and yet the spectator trembles – as much as the character himself trembles with violence – under the influence of his own contained violence.

In the second place, this originary violence, this violence of the impulse gradually penetrates a given milieu, a derived milieu, which it literally exhausts in a long process of degradation. Losey in this respect has a predilection for a 'Victorian' milieu, a Victorian city or house, where the drama takes place, and where the staircases assume a fundamental importance, inasmuch as they delineate a *line of the steepest slope*. The impulse scours the milieu, knowing no satisfaction other than that of taking possession of that which seems to be closed to it, to belong by rights to another milieu, to a higher level. Hence perversion in Losey, which consists both in this propagation of degradation and in the election or choice of the 'fragment' which is the most difficult to attain. *The Servant* illustrates this investment of the master and the house by the servant. It is a world of predators: *Secret Ceremony* brings several types of predator into confrontation, the lion, the two birds of prey and the hyena, humble, affectionate and vengeful. *The Go-Between* multiplies this process, since the farmer not only takes possession of the daughter of the house, but the two lovers take possession of the child, constrained and fascinated, petrifying him in his role as go-between, subjecting him to a strange violation which redoubles their pleasure. In Losey's world of impulses, perhaps one of the most important is 'servility', raised to the state of true elementary human impulse: 'in act' [*en acte*] in the servant, but latent and erupting in the master, the lovers and the child (even *Don Giovanni* is not exempt from this).[14] Like parasitism in Buñuel, servility is a feature of master as well as servant. Degradation is the symptom of this unversal impulse to servility, to which correspond the ensnaring mirrors and spell-working statues, like so many fetishes. Fetishes even appear in the disturbing form of 'vults', with *Mr Klein*'s Kabbala, or, above all, the belladonna of *The Go-Between*.

If naturalist degradation went through a kind of entropy in Stroheim, and through a cycle or repetition in Buñuel, it now takes on another configuration. This is what might be called – in the third place – the reversal against self. Here this notion takes on a simple meaning, peculiar to Losey. The originary violence of impulses is always 'in act', but it is too great for action. We might say that there is no action great enough to be its equivalent in the derived milieu. A prey to the violence of the impulse himself, the character trembles on to himself, and in this sense he becomes the prey, the victim of his own impulse. Losey thus sets traps which are so many psychological misinterpretations of his work. The character may give the impression of being a weakling who compensates for his weakness by an apparent brutality, to which he abandons himself when he no longer knows what to do, even though he may break down immediately afterwards. This already seemed to be the case in *Time without Pity*, and, more recently, in *The Trout*. Each time the adult kills in a position of impotence and breaks down like a child. But, in reality, Losey is not describing any psychological mechanism; he is inventing an extreme logic of impulses. It is pointless to talk of masochism. Fundamentally there is the impulse, which, by nature, is too strong for the character, whatever his personality. This violence is within him and is far from being an appearance, but it cannot be awakened – that is, reveal itself in the derived milieu – without shattering the character at a stroke, or entangling him in a becoming which is that of his own degradation and death. Losey's characters are not bogus hard men, but bogus weaklings: they are condemned in advance by the violence which dwells in them and which impels them to go to the limit of a milieu which the impulse explores, but at the price of making them disappear themselves with their milieu. *Mr Klein* is, to a greater extent than any of Losey's other films, the prime example of such a becoming, which sets the trap of psychological or psychoanalytical interpretations. The hero is indeed that keg of violence which we always find in Losey (Alain Delon has that static violence which a Losey actor needs). But what is peculiar to *Mr Klein* is that the violence of the impulses which dwell in him draw him into the strangest becoming: taken for a Jew, mistaken for a Jew under the Nazi occupation, he begins by protesting, and puts all his gloomy violence into a court inquiry, in which he wants to denounce the injustice of that assimilation. But it is not in the name of the law, or of a recognition of a more fundamental justice, but purely in the name of the violence within him that he gradually makes a decisive discovery: even if he *was* a Jew, all his impulses would still be opposed to the derived violence of an order which is not theirs, but the social order of a dominant régime. So that the character begins to assume that state of Jewishness which is not his own and consents to his disappearance among the mass of Jews led off to their deaths. It is exactly the becoming-Jew of a non-Jew.[15] The role of the double, and the course of the court inquiry in *Mr Klein* has been widely commented on. To us these themes appear secondary and subordinate to the impulse-image, that is, to the static violence of the character, whose only outlet in the derived milieu is a reversal against himself, a becoming which leads him to disappearance, as to the most overwhelming assumption of responsibility.

Is there a salvation in Losey, even one as ambiguous as in Stroheim or Buñuel? If there is one, we would have to look for it in the women. It seems that the world of impulses and the milieu of symptoms, enclose the men hermetically, delivering them up to a sort of male homosexual game from which they do not emerge. On the other hand, there is no originary woman in Losey's naturalism (except *Modesty Blaise*, woman of impulses and fetishes, but who is presented as a parody). Often women in Losey seem in advance of the milieu, in revolt against it and outside the originary world of the men – of which they will only be the victim, or the user. It is they who trace a line of exit, and who win a freedom which is creative, artistic, or simply practical: they have neither shame, nor guilt, nor static violence which would reverse itself against them. This is the case with the sculptress in *The Damned*, but also *Eve* and the new Eve whom Losey discovers in *The Trout*. They leave naturalism to reach lyrical abstraction. These advanced women are rather similar to Thomas Hardy's, with analogous functions.

Inseparable from derived milieux, Losey's originary worlds have particular features which belong to his style. These are the strange, flat spaces, often, but not always, overhanging, rocky or pebbly, criss-crossed with canals, galleries, trenches, tunnels which form a horizontal labyrinth: the cliff of *The Damned*, the high plateaux of *Figures in a Landscape*, the lofty terrace of *Boom!* But, on a lower level, they can be the 'nearly prehistoric' ghost town, the Venice of *Eve*, a peninsula which resembles an outer edge of the world, the Norfolk of *The Go-Between*, an Italianate garden for *Don Giovanni*, a one-time park, like that in which the hero of *Time without Pity* has set up his business and racing-track, a simple gravelly square, as in *The Servant*, a cricket pitch (which Losey loves filming, although he does not like the game), a winter cycle-racing track with its tunnels in *Mr Klein*. The originary world is thronged with grottoes and birds, but also with fortresses, helicopters, sculptures, statues; and we do not know if its canals are artificial or natural, lunar. Thus the originary world does not oppose Nature to the constructions of man: it is oblivious to this distinction, which is valid only in derived milieux. But, rising up between a milieu which has not finished dying and another which does not succeed in being born, it appropriates both the remains of the former and the outlines of the latter, to make them into its 'morbid symptoms', as Gramsci puts it in a formula which serves as exergue to *Don Giovanni*. The originary world embraces futurism and archaism. All that is act or gesture of the impulse belongs to it, as to the mad master of the cliff. And, from heights to depths, along the sloping paths which are this time vertical, or from the outside to the inside, the originary world communicates with the derived milieux, both as predator which choses its prey there and as parasite which hastens its degradation. The milieu is the Victorian house, just as the originary world is the wild region which overhangs and surrounds it.

This is how the four co-ordinates of naturalism are organised in Losey. He clearly shows it himself in relation to *The Damned*, by defining a double juxtaposition: on one hand the Portland cliffs, 'their primitive landscape and their military installations', their mutant, radioactive children (originary world), but also 'the pathetic Victorian style of the little holiday resort of Weymouth' (derived milieu); on the other hand, the great figures of birds and helicopters and the sculptures (images and acts of impulses), but also the motorbike gang whose handlebars are like wings (perverse actions in the derived milieu).[16] The four dimensions vary from film to film and enter into various relationships of opposition and complementarity, depending on what Losey wants to say and show.

9 The action-image
The large form

1 From situation to action: 'secondness'

We are approaching a domain which is easier to define: derived
milieux assert their independence and start to become valid for
themselves. Qualities and powers are no longer displayed in any-
space-whatevers, no longer inhabit originary worlds, but are
actualised directly in determinate, geographical, historical and social
space-times. Affects and impulses now only appear as embodied in
behaviour, in the form of emotions or passions which order and
disorder it. This is Realism. It is true that there are all kinds of
possible transitions. There was already a tendency for German
Expressionism to install its shadows and its chiaroscuro in physically
and socially defined spaces (Lang, Pabst). Conversely, a determinate
milieu can actualise so much power that it is itself valid as an originary
world or an any-space-whatever: we can see this in Swedish lyricism.
It is nevertheless true that realism is defined by its specific level. On
this level, it does *not* exclude fiction or even the dream. It can include
the fantastic, the extraordinary, the heroic and above all melodrama.
It can include exaggeration and lack of moderation, as long as these
are of its own type. What constitutes realism is simply this: milieux
and modes of behaviour, milieux which actualise and modes of
behaviour which embody. The action-image is the relation between
the two and all the varieties of this relation. It is this model which
produced the universal triumph of the American cinema, to the point
of acting as a passport for foreign directors who contributed to its
formation.

The milieu always actualises several qualities and powers. It carries
out a global synthesis of them, it is itself the Ambiance or the
Encompasser [*Englobant*], whilst the qualities and the powers have
become *forces* in the milieu. The milieu and its forces incurve on
themselves, they act on the character, throw him a challenge, and
constitute a situation in which he is caught. The character reacts in his
turn (action properly speaking) so as to respond to the situation, to
modify the milieu, or his relation with the milieu, with the situation,
with other characters. He must acquire a new mode of being (*habitus*)
or raise his mode of being to the demands of the milieu and of the

situation. Out of this emerges a restored or modified situation, a new situation. Everything is individuated: the milieu as a particular space-time, the situation as determining and determinate, the collective as well as the individual character. And, as we have seen, according to Peirce's classification of images, it is the reign of 'secondness'; everything here is two by itself. Already, in the milieu, we distinguish the power-qualities and the state of things which actualises them. The situation, and the character or the action, are like two terms which are simultaneously correlative and antagonistic. The action in itself is a duel of forces, a series of duels: duel with the milieu, with the others, with itself. Finally, the new situation which emerges from the action forms a couple with the initial situation. This is the set [*ensemble*] of the action-image, or at least its first form. It constitutes the organic representation, which seems to be endowed with breath or respiration. For it expands towards the milieu and contracts from the action. More precisely, it expands or contracts on either side, according to the states of the situation and the demands of the action.

In the set, nevertheless, it can be said that there are, as it were, two inverse spirals, of which one narrows towards action and the other broadens towards the new situation: a form like an hour-glass, or an egg-timer, which includes both space and time. This organic and spiral representation has, as its formula, SAS' (from the situation to the transformed situation via the intermediary of the action). This formula seems to us to correspond to what Burch called 'the large form'.[1] This action-image or organic representation has two poles, or rather two signs, of which one refers primarily to the organic, and the other to the active or functional. We call the first *synsign*, in partial conformity with Peirce: the synsign is a set of power-qualities as actualised in a milieu, in a state of things or a determinate space-time.[2] And we should like to call the other *binomial*, in order to designate every duel, that is to say, what is properly active in the action-image. There is a binomial as soon as the state of a force relates back to an antagonistic force, and particularly when – one (or both) of the forces being 'spontaneous' – it involves in its very exercise an effort to foresee the exercise of the other force: the agent acts as a function of what he thinks the other is going to do. Feints, parries and traps are therefore good illustrations of binomials. In a Western, the moment of the duel – when the street empties, when the hero comes out, walking with a very distinctive step, trying to guess where the other is and what he's going to do – is a binomial *par excellence*.

Take for example Sjöström's *The Wind* (his first American film).

The wind never stops blowing across the plain. It is almost an originary naturalist world, or even an Expressionist any-space-whatever, the space of the wind as affect. But there is also a whole state of things which actualises this power, combines it with that of the prairie, in a determinate space, Arizona: a realist milieu. A girl from the South arrives in this country, which she is not used to, and finds herself caught in a series of duels, a physical duel with the milieu, a psychological duel with the hostile family which takes her in, a sentimental duel with the rough cowboy who is in love with her, a bodily duel with the cattle dealer who tries to rape her. Having killed the dealer she tries desperately to bury him in the sand, but the wind uncovers the corpse each time. This is the moment at which the milieu throws down the strongest challenge to her, and where she reaches the essence [*fond*] of the duel. Reconciliation then begins: with the cowboy who understands and helps her, with the wind, whose power she comprehends as she feels a new mode of being growing within her.

How does this type of action-image develop through a number of great cinematographic genres? In the first place, the documentary. Toynbee has developed a pragmatic philosophy of history according to which civilisations were answers to the challenges thrown down by the milieu.[3] While the normal or rather normative case is that of communities confronting challenges which are great, but not great enough to absorb all the capacities of man, one can conceive two other cases: the one in which the challenges of the milieu are so strong that man can only respond to them or parry them using all his energy (civilisation of survival); and the one in which the milieu is so favourable that man can devote himself to living (civilisation of leisure). Flaherty's documentaries consider these cases, and discover the nobility of these extreme civilisations. He is therefore unconcerned by criticisms that he is Rousseauist, that he neglects the political problems posed by primitive societies and the role of Whites in the exploitation of these societies. This would be to introduce a third, a thirdness which has nothing to do with the conditions fixed by Flaherty: to capture in the raw a tête-à-tête with the milieu (ethology rather than ethnology). *Nanook of the North* begins with the exposition of the milieu, when the Eskimo approaches with his family. An immense synsign of the opaque sky and the ice slopes where Nanook wins his struggle for survival in a hostile milieu: the duel with the ice to build the igloo and above all, the famous duel with the seal. Here we have a grandiose SAS' structure, or rather SAS, since the grandeur of Nanook's actions lies less in modifying the situation than in surviving in an impervious milieu. Conversely, *Moana* shows us civilisation without challenge from Nature. But, as if man can only be man through effort and resistance to pain, he must compensate for an over-benevolent milieu by inventing for himself the trial of tattooing, which enables him to give himself up to a fundamental duel with himself.

In the second place, consider the psycho-social film: in the whole realist part of his work King Vidor was able to set up great global syntheses, moving from the collectivity to the individual and from the individual to the collectivity. Such a form can be called 'ethical'. Moreover it imposes itself in every genre, inasmuch as the ethos designates simultaneously the location or the milieu, the stay in a milieu, and the habit or the habitus, the mode of being. This ethical or realist form, far from excluding the dream, embraces the two poles of the American Dream: on the one hand the idea of a unanimist community or of a nation-milieu, melting pot and fusion of all minorities (the unanimous burst of laughter at the end of *The Crowd*, or the same expression which breaks out on the face of a Chinaman, a Black and a White, in *Street Scene*); on the other hand the idea of a leader, that is, a man of this nation who knows how to respond to the challenges of the milieu as to the difficulties of a situation (*Our Daily Bread, An American Romance*). This well directed unanimism circulates even through the most serious crises and leaves a place only to be formed again elsewhere: lost by the city, it passes into the agricultural communities, then leaps 'from corn to steel', to large-scale industry. None the less the unanimity can be false and the individual left to his own resources. Was this not precisely the case in *The Crowd*, where the town was only a human, artificial and indifferent collectivity and the individual, an abandoned being, deprived of resources and of reactions? The figure SAS′, in which the individual modifies the situation, has as its opposite a situation, SAS, such that the individual no longer knows what to do and at best finds himself in the same situation once more: the American nightmare in *The Crowd*.

It may even be that the situation gets worse, and that the individual falls lower and lower, in a descending spiral: SAS″. The American cinema admittedly prefers to present characters who are already degraded, like Howard Hawks' alcoholics, whose struggle to rise again will form the story. But even when it shows the process of degradation the approach is clearly completely different from that of Expressionism or naturalism. It is no longer a matter of a fall into a black hole, nor of an entropy as a decline in impulse (although King Vidor came close to this naturalist point of view).

Realist degradation – in the American manner – was to slip into the milieu-behaviour, situation-action, mould. It does not express a destiny of the affect or a destiny of impulses but a pathology of the milieu and a behavioural disorder. It is heir to a dazzling literary tradition, that of Fitzgerald or Jack London: 'Drinking was one of the modes of existence that I was leading, a habit of the men with whom I was mixed up. . . .' Degradaton marks a man who frequents milieux without law, of false unanimity or false community, and can only maintain falsely integrated forms of behaviour, cracked ways of behaving which can no longer succeed in organising their own segments. This man is a 'born loser', 'takes it too hard'. It is the world of the bars in Wilder's *Lost Weekend* (in spite of the happy ending), it is the world of billiards in Rossen's *The Hustler*, and it is above all the criminal world linked to prohibition, which was to constitute the great genre of the *film noir*. From this point of view, the *film noir* describes the milieu, sets out situations, holds itself back in preparation for action and action which is precisely organised (the model of the hold-up for example), and finally emerges into a new situation, the most common being re-established order. But, in fact, if the gangsters are born losers – in spite of the power of their milieu and the effectiveness of their actions – it is because something eats away at both, reversing the spiral to their cost. On the one hand the 'milieu' is a false community, in fact a jungle where every alliance is precarious and reversible; on the other hand, the modes of behaviour, however studied they are, are not true habits, true responses to situations, but conceal a fault or cracks which cause them to disintegrate. This is the story of Hawks' *Scarface*, where all the hero's cracks, all the little faults which made him take it too hard, converge in the appalling crisis to which he succumbs on the death of his sister. Or , in a different way, in Huston's *Asphalt Jungle*, the doctor's extreme attention to detail and the killer's skill cannot resist the treason of a minor character who opens up in the one the little crack of eroticism, and in the other the nostalgia for his native country, and leads them both to failure or death. Are we to conclude that society is made in the image of its crimes, and that all milieux are pathological, and all modes of behaviour are cracked? This would be closer to Lang or Pabst. But the American cinema had the means to save its dream by passing through nightmares.

The Western is a fourth great genre, and is solidly anchored in a milieu. Since Ince, and according to the formula SAS' (we will see that this is not the only formula of the Western), the milieu is the Ambiance or the Encompasser. Here, the principal quality of the image is breath, respiration. It not only inspires the hero, but brings things together in a whole of organic representation and contracts or expands depending on the circumstances. When colour takes possession of this world, it follows a chromatic scale where it diffuses, and where the saturated [*saturé*] resonates with the faint [*lavé*] (we will rediscover this ambiant colour in the artificial sets [*décors*] of Ford's *How Green Was My Valley*). The ultimate encompasser is the sky and its pulsations, not only in Ford, but also in Hawks who makes one of the characters in *Big Sky* say: it is a big country, the only thing which is bigger is the sky. . . . Encompassed by the sky, the milieu in turn encompasses the collectivity. It is as representative of the collectivity that the hero becomes capable of an action which makes him equal to the milieu and re-establishes its accidentally or periodically endangered order: mediations of the community and of the *land*[4] are necessary in order to form a leader and render an individual capable of such a great action. We recognise the world of Ford, with the intense collective moments (marriage, festival, dances and songs), the constant presence of the land and the immanence of the sky. Some have concluded from this that there is a closed space in Ford, without real movement or time.[5] It seems to us, rather, that movement is real but, instead of happening from part to part, or in relation to a whole whose change it would express, it happens *in* an encompasser, whose respiration it expresses. The outside encompasses the inside, both communicate, and we advance by passing from the one to the other in both directions, as in the images of *Stagecoach* where the diligence inside alternates with the diligence seen from the outside. One can go from a known to an unknown point, the promised land, as in *Wagonmaster*: the essential point remains the encompasser which includes both and which expands as one advances painfully and contracts when one stops and rests. Ford's originality lies in the fact that only the encompasser gives measure to movement, or the organic rythmn. It is thus the melting pot of minorities, that is, what brings them together, what reveals their correspondences even when they appear to be opposed, what already shows the fusion between them necessary for the birth of a nation: for example, the three groups of persecuted people who meet in *Wagonmaster* – the Mormons, the travelling players and the Indians.

If one remains at this first approximation, one is in an SAS structure which has become cosmic or epic – the hero becomes equal to the milieu via the intermediary of the community, and does not modify the milieu, but re-establishes cyclic order in it.[6] However, it would be dangerous to reserve an epic genius for Ince and Ford, attributing to other more recent directors the invention of a tragic or even a romantic Western. The application of Hegel's and Lukács' formula of the succession of these genres works badly for the Western: as Mitry has shown, from the outset the Western explores all the directions – epic, tragic, romantic – with cowboys who are already nostalgic, solitary, ageing, or even born losers, or rehabilitated Indians.[7] Throughout his work, Ford constantly grasps the evolution of a situation, which introduces a perfectly real time. There is certainly a great difference between the Western and what can be called the neo-Western; but it is not explicable in terms of a succession of genres, or of a transition from the closed to the open in space. In Ford, the hero is not content to re-establish the episodically threatened order. The organisation of the film, the organic representation, is not a circle, but a spiral where the situation of arrival differs from the situation of departure: SAS′. It is an ethical rather than an epic form. In *The Man Who Shot Liberty Valance* the bandit is killed and order re-established: but the cowboy who has killed him allows us to think that it is the future senator, thus accepting the transformation of the law which ceases to be the tacit epic law of the West in order to become the written or novelistic law of industrial civilisation. Similarly, in *Two Rode Together*, where this time the sheriff gives up his job and refuses to accept the evolution of the small town.[8] In both cases Ford invents an interesting procedure, which is the modified image: an image is shown twice, but the second time, it is modified or completed in such a way as to make us feel the difference between S and S′. In *Liberty Valance* the end shows the true death of the bandit and the cowboy who shoots, whilst we had previously seen the truncated image which the official version would stick to (it is the future senator who killed the bandit). In *Two Rode Together*, we are shown the same silhouette of the sheriff in the same posture, but it is no longer the same sheriff. It is true that between the two, between S and S′, there is a lot of ambiguity and hypocrisy. The hero of *Liberty Valance* is bent on cleansing himself of the crime in order to become a respectable senator, whilst the journalists are bent on leaving him his legend, without which he would be nothing. And as Roy has shown, *Two Rode Together* has as its subject the spiral of money which, from the start, undermines the community and goes on to enlarge its empire.

But one might say that, in both cases, what counts for Ford is that the community can develop certain illusions about itself. This would be the great difference between healthy and pathogenic milieux. Jack

London wrote fine passages in order to show that, finally, the alcoholic community has no illusions about itself. Far from producing dreams, alcohol 'refuses to let the dreamer dream', it acts as a 'pure reason' which convinces us that life is a masquerade, the community a jungle, life a despair (hence the sneering of the alcoholic). The same could be said of criminal communities. On the contrary, a community is healthy in so far as a kind of consensus reigns, a consensus which allows it to develop illusions about itself, about its motives, about its desires and its cupidity, about its values and its ideals: 'vital' illusions, realist illusions which are more true than pure truth.[9] Ford also took this point of view, and in *The Informer*, showed the almost Expressionist degradation of a treacherous informer in so far as he can no longer have any illusions. One cannot, therefore, criticise the American dream for being only a dream: this is what it wants to be, drawing all its power from the fact that it is a dream. For Ford, as for Vidor, society changes, and does not stop changing, but its changes take place in an Encompasser which covers them and blesses them with a healthy illusion as continuity of the nation.

Finally, the American cinema constantly shoots and reshoots a single fundamental film, which is the birth of a nation-civilisation, whose first version was provided by Griffith. It has in common with the Soviet cinema the belief in a finality of universal history; here the blossoming of the American nation, there the advent of the proletariat. But, with the Americans, organic representation is obviously unaware of dialectical development; it and it alone is the whole of history, the germinating stock from which each nation-civilisation detaches itself as an organism, each prefiguring America. This is the origin of the deeply analogical or parallelist character of this conception of history, as it is found in Griffith's *Intolerance* which intersperses four periods, or in the first version of Cecil B. De Mille's *Ten Commandments*, which puts two periods into parallel, the latter being America. The decadent nations are sick organisms, like Griffith's Babylon or De Mille's Rome. If the Bible is fundamental to them, it is because the Hebrews, then the Christians, gave birth to healthy nation-civilisations which already displayed the two characteristics of the American dream: that of a melting pot in which minorities are dissolved and that of a ferment which creates leaders capable of reacting to all situations. Conversely, Ford's Lincoln recapitulates biblical history, judging as perfectly as Solomon, bringing about, like Moses, the transition from the nomadic to the written law, from nomos to logos, entering the city on his ass like

Christ (*Young Mr Lincoln*). And if the historical film thus forms a great genre of the American cinema, it is perhaps because, in the conditions peculiar to America, all the other genres were already historical, whatever their degree of fiction: crime with gangsterism, adventure with the Western, had the status of pathogenic or exemplary historical structures.

It is easy to make fun of Hollywood's historical conceptions. It seems to us, on the contrary, that they bring together the most serious aspects of history as seen by the nineteenth century. Nietzsche distinguished three of these aspects, 'monumental history', 'antiquarian history' and 'critical', or rather ethical, history.[10] The monumental aspect concerns the physical and human encompasser, the natural and architectural milieu. Babylon and its defeat, in Griffith, the Hebrews, the desert and the sea which opens; or, in Cecil B. De Mille, the Philistines, Dagon's temple and its destruction by Samson, are immense synsigns which make the image itself monumental. The treatment can be very different; whether great frescos in *The Ten Commandments*, or a series of engravings in *Samson and Delilah*, the image remains sublime, and although the temple of Dagon can trigger off our laughter, it is an Olympian laughter which takes hold of the spectator. According to Nietzsche's analysis, such an aspect of history favours the analogies or parallels between one civilisation and another: the great moments of humanity, however distant they are, are supposed to communicate via the peaks, and form a 'collection of effects in themselves' which can be more easily compared and act all the more strongly on the mind of the modern spectator. Monumental history thus naturally tends towards the universal, and finds its masterpiece in *Intolerance*, because the different periods do not simply follow one another, but alternate through an extraordinary rhythmic montage (Buster Keaton gives a comic version of it in *Three Ages*). And, in whatever manner it proceeded, a confrontation of periods continued to be the dream of the monumental history film even in Eisenstein.[11] This conception of history has, however, a big disadvantage: that of treating phenomena as effects in themselves, separate from any cause. Nietzsche had already pointed this out and it is what Eisenstein criticises in the American historical and social cinema. Not only are civilisations considered to be parallel, but the principal phenomena of a single civilisation, for example, the rich *and* the poor, are treated as 'two parallel independent phenomena', as pure effects that are observed, if necessary with regret, but nevertheless without having any cause assigned to them. Hence, it is inevitable that causes are rejected from another perspective, and only appear in the form of individual duels which sometimes oppose a representative of the poor and a representative of the rich, sometimes a decadent and a man of the future, sometimes a just man and a traitor, etc. Eisenstein's strength thus lies in showing that the principal *technical aspects* of American montage since Griffith – the alternate parallel montage which makes up the situation, and the alternate concurrent montage which leads to the duel – relate back to this social and bourgeois historical conception. It is this essential defect that Eisenstein wants to remedy: he demands a presentation of true causes, which would have to subject the monumental to a 'dialectical' construction (in any event, the struggle of classes instead of that of a traitor, a decadent or an evildoer).[12]

If monumental history considers effects in themselves, and if the only causes it understands are simple duels opposing individuals, antiquarian history must occupy itself with these as well, and reconstitute their forms which are habitual to the epoch: wars and confrontations, gladiator combats, chariot races, tournaments, etc. And antiquarian history is not satisfied with duels in the strict sense, it stretches out towards the external situation and contracts into the means of action and intimate customs, vast tapestries, clothes, finery, machines, weapons or tools, jewels, private objects. The orgy allows gigantism and intimacy to coexist. The antiquarian runs parallel to the monumental. Here again facile ironical remarks are made about Hollywood reconstructions, and the 'brand-new' appearance of the props: the new is, as in the antiquarian, the sign of the actualisation of the epoch. The fabrics become a fundamental element of the historical film, especially with the colour-image, as in *Samson and Delilah*, where the display of cloth by the merchant and Samson's theft of the thirty tunics, constitute the two peaks of colour. Machines also form a peak, whether they give birth to a new nation-civilisation, or whether on the contrary they announce its decline or disappearance. In his only historical film strictly speaking, *Land of the Pharaohs*, Hawks only seems to be interested in one moment, the whole ending, where the architect has become an engineer as well, and has set up an extraordinary new machine for the Pharaoh which combines sand and stone, flowing sand and descending stone, so that the pyramid's funeral chamber can be absolutely hermetically closed.

Finally, it is true that the monumental and antiquarian conceptions of history would not come together so well without the ethical image which measures and organises them both. As Cecil B. De Mille says, it is a matter of Good and Evil, with all the temptations or the horrors of Evil (the barbarians, the unbelievers, the intolerant, the orgy, etc.). The ancient or recent past must submit to trial, go to court, in order to disclose what it is that produces decadence and what it is that produces new life; what the ferments of decadence and the germs of new life are, the orgy and the sign of the cross, the omnipotence of the rich and the misery of the poor. A strong ethical judgement must condemn the injustice of 'things', bring compassion, herald the new civilisation on the march, in short, constantly rediscover America . . . more especially as, from the beginning, all examination of causes has been dispensed with. The American cinema is content to illustrate the weakening of a civilisation in the milieu, and the intervention of a traitor in the action. But the marvel is that, with all these limits, it has succeeded in putting forward a strong and coherent conception of universal history, monumental, antiquarian and ethical.[13]

2 The laws of organic composition

What are the laws of the action-image across all these genres? The first concerns the action-image as organic representation in its entirety [*ensemble*]. It is structural because the places and the moments are well defined in their oppositions and their complementarities. From the point of view of the situation (S), from the point of view of space, of the frame and of the shot, it organises the way in which the milieu carries several powers into effect, the weight given to each one. For example, in Ford's skies, the conflict or the agreement of these powers, the particular role of the earth, of the land, which is both one power among others, and the location of confrontation or of reconciliation of all of them; but also the way in which the whole incurves itself around the group, the character or the home, constituting an encompasser from which the hostile or favourable forces are detached, the way in which the Indians appear on top of a hill, at the boundary between earth and sky. . . . And, from the point of view of time or of the succession of shots, it organises the passage from S to S', the great respiration, the alternation of moments of contraction and of expansion, the alternations of outside and inside, the division of the principal situation into secondary situations which are like so many little local missions within the global mission. In all these respects, organic representation is a spiral of development which includes spatial and temporal caesuras. We rediscover this conception in Eisenstein, although he conceives of the distribution and succession of vectors on the spiral entirely differently. For Griffith and the American cinema, alternate parallel montage is sufficient to organise empirically the mutual link between the vectors.

Alternate montage includes another figure, no longer parallel, but concurrent or convergent. The passage from S to S′ takes place through the intermediary of A, the decisive action, most often placed very close to S′. The synsign must contract into a binomial or duel in order for the powers which it actualises to be redistributed in a new way, to be pacified or to recognise the triumph of one of them. The second law therefore governs the passage from S to A. Now the decisive action or the duel can only arise if, from various points of the encompasser, lines of action emanate converging on this occasion to make possible the ultimate individual confrontation, the modifying reaction. These are the lines of action which are the object of alternate convergent montage, the second figure of montage in Griffith. But perfection was, perhaps, achieved by Lang, in *M* (which, in fact, prepared Lang's departure for America). It is in analysing the convergent montage of this film that Noël Burch advances the notion of 'large form'. Indeed, the global situation is first of all displayed in a determined and individuated space-time: the courtyard of the building in the town, the landing and the kitchen of an apartment in the building, the journey from the apartment to the school, the posters on the walls, people's excitement. . . . But very quickly two points emerge from this milieu, then two lines of action which will alternate constantly in converging, with continual 'rhymes' from one to the other and form a pincer to grab the criminal: the line of the police and the line of the underworld (which fears that the child-killer will harm its activities). It will be noted that, by virtue of the strongly structural character of organic representation, the negative or positive hero's place has been prepared long before he comes to occupy it and even before he knows he is to occupy it: hence the progressive unmasking of the murderer. And it is when the underworld lays hands on him that we witness the real action and really know the murderer. It is *M*'s duel with the tribunal of bandits and beggars. The double line with its caesuras and its rhymes has led us to the situation of the duel, from the synsign to the binomial. The organic representation, it is true, retains its final ambiguity: for, when the police catch up with the underworld, and snatch the killer from it to bring him before a legal tribunal, we do not know whether the situation will emerge from it modified, re-established, cleansed of the crime, or whether nothing will be like it was before, and crime, always destined to take on new forms ('now, we will have to keep a closer eye on the little ones'): S' or S?

The third law is like the reverse of the second. In fact, while alternate montage is absolutely necessary to the passage from situation to action, it seems that in the action which is thus compressed, at the very root of the duel, there is something which rebels against any montage. We might call this third law, Bazin's law or the law of 'forbidden montage'. André Bazin showed that if two independent actions which coincide at the production of an effect are amenable to montage, then in the effect produced there must be a moment where two terms confront each other face to face and must be seized in an irreducible simultaneity, without the possibility of resorting to a montage, or even to a shot-reverse shot. Bazin cites as an example Chaplin's *The Circus*: all trick shots are permitted, but Charlie really has to go into the lion's cage and be with the lion in a single shot. Nanook and the seal must also confront one another in the same shot.[14] This law of the binomial no longer concerns SS', nor SA, but A for itself.

The duel is moreover not a unique and localised moment of the action-image. The duel stakes out the lines of action, always marking the necessary simultaneities. The passage from situation to action is thus accompanied by a dovetailing of duels in each other. The binomial is a polynomial. Even in the Western, which presents the duel in its purest state, it is difficult to mark out its boundaries in the final instance. Is the duel that of the cowboy with the bandit or the Indian? Or with the woman, with the boyfriend, with the new man who will supersede him (as in *Liberty Valance*)? In *M*, is the real duel between M and the police or society, or rather between M and the underworld which does not want him? Does not the real duel remain elsewhere? Finally, it might be external to the film, although internal to the cinema. In the scene of the underworld tribunal, the bandits and the beggars vindicate the rights of the crime habitus or mode of behaviour, crime as rational organisation, and criticise M for acting through passion. To which M replies that this is what makes him innocent: he cannot do otherwise, he only acts through impulse or affect, and at precisely this moment, and only at this moment the actor acts in an Expressionist way. Finally, is not the true duel in *M* between Lang himself and Expressionism? It is his farewell to Expressionism, it is his entry into realism as *The Testament of Dr Mabuse* will confirm (in which Mabuse disappears, giving way to the frigid realist organisation).

But if there is in this way a whole dovetailing of duels, it is by reason of a fifth law: there is necessarily a *big gap* between the encompasser and the hero, the milieu and the behaviour which modifies it, situation and action, which can only be bridged progressively, throughout the length of the film. One can imagine a situation which would become instantaneously converted into a duel, but this would be 'burlesque'. In a short masterpiece (*The Fatal Glass of Beer*), Fields opens the door of his cabin in the frozen North at regular intervals protesting 'it's not fit to put a dog out', and immediately receives two anonymous snowballs right in the face. But, normally, the path from the milieu to the final duel is a long one. This is because the hero is not immediately ripe for action; like Hamlet, the action to be undertaken is too great for him. It is not that he is weak: he is, on the contrary, equal to the encompasser but only potentially. His grandeur and his power must be actualised. He must give up his withdrawal and his internal peace, or he must rediscover the strengths of which the situation has deprived him, or he must await the favourable moment when he will receive the necessary support of a community and of a team. Indeed, the hero needs a people, a fundamental group which gives him its blessing, but also a makeshift group which helps him, which is smaller and more heterogeneous. He must cope with the failings and the betrayals of the one as with the evasions of the other. These are variables that are found in the historical film as well as in the Western. Even in Eisenstein, what Soviet critics did not appreciate was the Hamletian character of *Ivan the Terrible*: the two great moments of doubt through which he passes, like two caesuras of the film; and also his aristocratic nature which means that the people cannot serve as the fundamental group for him, but only as a makeshift group which he uses as a tool. In general the hero must pass through moments of impotence, internal or external. What produces the intensity of Cecil B. De Mille's *Samson and Delilah* are the images which show Samson blind and turning the millstone, then weighed down with chains and pushed into the temple enclosure, groping his way along, hopping about under the gnashing jaws of the cats who are being excited by the grotesque dwarves; finally, all his power regained, making the enormous column of the temple slide on its plinth, in an image which 'rhymes' with that of his extreme powerlessness, when he makes the grinding millstone turn. Conversely, the cat's jaws which bite the powerless Samson rhyme with the ass's jawbone which the powerful Samson used at the beginning to knock out his attackers. In short, a whole spatio-temporal advance is intertwined with the process of actualisation, by which the hero becomes 'capable' of action; and his power becomes equal to that of the encompasser. Occasionally one even sees a relay between two characters, such that the one loses his capability as the state of things itself evolves, whilst the other gains that capability: from Moses to Joshua. Ford is fond of this dualist structure which indicates another binomial: the man of law who takes over from the man of the West in *Liberty Valance*; or, in *The Grapes of Wrath*, the matriarchal mother of the agricultural family, who ceases 'to see clearly' as the group decays, while the son begins to see clearly as he understands the meaning and significance of the new fight. From all these points of view, organic representation is ruled by this last law of development: *there must be a big gap between the situation and the action to come, but this gap only exists to be filled*, by a process marked by caesuras, as so many retrogressions and progressions.

3 The sensory-motor link

The action-image inspires a cinema of behaviour (behaviourism), since behaviour is an action which passes from one situation to another, which responds to a situation in order to try to modify it or to set up a new situation. Merleau-Ponty saw in this rise of behaviour a sign common to the modern novel, to modern psychology and to the spirit of the cinema.[15] But from this perspective, the sensory-motor link must be very strong, behaviour must be truly structured. The great organic representation, SAS', must not only be composed, but engendered: on the one hand the situation must permeate the character deeply and continuously, and on the other hand the character who is thus permeated must burst into action, at discontinuous intervals. This is the formula of realist violence, completely different from naturalist violence. The structure is that of an egg: a vegetable or vegetative pole (permeation) and an animal pole (acting-out). We know that the action-image, in this sense, found its systematisation in the Actors Studio and in Kazan's cinema. It is here that a sensory-motor schema takes possession of the image, and that a genetic element tends to emerge. From the outset, the rules of the Actors Studio applied not only to the actor's acting out but also to the conception and unfolding of the film, its framings, its cutting, its montage. We must infer the one from the other, the realist nature of the film from the acting of the actor and conversely. Now it is clear that the actor is never neutral, and never stationary. When he is not bursting out he is being permeated and never remains tranquil. For the actor as for the character, the basic neurosis is hysteria. The vegetative pole's movement on the spot is in fact just as great as the violent movement of the animal pole. Spongy permeation has as much intensity as acting-out, as sudden extension. For this very reason this structural and genetic representation of the action-image gives rise to a formula whose applications are truly infinite. Kazan advised that people in conflict should be made to eat together: the common absorption would make the eruption of duels even stronger. Let us consider a recent film which applies the Method or the System: Arthur Penn's *Georgia*. One scene shows a dinner which brings together the girl's multi-millionaire father and the immigrant proletarian fiancé; we see the tension being internalised in the protagonists; then the father says, 'I'm not in the habit of giving away what belongs to me', and these words are like an explosion which modify the situation because they introduce the new element of an incestuous relation between father and daughter. Later, at the engagement party, the father, almost imperceptible, blurred behind a great bay window, seems to become permeated with the situation like a poisonous plant; only a small child notices and waits for him; and the father rushes outside, kills his daughter and gravely wounds the fiancé, again modifying the situation by this animal acting-out.

This is like the differentiation of life according to Bergson: the plant, or the vegetable, undertakes the task of accumulating the explosive, on the spot, whilst the animal undertakes its detonation, in sudden movements.[16] Fuller's originality was perhaps to have taken this differentiation as far as it would go, even if it meant proceeding by fits and starts and breaking up sequences. The war film favours this with its interminable waiting and its permeations of atmosphere on the one hand and on the other its brutal explosions and its acting-out. At the limit Fuller was to find the figures of his violence in the vegetative madmen who stand like plants in the corridor of *Corridor Shock* and in the racist dog of *White Dog* which explodes in acts of attack. It is true that madmen have their own unforeseeable detonations, and that the dog had its long mysterious period of permeation. 'I explained to the dog that it was an actor. . . .' But Fuller also knows how to explain it to plants. What counts for him is this extreme dissociation which renews and augments each of the two aspects of the violence, and which sometimes carries out an inversion of the poles: it is the situation which then attains a sombre naturalism.

Kazan is also able to dissociate the poles, and *Baby Doll* is one of the finest vegetative films, expressing both the slow and poisonous life of the South and the vegetable existence of the young woman at the cradle. But what interests Kazan, and what determines the evolution of his work, is the linking of permeations and explosions so as to obtain a continuous structuring rather than a structure with two poles. The elongated format of cinemascope reinforces this tendency. And this is the orthodoxy of the Actors Studio: a great 'global mission', SAS', is divided into successive and continuous 'local missions' (s1, a1, s2, a2, s3 . . .). In *America, America* each sequence has its geography, its sociology, its psychology, its tonality, its situation which depends on the preceding action, and which gives rise to a new action, drawing the hero in turn into the succeeding situation, each time by permeation and explosion, until the final explosion (involving the New York waterfront). Plundered, prostituted, murderer, fiancé, traitor, the hero moves through these sequences which are all encompassed in the great mission which is present throughout, to escape Anatolia (S) in order to reach New York (S'). And the encompasser, the great mission, sanctifies the hero or at least acquits him of all he had to do both here and there: dishonoured externally, he has saved his inward honour, the purity of his heart and the future of his family. Not that he finds peace. It is the world of Cain, it is the sign of Cain, which knows no peace, but makes innocence and guilt, shame and honour correspond to each other in a hysterical neurosis: what is and remains humiliation in a particular local situation is also the heroism required by the great global situation, the price that must be paid. *On the Waterfront* abundantly develops this theology: if I don't betray others, I betray myself and I betray justice. One has to go through many dirty permeating situations, and through many humiliating explosions, in order to catch a glimpse through them of the impression which cleanses us and the detonation which saves or pardons us. *East of Eden* is the great biblical film, the story of Cain and of betrayal, which obsesses, in different ways, Nicholas Ray and Samuel Fuller.[17] This theme had always been there in the American cinema and in its conception of History, sacred and profane. But now it has become the essential point: Cain has turned realist. What is curious, with Kazan, is the way in which the American Dream and the action-image grow tougher together. The American Dream is affirmed more and more to be a dream, nothing other than a dream, contradicted by the facts; but it draws from this a sudden burst of increased power since it now encompasses actions such as betrayal and calumny (the very ones that the dream had the purpose of excluding according to Ford). And it is precisely after the war – at the very moment when the American Dream is collapsing, and when the action-image is entering a definitive crisis, as we will see – that the dream finds its most fertile form, and action its most violent, most detonating, schema. This is the final agony of the action cinema, even if films of this type go on being made for a long time yet.

The cinema of behaviour is not content with a simple sensory-motor formula, even of the conditioned reflex arc type. It is a much more complex behaviourism which essentially took into account internal factors.[18] Indeed, what must appear on the outside is what happens inside the character, at the intersection of the situation which permeates and the action which is to detonate. This is the rule of the Actors Studio: *only the inner counts*, but this inner is not beyond or hidden, it is not the same as the genetic element of behaviour, which must be shown. This is not a perfecting of action, it is the absolutely necessary condition of the development of the action-image. This realist image indeed never forgets that it is presenting by definition, fictitious situations and sham action: one does not 'really' find oneself in a desperate situation and one does not kill or one does not 'really' drink. It is only theatre or cinema. The great realist actors are perfectly conscious of this and the Actors Studio offers them a method. On the one hand a sensory contact must be established with the objects adjacent to the situation: even an imaginary contact with a material, with a glass, a particular sort of glass, or a fabric, a costume, an instrument, some chewing gum to chew. On the other hand the object must, in this way, awaken an affective memory, reactualise an emotion which is not necessarily identical, but is analogous to that which the role calls up.[19] Handling a nearby object, awakening an emotion corresponding to the situation – it is by this internal link between the object and the emotion that the external linking of the fictitious situation and the sham action will take place. The Actors Studio does not invite the actor to identify himself with his role any more than any other method; what characterises it is the reverse operation, by which the realist actor is supposed to identify the role with certain inner elements that he possesses and selects in himself.

But the inner element is not merely the actor's training, it appears in the image – hence the constant agitation of the actor. It is in itself, and directly, an element of behaviour, sensory-motor training. It adjusts permeation and explosion to each other. The pair of object and emotion thus appears in the action-image as its genetic sign. The object will be grasped in all its virtualities (used, sold, bought, exchanged, broken, accepted, rejected . . .) at the same time as the corresponding, actualised, emotions: for example in *America, America*, the knife given by the grandmother, the abandoned shoes, the fez and the straw hat which correspond to S and S'. There is in all these cases an emotion/object pair which belongs to realism alone, but is equivalent in its own way to that of the impulse and the fetish, or of the affect and the face. Not that cinema of behaviour necessarily avoids the close-up (Tailleur analyses a very fine image in *Baby Doll* where the man literally 'enters' the close-up of the young woman, his hand venturing across the face, his lips at the edge of the hair).[20] It is nevertheless true that the emotional handling of an object, an act of emotion in relation to the object, can have more effect than a close-up in the action-image. In a situation in *On the Waterfront*, where the woman behaves ambivalently, and where the man feels timid and guilty, he picks up the glove that she has dropped, keeps it and plays with it, finally slipping it on to his hand.[21] It is like a genetic or embryonic sign for the action-image, that could be called *Impression* (emotional object) and which already functions as a 'symbol' in the sphere of behaviour. It simultaneously brings together, in a strange way, the unconscious of the actor, the personal guilt of the director, the hysteria of the image, such as the burnt hand, for example, the impression which constantly arises in Dmytryk's films. In its most general definition, the impression is the inner, but visible, link between the permeating situation and the explosive action.

10 The action-image
The small form

1 From action to situation

We must now consider a completely different aspect of the action-image. As the action-image on all its levels always brings together 'two', it is not surprising that it should have two different aspects itself. The large form – SAS' – moved from the situation to the action, which modified the situation. But there is another form, which, on the contrary, moves from the action to the situation, towards a new action: ASA'. This time it is the action which discloses the situation, a fragment or an aspect of the situation, which triggers off a new action. The action advances blindly and the situation is disclosed in darkness, or in ambiguity. From action to action, the situation gradually emerges, varies, and finally either becomes clear or retains its mystery. We have called the action-image which moves from the situation as encompasser (synsign) to the action as duel (binomial) the 'large form'. For convenience, we will given the name 'small form' to the action-image which moves from an action, a mode of behaviour, or a 'habitus', to a partially disclosed situation. It is a reversed sensory-motor schema. A representation like this is no longer global but local. It is no longer spiral but elliptical. It is no longer structural but constructed round events [événementielle]. It is no longer ethical, but comedic (we say 'comedic', because this representation gives rise to a comedy, although it it not necessarily comic, and may be dramatic). The sign of which this new action-image is made up is the index.

This action-image seems to have become particularly self-conscious in *Public Opinion*, the film which Chaplin directed, but did not appear in, and in the whole of Lubitsch's work. Even at the level of a superficial analysis, we can see that there are two sorts or two poles of the index. In a first case, an action (or an equivalent of action, a simple gesture) discloses a situation which is not given. The situation is thus deduced from the action, by immediate inference, or by relatively complex reasoning. Since the situation is not given for itself, the index here is an index of lack; it implies a gap in the narrative, and corresponds to the first sense of the French word *'ellipse'*.[1] For example, in *Public Opinion*, Chaplin insisted on the gap of a year, which was not filled by anything, but which we can infer from the new behaviour and clothes of the heroine, who has become a rich man's mistress. Similarly, the faces did not merely have an autonomous expressive or affective value, but neither did they simply indicate what was going on off screen: they really did function as indices of a global situation. Thus the famous image of the train, whose arrival we only see from the lights which pass across the woman's face, or the erotic images which we can only infer from the spectators. The examples are even more striking when the index involves a process of reasoning, however rapid it may be: thus 'a chamber maid opens a chest of drawers, and a man's collar accidentally falls on the floor, revealing Edna's liaison'.[2] In Lubitsch, we constantly find these rapid reasoning processes introduced into the image itself, which then functions as an index. In *Design for Living*, a film which has retained all its audacity, since the heroine lays claim ingenuously or unaffectedly to the right to live and cohabit with two lovers, one of them sees the other in the early morning in a dinner jacket. He concludes from this index (and so does the spectator), that his friend has spent the night with the young woman. The index thus consists in the following: that one of the characters is 'too' dressed up, too well-dressed in evening clothes, for him not to have spent the night in a very intimate situation which has not been shown. This is a reasoning-image.

There is a second, more complex type of index, an index of equivocity, which corresponds to the second (geometrical) sense of the word 'ellipse'. In *Public Opinion*, many indices of the first type lead us to think that the heroine is not very attached to the man who loves her (her little enigmatic smiles). On the other hand, she has a more equivocal relationship with her rich lover, which leads the spectator to wonder constantly whether she is attached to him by fortune, luxury, and a certain complicity, or whether she loves him with a much more profound and all-embracing love. The same question arises in Lubitsch's *Bluebeard's Eighth Wife*. In these cases, we are made to hesitate by a whole world of details, another type of indices; not because of something which is lacking, or which is not given, but by virtue of an equivocity which completely belongs to the index (thus the scene of the necklace thrown off and recovered in *Public Opinion*). It is as if an action, a mode of behaviour, concealed a slight difference, which was nevertheless sufficient to relate it simultaneously to two quite distant situations, situations which are worlds apart. Or as if two actions, two gestures, were very slightly different, and nevertheless in their infinitesimal difference, referred to two opposable or opposing situations. The two situations may be such that one is real and the other apparent or illusory, but they may both be real and finally, they can interchange to such an extent that the one becomes real and the other apparent, and vice versa. Some of these cases are commonplace in any kind of film: for example the innocent man assumed to be guilty (a man holds a knife by a corpse: is it because he has killed him, or has he just pulled the knife out?). The more complex cases which we have just mentioned are more interesting. They allow us to identify the law of the new index: *a very slight difference in the action, or between two actions, leads to a very great distance between two situations*. This is an *ellipse*, in the second sense of the word – a geometrical figure – since the distant situations are like a double centre. It is an index of equivocity, or of distance, rather than being one of lack. It matters little that one of these situations is contradicted or denied, for this happens only after its function has been exhausted, and never to such an extent that it eliminates the equivocity of the index and the distance between the situations which are evoked. In *To Be Or Not To Be* Lubitsch undoubtedly achieves a perfect handling of these complex indices. Sometimes in irresolvable images, for example, when a spectator leaves his seat as soon as the actor begins his monologue: is it because he has had enough, or because he has a rendezvous with the actor's wife? Sometimes in relation to the whole [*ensemble*] of the plot, which brings all the montage into play: the very slight difference in the gesture, but also the enormity of the distance between two situations, depending on whether the troupe of actors is playing the role of Germans in front of a theatre audience or, on the contrary, is 'doing' Germans in front of Germans who, consequently, seem to be playing their own role. A question of life or death: the distance between the situations is proportionate to the extent to which the characters know that all hangs on very small differences in behaviour.

In any case, in the small form, we deduce the situation, or the situations, from the action. This form seems to be less expensive in principle, more economical. Thus Chaplin explains that he has kept the light and shadow reflected from the train on a face because he did not have a real French train to show directly. . . . This ironical remark is important, because it raises a general problem: the effect that B movies or low budget films had on the inventions of the image in the cinema. Economic constraints undoubtedly gave rise to flashes of inspiration and images dreamed up with a view to economy could have universal repercussions. There were to be many examples of this in neo-realism and in the new wave, but it applies to all periods, and we can often see the B movie as an active centre of experimentation and creation. Nevertheless, the 'small form' does not necessarily have its origin and certainly does not find its full expression, in low budget films. It finds as many factors of expression in cinemascope, in colour, in lavish staging and in sets as the large form itself. Although we call it the small form, this is in itself inadequate: we do so merely to contrast the two forms of the action-image – SAS' and ASA'. In other words, to contrast the univocal large organism which embraces the organs and functions to the actions and organs which are gradually formed in an equivocal organisation.

It is, therefore, easy to work out which genres or states of genre correspond to the two formulas of the action-image and are inspired by them. What we have just seen is the comedy of manners of the small form ASA, considered as distinct from the psycho-social film of the large form SAS. But an analogous distinction or opposition is applicable in the most varied areas. Let us first of all return to the great SAS historical film, the film of monumental and antiquarian history. To this is opposed a type of film which is no less historical – an ASA film – which has aptly been called the 'costume film'. In this case the costume, the dress and even the fabrics function as modes of behaviour or 'habitus' and are indices of a situation which they disclose. This is quite different from the historical film where – as we have seen – the fabrics and costumes have great importance, but only in so far as they are integrated into a monumental and antiquarian conception. Here it is a modist or modellist conception, as though the dressmaker, the designer had taken the place of the architect and the antiquarian. In the costume film, as in the comedy of manners, the 'habitus' are inseparable from the outfits [*habits*], the actions are inseparable from the state of the costumes which constitute their form, and the situation which follows from this is inseparable from the fabrics and hangings. It is not surprising that Lubitsch in his earliest work – his German Expressionist period – should have made costume films (*Anne Boleyn, Madame Dubarry* and, above all, the oriental fantasy *Sumurun*) which already bore the imprint of his particular genius – the fabrics, the outfits, the states of dress whose texture, matt or luminous, he was able to reproduce in the image and which functioned as indices.[3]

In the field of the documentary, the English school of the 1930s was opposed to the great Flaherty-documentary. Grierson and Rotha criticised Flaherty for his social and political indifference. Instead of starting from an encompasser, from a milieu from which the behaviour of men was naturally deduced, it was necessary to start from modes of behaviour, to infer from them the social situation which was not given as an in-itself, but which itself referred back to struggles and modes of behaviour which were always in action or in transformation. The 'habitus' thus indicated differences of civilisation, and differences within a single civilisation. Thus one moved from the behaviour to the situation in such a way that, from the one to the other, there was the possibility of a 'creative interpretation of reality'. This movement would be taken up again in other conditions by direct cinema and cinéma-vérité.

There is also the detective film, as distinct from the crime film. There may, of course, be detectives in the crime film, just as there may not be any in the detective film. What distinguishes the two types is that in the crime formula – SAS – one moves from the situation, or the milieu, towards actions which are duels, while in the detective formula – ASA – one moves from blind actions, as indices, to obscure situations which vary entirely or which fluctuate completely, depending on a minuscule variation in the index. The novelist Hammett's formula expresses this type of image exactly: 'putting a spanner in the works'. It is the blind gesture which shatters the completely black situation, tears away the shreds of the situation. Some fine films resulted from this: Hawks' *The Big Sleep*, Huston's *The Maltese Falcon* (the same directors who also excelled themselves in the large form of the crime film). Lang perhaps achieved the masterpiece of the genre in *Beyond a Reasonable Doubt*: the hero, in the context of a campaign against a judicial error, fabricates false indices which accuse him of a crime, but since the evidence of the fabrication has disappeared, he finds himself in the situation of being arrested and sentenced. However, on the verge of being reprieved, during a final visit by his fiancée, he gives himself away, and lets slip an index which makes her realise that he is guilty, and has genuinely committed murder. The fabrication of the false indices was a way of obliterating the true ones, but resulted, by a roundabout route, in the same situation as the true ones. No other film surrenders itself to this dance of indices with such mobility and convertibility of opposed distant situations.

2   The Western in Hawks: functionalism

Finally, the Western poses the same problem in particularly fertile conditions. We have seen that the large 'respiration' form was not content with the epic but, throughout its varieties, sustained an encompassing milieu, a global situation, which would give rise to an action, capable in its turn of modifying the situation from within. This great organic representation – for example in Ford – had precise characteristics: it comprised one or several fundamental groups, each well-defined, homogeneous, with its locations, its interiors, its customs (thus, the five groups in *Wagonmaster*); it also comprised a makeshift group, thrown together by chance or circumstance, more heterogeneous, incongruous, but functional. Finally, *there was a big gap between the situation and the action to be undertaken, but this gap only existed to be filled.* The hero had to actualise the power which made him equal to the situation, he had to become capable of the action, and became so gradually in so far as he represented the 'good' fundamental group and found the necessary support in the makeshift group (the alcoholic doctor, the whore with a heart of gold, etc. proved to be effective). And it is remarkable that Hawks subscribes to this organic representation, but subjects it to such a treatment that it emerges profoundly affected, deformed. In its full expression, as at the start of *Red River*, where the couple outlined against the sky is equal to the whole of Nature, the image is too strong to be able to last. And, when it does last, it is in another mode: the image needs to become fluid, the horizon joins with the river, as much in *Red River* as in *The Big Sky*. We might say that in Hawks the earthly organic representation tends to empty itself, leaving nothing but almost abstract fluid functions which come to the forefront.

First of all, the locations lose the organic life which encompassed them, traversed them and situated them in a set: the purely functional prison in *Rio Bravo* does not even need to show us its prisoner; the church in *El Dorado* no longer bears witness to anything but an abandoned function; the town of *Rio Lobo* is reduced to 'a diagram, now only showing functions, a bloodless town condemned by the weight of a past'. At the same time, the fundamental group becomes very vague, and the only community which is still well-defined is the incongruous makeshift group (an alcoholic, an old man, a young boy . . .); it is a functional group which no longer has its foundation in the organic. It finds its motivations in a debt to be discharged, a mistake to be redeemed, a downhill slope into degradation to be climbed again, and its forces or means in the invention of an ingenious machine, rather than in the representation of a collectivity (the catapult-tree in *The Big Sky*, the final fireworks in *Rio Bravo* and, leaving Westerns, from the scientists' machine in *Ball of Fire* to the great invention in *Land of the Pharaohs*).[4] In Hawks, pure functionalism tends to replace the structure of the encompasser. The claustrophilia of certain of Hawks' films has often been noticed: notably *Land of the Pharaohs*, where the invention consists in locking the funeral chamber from the inside, but also in *Rio Bravo*, which could be called a 'chamber Western'. This is because in the obliteration of the encompasser, there is no longer (as in Ford) communication between an organically situated interior and an outside which surrounds it, giving it a living milieu which is a source of assistance as much as aggression. Here, on the contrary, the unexpected, the violent, the event, come from the interior whilst the exterior is rather the location of the customary or premeditated action, in a curious reversal of the outside and the inside.[5] Everyone enters and passes through the room where the sheriff is having a bath, as though it were a public place (*El Dorado*). The external milieu loses its curvature and assumes the figure of a tangent from a point, or from a segment which functions as interiority. The outside and the inside thus become external *to one another*, they enter into a purely linear relationship, which makes possible a functional permutation of the opposites. Hence the constant mechanism of reversals in Hawks which operates quite openly, independently of a symbolic background, even when they do not just relate to the outside and the inside but, as in the comedies, concern all the binary relations. If the outside and the inside are pure functions the inside can assume the function of the outside. But the woman can also assume the function of the man in the relationship of seduction, and the man that of the woman (*Bringing up Baby, I Was a Male War Bride*, and the female roles in Hawks' Westerns). The adults or old people have the functions of children, and the child a monstrous function of the mature adult (*Ball of Fire, Gentlemen Prefer Blondes*). The same mechanism can come into play between love and money, noble language and slang. As we shall see, these reversals, as functional permutations, form veritable *Figures* ensuring a transformation of the form.

Hawks surrenders himself to a topological deformation of the large form. This is why Hawks' films preserve a great 'respiration' (as Rivette calls it), although it has become fluid, expressing the continuity and permutation of functions more than the unity of an organic form.[6] But, despite its debt to Hawks, the neo-Western takes another direction: it borrows the 'small form' directly, even on the big screen. The ellipse reigns and replaces the spiral and its projections. It is no longer a matter of the global or integral law SA (a big gap which only exists to be filled), but a differential law AS: the smallest distance, which exists only to be increased, to give rise to very distant or opposable situations. In the first place, the Indians no longer appear at the top of the hill outlined against the sky, but spring up from the tall grass, from which they were indistinguishable. The Indian almost blends into the rock behind which he waits (Martin Ritt's *Hombre*), and the cowboy has something mineral about him which makes him blend into the landscape (Anthony Mann's *Man of the West*).[7] Violence becomes the principal impetus, and gains from this as much in intensity as in unexpectedness. In Boetticher's *Seminole*, people die from the blows of an invisible adversary hidden in the swamps. Not only has the fundamental group disappeared in favour of increasingly incongruous and mixed makeshift groups but the latter, in proliferating, have lost the clear distinction which they still had in Hawks: there are so many relations and such complex alliances between men in the same group and those in different groups that they are scarcely distinguishable and their oppositions constantly shift (Peckinpah's *Major Dundee* and *The Wild Bunch*). The difference between the hunter and the hunted, but also between White Man and Indian, becomes smaller and smaller: in Mann's *The Naked Spur*, the bounty-hunter and his prey do not seem very different; and in Penn's *Little Big Man*, the hero is constantly white with the White Men, Indian with the Indians, crossing a minuscule frontier in both directions, at the prompting of actions which are barely distinguishable from one another. This is because the action can never be determined by and in a preceding situation – it is, on the contrary, the situation which flows progressively from the action – Boetticher used to say that his characters are not defined by a 'cause', but by what they do to defend it. And, when Godard analysed form in Anthony Mann, he extracted a formula ASA′, which he opposed to the large form SAS′: the *mise-en-scène* 'consisted in discovering *at the same time as* specifying, while, in a classical Western, the *mise-en-scène* consists in discovering, *then* in specifying'. But, if the situation itself depends on the action in this way, the action in its turn must necessarily be related to the moment of its birth, to the instant, the second, the smallest interval as the differential which serves as its impetus.

In the second place, this law of the slight difference is only valid in so far as it produces situations which are logically very distant. The situation of *Little Big Man* really changes entirely depending on whether it is impelled by the Indians or the White Man. And, if the instant is the differential of the action, at each of these instants the action can swing into a completely different or opposed situation. Nothing is ever won. Thus, failings, doubts, fear no longer have the same sense as they do in the organic representation: they are no longer the steps – even painful ones – which fill the gap, through which the hero rises to the demands of the global situation, actualises his own power and becomes capable of such a great action. For there is no longer any grandiose action at all, even if the hero has retained extraordinary technical qualities. At the limit, he is one of the 'losers', as Peckinpah presents them: 'they have no façade, they have not a single illusion left: thus they represent disinterested adventure, from which no advantage is to be gained except the pure satisfaction of remaining alive.' They have kept nothing of the American dream, they have only kept their lives, but at each critical instant, the situation to which their action gives rise can rebound against them, making them lose the one thing they have left. In short, the action-image has signs as indices, which are both indices of lack – illustrated by the brutal ellipses in the story – and indices of distance or equivocity – illustrated by the possibility and reality of sudden reversals of the situation.

It is not merely a case of hesitation between two situations which are distant or opposed, but simultaneous. The successive situations, each of which is already equivocal in itself, will form in turn with one another, and with the critical instants which give rise to them, a broken line whose path is unpredictable, although necessary and rigorous. This is as true of locations as of events. In Peckinpah, there is no longer a milieu, a West, but Wests: including Wests with camels, Wests with Chinamen, that is, totalities [*ensembles*] of locations, men and manners which 'change and are eliminated' in the same film.[8] In Mann and also in Daves, there is a 'shorter route', which is not the straight line, but which brings together actions or parts, A and A', each one of which retains its independence, each one of which is a heterogeneous critical instant, 'a present sharpened to its own extreme point'.[9] It is like a knotted rope, twisting itself at each take, at each action, at each event. Thus contrary to the *respiration-space* of the organic form, a quite different space is formed: a *skeleton-space*, with missing intermediaries, heterogeneous elements which jump from one to the other, or which interconnect directly. It is no longer an ambient space, but a vectorial space, a vector-space, with temporal distances. It is no longer the encompassing stroke of a great contour, but the broken stroke of a line of the universe, across the holes. The vector is the sign of such a line. It is the genetic sign of the new action-image, whilst the index was the sign of its composition.

3 The law of the small form and burlesque

We have seen how the classical genres of the cinema could, in a summary fashion, be assigned to one of the two forms of the action-image. There is one genre which seems to be exclusively devoted to the small form, to the extent of having created it, and of having served as the condition for the comedy of manners – the burlesque. In it the formula of the form AS is most fully developed: a very slight difference in the action, or between two actions, which brings out an infinite distance between two situations, and which exists only to bring out that distance. Let us take some famous examples from the Charlie Chaplin series: viewed from behind, Charlie, deserted by his wife, seems to be shaking with sobs, but as soon as he turns round we see that he is in fact shaking himself a cocktail. Similarly, in battle, Charlie scores a point for himself each time he fires a shot: but then an enemy bullet replies, and he subtracts a point. The important element, the burlesque process itself, consists in this: the action is filmed from the angle of the smallest difference from another action (firing a gun – playing a shot), but in this way it discloses the enormity of the distance between two situations (game of billiards – war). When Charlie hangs on to a sausage suspended in a butcher's shop, he draws an analogy which equally evokes all the distance which separates a butcher's shop from a tramcar. This is what we find in most diversions of everyday objects: a very slight difference introduced into the object will induce opposable functions or opposed situations. This is the potentiality of tools: and even when Charlie comes face to face with machines, he clings to the idea of a huge tool which is automatically converted into the opposing situation. Hence Chaplin's humanism, demonstrating that a 'mere nothing' is enough to set the machine against man, to make it an instrument of imprisonment, immobilisation, frustration and even torture, at the level of the most elementary needs (the two great machines of *Modern Times* confront man's simple need to eat by setting up insuperable difficulties). In the Charlie series, we do not merely discover the laws of the small form, rather we grasp them at their source: confusion, identification with the milieu (Charlie in the sand, Charlie-statue, Charlie-tree, re-incarnating the prophecy of Macbeth . . :); the slight difference which makes the situation fluctuate, like the personality split of a pivotal character in *Gold Rush* or *City Lights*; the instant as critical moment of opposable situations. Charlie caught in the instant, moving from one instant to the next, each requiring his full powers of improvisation; finally, the line of the

universe which he describes in this way, the broken stroke which
makes itself felt even in the angular swerves of his walk, which only
finally brings its segments and directions together by aligning them
on the long road, where Charlie, seen from the rear, plunges between
telegraph poles and leafless trees; or else zigzagging along the frontier
between America, where the police are on the lookout for him, and
Mexico, where bandits are waiting for him. The sign of the burlesque
is thus constituted by the whole play of indices and vectors; the
'ellipse' in both senses.

Indeed, the law of the index – the slight difference in the action
which brings out an infinite distance between two situations – seems
to be omnipresent in burlesque in general. Harold Lloyd, particularly,
develops a variant which moves the process on from the action-image
to the pure perception-image. A first perception is given to us, for
example Harold in a luxurious car, brought to a standstill at a stop
sign; then a second perception appears when the car starts up,
revealing Harold on a poor man's bicycle. He had only been framed
in the car window, and the infinitely small difference between the
two perceptions brings home to us all the more fully the infinite
distance between the two situations of rich–poor. Similarly in an
excellent scene from *Safety Last*, a first perception gives us a seated,
hunched-up man, bars, a dangling slip-knot, a woman crying, a
pleading priest; while the second perception reveals that it is only
a goodbye on a station platform, where each element has its proper
place.

If we want to define Chaplin's originality, to find what gave him
an incomparable place in the burlesque, we must look elsewhere. For
Chaplin knew how to select gestures which were close to each other
and corresponding situations which were far apart, so as to make
their relationship produce a particularly intense emotion at the same
time as laughter, and to redouble the laughter through this emotion.
If a slight difference in the action induces very distant or opposable
situations – S and S' – and makes them alternate, one of these situations
will be 'really' touching, horrific and tragic (and not merely through
an optical illusion, as in Harold Lloyd). In the previous example of
Shoulder Arms, war is the real and present situation, whereas the game
of billiards recedes to infinity. However it does not recede enough to
stop us laughing: conversely, our laughter does not stand in the way
of emotion before the image of war which imposes itself and
develops, even into the flooded trenches. In short, the infinite
distance between S' and S'' (the war and the game of billiards) moves
us all the more as the convergence of the two actions, the slight

difference in the action makes us laugh more. Because Chaplin knows how to invent the minimum difference between two well-chosen actions, he is also able to create the maximum distance between the corresponding situations, the one achieving emotion, the other reaching pure comedy. It is a laughter-emotion circuit, in which the one refers to the slight difference, the other to the great distance, without the one obliterating or diminishing the other, but both interchanging with one another, triggering each other off again. No case can be made for a tragic Chaplin. There is certainly no case for saying that we laugh, whereas we should cry. Chaplin's genius lies in doing both together, making us laugh as much as moving us. In *City Lights* the blind girl and Charlie do not divide up the roles between them. In the unravelling scene – between the unseeing action which tends to eradicate any difference between one thread and another, and the visible situation, which is completely transformed depending on whether a Charlie, assumed to be rich, is holding the skein, or a poverty-stricken Charlie is losing his rag of clothing – the two characters are on the same circuit, both of them comic and moving.

Chaplin's last films both discover sound and put Charlie to death (it is not merely that Verdoux becomes Charlie when he goes to his death, but the dictator who mounts the rostrum merges into Charlie ascending the scaffold). Here the same principle seems to gain a new power. Bazin insisted that *The Great Dictator* would not have been possible had Hitler not, in reality, appropriated and stolen Charlie's moustache.[10] The difference between the little Jewish barber and the dictator is as slight as that between their two moustaches. However, two situations arise from this which are infinitely far apart, as opposable as those of the victim and the executioner. Likewise in *Monsieur Verdoux* the difference between the two aspects or modes of behaviour of the same man – the woman-killer and the loving husband of an invalid – is so slender that his wife needs all her intuition to sense when he has 'changed'. As Mireille Latil says, it was not through incapacity, but by a stroke of fortune that Chaplin 'scarcely varied the appearance of the character, and never changed his style of acting' in portraying Verdoux's two aspects.[11] A great distance between the opposing situations emerges from the slight, evanescent difference, illustrated by the frenetic comings and goings between the false domiciles and the true home. In these two films, does Chaplin want to tell us that there is a Hitler, a potential murderer in each of us? And that it is only situations which make us good or evil, victims or executioners, capable of loving or destroying? Whether or not such ideas are profound or platitudinous, this does not seem consistent with Chaplin's way of looking at things, except in a very secondary way. For what is still more important than the two opposing situations of good and evil are the underlying *discourses*, which are expressed as such at the end of these films. For this very reason these films proceed simultaneously to a progressive conquest of the talkie, and to a progressive elimination of Charlie. What the discourses say, in *The Great Dictator* and *Monsieur Verdoux*, is that Society puts itself in the situation of making any powerful man into a bloody dictator, any businessman a murderer, literally a murderer, because it gives us too much incentive to be evil, instead of giving rise to situations where freedom and humanity would be bound up with our interest or our *raison d'être*. This is an idea close to Rousseau, and to a Rousseau whose social analysis was fundamentally realist. Consequently we see what has changed in Chaplin's last films. Discourse brings them a completely new dimension, and constitutes 'discursive' images.

We are no longer merely dealing with two opposing situations which appear to be born out of minuscule differences between actions, between men, or in the same man. It is a case of two states of society, two opposable Societies, one of which makes the slight difference between men into the instrument of an infinite distance between situations (tyranny), and the other which would make the slight difference between men the variable of a great situation of community and communality (Democracy).[12] In the series of silent Charlie films, Chaplin could only reach this theme through idyllic or dream images (the great dream in *Easy Street* or the idyllic image of *Modern Times*). But it is the talkie, in the form of discourse, which was to give this theme a realist force. We might say that Chaplin is at once one of the directors who most mistrusted the talkie, and one of those who made a radical, original use of it. Chaplin uses it to introduce the Figure of discourse into the cinema, thus transforming the initial problems of the action-image. Hence the particular importance of *The Great Dictator*, where the final discourse (whatever its intrinsic value) is identified with all human language, represents everything that man can say, in comparison with the false language of nonsense and terror, sound and fury that Chaplin has the genius to invent and put into the mouth of the tyrant. The small burlesque form lacked nothing; but, in his last films, Chaplin pushes it to a limit which links it up again with a large form which no longer needs the burlesque, but which retains its power and its signs. Indeed, it is always the slight difference which appears in two incommensurable or opposing situations. (This gives rise to *Limelight*'s incisive question: what is this 'mere nothing', this fracture of age, this slight difference of wear and tear which turns an excellent clown's act into a lamentable spectacle?) But, in the last films, and again particularly in *Limelight*, the slight differences between men, or in the same man, become states of life on their own account, even at the lowest level, variations of a vital force that the clown can mimic, while the opposable situations become two states of society, the one pitiless and life-denying; the other, which the dying clown can still foresee and communicate to the cured woman. And it is again in *Limelight* that everything is conveyed through the introduction of the discourse, in a Shakespearian mode, the most Shakespearian of Chaplin's three discourses. Chaplin was to recall this when *A King in New York* launches into Hamlet's discourse, which is like the reverse or diametrical opposite of American society (democracy has become 'kingdom' since America has become a society of propaganda and police).

Buster Keaton's position, however, is very different. Keaton's paradox is that of inserting burlesque directly into a large form. While it is true that the burlesque belongs essentially to the small form, there is in Keaton something which is incomparable, even with Chaplin who only conquers the large form through the figure of discourse and the relative effacement of the burlesque character. Buster Keaton's profound originality lies in giving the large form a burlesque content which it appeared to challenge, in having reconciled – against all the odds – the burlesque and the large form. The hero is like a minuscule dot encompassed by an immense and catastrophic milieu, in a transformation-space [*espace à transformation*]: vast, changing landscapes and deformable geometric structures, rapids and waterfalls, a great ship drifting on the seas, a town swept by the cyclone, a bridge collapsing like a flattened parallelogram. . . . Keaton's gaze, as Benayoun describes it, seen full on or in profile, sometimes sees everything, in a periscope position, sometimes sees far, in a sentinel's position.[13] It is a gaze made for great internal or external spaces. At the same time, a type of images which are unexpected in the burlesque rise up before our very eyes. For example, the opening sequence of *Our Hospitality*, with the night, the thunderstorm, the lightning, the double murder and the terrified woman: pure Griffith. Also the cyclone in *Steamboat Bill Junior*, the diver's suffocation at the bottom of the sea in *The Navigator*, the crushing of the train and the flood in *The General*, the terrible boxing match in *Battling Butler*. Occasionally it is, in particular, an element of the image: the sabre-blade about to be thrust into an enemy's back, in *The General*, or the knife which *The Cameraman* slips into the hand of a Chinese demonstrator. Take, for example, the boxing match, since all burlesques have used this theme. Charlie Chaplin's matches correspond well to the law of the slight difference: a ballet-match, or domestic-match. But in *Battling Butler* there are three contests: a match which appears to be genuine, perceived in all its violence; a training session, treated in a traditional burlesque fashion, with Keaton like an excited child leaping around, then being threatened by the father-trainer; then finally the settling of scores between Keaton and the champion in all its ugliness: the bodies tossed about, the distortion and crumpling of flesh under the blows, the hatred which appears on their faces. It is one of the greatest indictments of boxing. One of Keaton's anecdotes thus becomes clearer: wanting to include a flood, he ran up against the producer's objection that things like that do not make people laugh. He replied that Chaplin had got laughs out of the First World War, but the producer held fast and only accepted a cyclone (because he did not seem to have realised the number of deaths which cyclones can cause).[14] This producer's intuition was correct: for if Chaplin could get laughs from the First World War, it is because, as we have seen, he relates the terrible situation to a slight difference which is itself ludicrous. Keaton, however, gives himself a scene or situation outside the burlesque, a limit-image: in the cyclone as much as in the fight. It is no longer a case of a slight difference which brings out the opposable situations, it is a case of a large gap between the given situation and the anticipated comic action (law of the large form). How will the gap be breached, not just so that the comic action is 'incidentally' produced, but so that it dominates and carries along the situation in its entirety, and coincides with it? One would not say of Keaton, any more than of Chaplin, that he is tragic. But the problem is quite different in both directors.

What is unique to Buster Keaton is the way in which he raises the burlesque directly to the large form. However, he uses several methods. The first is what David Robinson calls the 'trajectory gag', which brings into play a whole art of rapid montage: thus as early as in *The Three Ages* the hero (as ancient Roman) escapes from a dungeon, seizes a shield, runs up a staircase, grabs a lance, jumps on to a horse, and standing up leaps through a high window, pushes aside two pillars, bringing the ceiling down, carries off the girl, slides along the lance and jumps into a litter which is just being carried off. Or else the modern hero leaps from the top of one house to another, but falls, saving himself by grabbing hold of a canopy, tumbles down a pipe which comes loose, projecting him down two storeys into a fire station, where he slides down the pole to jump on to the back of the fire-engine, which is about to set off. In other burlesques, including those of Chaplin, there are very fast chases and races, with continuity in the variety, but Buster Keaton is perhaps alone in carrying out pure continuous trajectories. The fastest such trajectory is achieved in *The Cameraman*, where the girl telephones the hero, who rushes into New York and is already at her place when she puts the receiver down. Or in *Sherlock Junior* where, without montage, in a single shot, Keaton gets on to the roof of the train through a trap door, leaps from one carriage to the next, grabs the cord of a water tank that we saw at the start, is carried down on to the track by the torrent of water which he unleashes, and runs off into the distance, while two men arrive on the scene and get drenched. Or, yet again, the trajectory gag is achieved by a change of shot, the actor remaining immobile: thus the famous dream-sequence in *Sherlock Junior*, where cutting gives us successively the garden, the street, the precipice, the sand-dune, the reef washed by the sea, the snowy plain, and finally the garden once again (likewise the passage through a change of scenery into a stationary car).[15]

Another method might be called the machine gag. Keaton's biographers and commentators have emphasised his liking for machines, and his affinity in this respect with Dadaism rather than Surrealism: the house-machine, the ship-machine, the train-machine, the cinema-machine. . . . Machines and not tools: this is the first important aspect of his difference from Chaplin, who advances by means of tools, and *is opposed to* the machine. But, in the second place, Keaton makes machines his most precious ally because his character invents them and becomes part of them, machines 'without a mother' like those of Picabia. They may get out of control, become absurd, or be absurd from the start, complicate the straightforward, but they never cease to serve a secret higher finality which is at the heart of Keaton's work. The model house in *One Week*, whose parts have been put together in disorder and which becomes a maelstrom; *The Scarecrow*, where the single-roomed house 'without a mother' muddles each potential room with another, each cogwheel with another, stove and gramophone, bath and couch, bed and organ. These are the house-machines which Keaton, the Dadaist architect *par excellence*, designs. But; in the third place, they themselves lead us to the question; what is this finality of the absurd machine, this distinctive form of nonsense in Keaton? They are both geometrical structures and physical causalities. But, in the whole of Keaton's work, their particularity is that they are geometrical structures with a 'minoring' function, or physical causalities with a 'recurrent' function.

In *The Navigator* the machine is not merely the great liner by itself: it is the liner apprehended in a 'minoring' function, in which each of its elements, designed for hundreds of people, comes to be adapted to a single destitute couple. The limit, the limit-image is thus the object of a series which does not set out to breach it, or even to reach it, but to attract it, to polarise it. By which system can a little egg be cooked in a huge pot? In Keaton, the machine is not defined by immensity. It implies immensity, but in inventing the 'minoring' function which transforms it, by virtue of an ingenious system which is itself machinic, based on the mass of pulleys, wires and levers.[16] Likewise, in *The General*, one should not just think that the girl who feeds the train's boiler with little pieces of wood is behaving in a clumsy and inept way. This is of course true, but she also brings to realisation Keaton's dream of taking the biggest machine in the world and making it work with the tiniest elements, thus converting it for the use of each one of us, making it the property of everyone. Keaton sometimes passes directly from the great, real machine to its reproduction as toy, for example, at the end of *The Blacksmith*. *Go West* effects very varied 'minorations'; from the minuscule revolver to the little calf who has the task of rounding up the vast herd. This is the finality of the machine itself: it does not just comprise its main parts and mechanisms; it comprises its conversion into miniature, its conversion to the miniature, the mechanism of a transformation which adapts it to a solitary man, to a lost couple, beyond skills and specialisations. This *must* form part of the machine: in this respect we cannot be certain that Keaton lacks a political vision that is, on the contrary, present in Chaplin. There are rather two very different 'socialist' visions, the one communist-humanist in Chaplin, the other anarchistic-machinic in Keaton (rather like Illich, who was to lay claim to the right to use, or the 'minoration' of big machines).

These 'minorations' can only take place through the processes of physical causality, which pass through detours, extensions, indirect paths, liaisons between heterogeneous elements, providing the absurd element which is indispensable to the machine. Already in the 'Malec' series, *The High Sign* puts forward a bizarre abridgement of the causal series: a shooting machine in which the hero presses his foot on a hidden lever, so that a system of wires and pulleys brings down a bone which a dog tries to reach by pulling a cord so that the bell on the target rings (a cat is enough to throw the mechanism out of gear). We are reminded of the drawings of Rube Goldberg – also Dadaist – the prodigious causal series where 'posting a letter', for example, passes through a long succession of disparate mechanisms, each engaging with the others, beginning with a boot which sends a rugby ball into a tub, and, passing through interlocking mechanisms, finishes by unravelling before the sender's eyes a screen on which is written *You Sap Mail that Letter*. Each element of the series is such that it has no function, no relationship to the goal, but acquires one in relation to another element which itself has no function or relation. . . . These causalities operate through a series of disconnections: like Keaton's, some of Tinguely's machines string together several structures, each including an element which is not functional but which becomes so in the one that follows (the grandmother who pushes the pedals in the car does not make the vehicle move forward, but triggers off an apparatus for sawing wood . . .). These recurrent causalities make possible the appropriation of large geometrical structures and the development of great trajectories. A structure is the sketch of a trajectory, but a trajectory is no less the outline of a machine. Each trajectory itself constitutes a machine, in which man is a cog between the different elements: like the mechanic seated on the driving shaft of the locomotive which draws his motionless body into a series of arcs of a circle. The two essential forms of the gag in Keaton – the trajectory-gag and the machine-gag – are two aspects of a same reality, a machine which produces man 'without a mother', or the man of the future. The big gap between the immense situation and the minuscule hero will be filled by these 'minoring' functions and these recurrent series which make the hero equal to the situation. In this way, Keaton invents a burlesque which defies all the apparent conditions of the genre and naturally takes as its framework the large form.

11 Figures,
or the transformation of forms

1 The passage from one form to another in Eisenstein

The distinction between the two forms of action is in itself clear and simple, but its applications are more complicated. As we have seen, financial considerations could intervene, but were not determining, since the small form – as much as the large – needs a large screen, lavish sets and colours to express and develop itself. Here one should bear in mind that Small and Large are used in Plato's sense. He made two ideas correspond to them: and indeed the idea is first of all the form of action. This has consequences for the cinema. Some directors clearly have a preference or a vocation for one or other of the two forms. Nevertheless, from time to time they borrow the other form; whether to respond to new imperatives, or to change, to have a break, to test themselves in another way, or to try something out. Ford, for example, is a master of the large form, with synsigns and binomials: nevertheless he created masterpieces of the small form, using indices (as is the case in *The Long Voyage Home*, where the aeroplanes' attack is indicated only by the sound, and the unleashing of the sea by waves coming over the ship's forecastle). Other directors pass easily from one form to the other, as if they had no preference. We saw this in Hawks' *films noirs*, but this was because he knew how to invent an original form, a deforming form [*forme à déformation*], capable of playing on the two others, as his Westerns illustrate. We call the sign of such deformations, transformations or transmutations *Figure*. There are here all kinds of aesthetic and creative evaluations, which go beyond the question of the action-image, and which clearly arise not only in the context of the American cinema, but concern all epochs of the universal cinema.

The point is that Small and Large do not merely designate forms of action, but conceptions, ways of conceiving and seeing a 'subject', a story or a script. This second sense of the Idea, the conception, is all the more essential to the cinema in that it generally precedes the script and determines it, but, equally, it can come afterwards (Hawks stressed this point, the neutrality of the script which he could take ready-made). The conception harnesses a *mise-en-scène*, a cutting and a montage which are not simply dependent on the script. Mikhail

Romm records a conversation which he had with Eisenstein when he was making *Boule de suif*, based on Maupassant's short story.[1] Eisenstein began by asking which of the two parts of the story he was taking: Rouen, the German occupation and the whole range of characters, or the tale of the diligence? Romm replied that he was taking the diligence, the 'little tale'. Eisenstein said that he personally would have taken the former, the large one: this is a perfect alternative between the two forms of action-image, SAS' and ASA'. Then Eisenstein asked Romm for his 'explanation of the *mise-en-scène*'. Romm replied by explaining the script, but Eisenstein said that this was not what he had meant at all. The question was how Romm conceived of the script, how he saw the first image, for example. 'The corridor, the door, close-up, boots by the door', he said. Eisenstein concluded: 'Well, at least film the boots so that it makes a striking image, even if you do nothing else. . . .' This seems to us to mean: if you choose the small form ASA', then make an image which is really an index, which functions as an index. Perhaps Eisenstein was recalling a successful example of that genre, Pudovkin's shoes in *Storm over Asia*. Pudovkin himself explains this: he 'has the idea' of his film, he really conceives it, not from the script, but when he imagines an English soldier, upright and well-waxed, who is normally careful not to get his shoes dirty when he walks, but who later in the film goes down the same street squelching through the mud with complete disregard.[2] That is an 'explanation of the *mise-en-scène*'. Between the two modes of behaviour, A and A', something has happened: the soldier must have found himself in a disturbing, almost dishonourable situation (the Mongol's execution), whose index is A'. And this is the most general procedure in Pudovkin's work: however great the milieu presented, St Petersburg or the Mongolian plains, whatever the grandeur of the revolutionary action to be achieved, we move from a scene where modes of behaviour disclose an aspect of the situation, to another scene, each one marking a determined moment of consciousness, and connecting up with the others to form the progression of a consciousness which becomes equal to the whole [*ensemble*] of the disclosed situation. Romm is, to a far greater extent than he thinks, a disciple of Pudovkin (in a generation for whom the large form is often merely a relic, or a constraint imposed by Stalin). Romm's *Nine Days of One Year* proceeds by clearly distinguished days, each of which has its indices, and the whole of which is a progression in time. And, once again, what he wanted in *Ordinary Fascism* was a montage of documents, which could steer clear of a history of fascism or a reconstruction of great events: fascism would

need to be shown as a situation which disclosed itself through
ordinary behaviour, everyday events, people's attitudes, or the
gestures of the leader apprehended in their psychological content, as
moments of an alienated consciousness.

We have seen that Soviet film-makers were defined by a dialectical
conception of montage. This, however, was a nominal definition,
which was sufficient to distinguish them from the other great
tendencies in the cinema, but which did not prevent them from
having profound differences from each other, and even opposing
positions, since each one was interested in a particular aspect, or a
special 'law' of the dialectic. For them the dialectic was not a pretext,
neither was it a theoretical and *ex post facto* reflexion: it was primarily
a conception of images and their montage. What interests Pudovkin
is the law of quantity and quality, of the quantitative process and the
qualitative leap: what all his films show us are the moments and
discontinuous leaps of a dawn of consciousness, in so far as they
assume a continuous linear development and a progression in time,
but also react upon them. This is a small form – ASA' – with indices
and vectors, a skeleton, but full of dialectics: the broken line has
ceased to be unpredictable, and becomes the political and revolutionary
'line'. It is clear that Dovzhenko conceives of another aspect of the
dialectic, the law of the whole, set and parts: how the whole is already
present in the parts but must move from the in-itself to the for-itself,
from the potential to the actual, from the old to the new, from legend
to history, from dream to reality, from Nature to man. It is the song
of the earth, which is transmitted through all human songs – even the
saddest – and whose refrain returns in the great revolutionary hymn.
With Dovzhenko, the large form – SAS' – receives from the dialectic a
'respiration', an oneiric and symphonic power overflowing the
boundaries of the organic.

As for Eisenstein, he reckons himself to be the master of all of them,
because he is interested in a third law, that of opposition developed
and overcome (how One becomes two in order to produce a new
unity). Of course the others are not his disciples. But Eisenstein
rightly considers himself to have created a *transforming form* [*forme à
transformation*], capable of passing from SAS' to ASA'. Indeed he 'sees
big', as his conversation with Romm reminds us. But, starting out
from the large organic representation, from its spiral or respiration,
he subjects them to a treatment which relates the spiral to a cause or
law of 'growth' (golden section) and thus determines as many
caesuras within the organic representation as intervals of respiration.
And we can see how these caesuras mark crises or privileged instants

which, on their own account, enter into relationships with each other according to vectors. This is the pathetic, which undertakes the 'development' by carrying out qualitative leaps between two moments carried to their peak. This link between the pathetic and the organic, this 'pathetisation' as Eisenstein puts it, is as if the small form grafted itself from the inside on to the large form. The law of the small form (qualitative leaps) constantly combines with the law of the large form (the whole related to a cause). Consequently we pass from great duel-synsigns to vector-indices: in *Battleship Potemkin* the landscape and the ship's silhouette in the fog are synsigns, but the eyeglass of the captain who sways among the ropes is an index.

Eisenstein's transforming form often demands a more complex circuit: the transformation is indirect and thus all the more effective. Here we are concerned with the difficult question of 'montage of attractions'. We have already analysed and defined it by the insertion of special images; sometimes theatrical or scenographic representations, sometimes sculptural or plastic representations, which seem to interrupt the course of the action. Twice, in Part Two of *Ivan the Terrible*, the situation is taken over by a theatrical representation which replaces the action or prefigures the action to come: on one occasion, it is the boyars sanctifying their companions who have been beheaded; on another it is Ivan who provides his next victim with an infernal performance by clowns and circus. Conversely, an action can be extended in plastic and sculptural representations, which distance us from the present situation: the obvious example is the stone lions in *Battleship Potemkin*, but there is also the sculptural series of *October* (the counter-revolutionaries' appeal to religion, for example, is extended into a series of African fetishes, Hindu gods and Chinese Buddhas). In *The General Line*, this second aspect assumes its full importance: the action is suspended – is the creamer going to work? A drop falls, then a flood of milk, to be extended in images of streams of water and substitutive streams of fire (a fountain of milk, an explosion of milk). Psychoanalysis has subjected these famous images of the creamer and what follows to such puerile treatment that it has become hard to rediscover their simple beauty. The technical explanations which Eisenstein himself gives are a better guide. He says that it is a case of 'pathetising' something humble and everyday: it is no longer the situation of *Battleship Potemkin*, which was by itself pathetic. It is therefore necessary that the qualitative leap should no longer be purely material, relating to the content, but should become formal and pass from one image to a quite different mode of image which has only an *indirect reflexive relationship* with the initial image.

Eisenstein adds that he had the choice between a theatrical representation and a plastic representation for this other mode: but a theatrical representation, such as peasants dancing on Bald Mountain, would have been ridiculous and, moreover, he had already used the theatrical mode for an earlier scene in the same film. He therefore now needed a plastic representation strong enough to be able to return through its detour to the action. This was the role of the water and the fire.[3]

We must reconsider the two cases. On the one hand, in the theatrical representation, the real situation does not immediately give rise to an action which corresponds to it, but is expressed in a fictitious action which will merely prefigure a project, or a real action to come. Instead of S → A, we have: S → A' (fictitious theatrical action), A' consequently serving as index to the real action, A, which is being prepared (the crime). On the other hand, in the plastic representation, the action does not immediately disclose the situation which it envelops, but is itself developed in grandiose situations which encompass the implied situation. Instead of A → S, we have A → S' (plastic figuration), S' serving as synsign or encompasser of the real situation S, which will only be discovered through its intermediary (the rejoicing of the village). In one case, the situation refers back to an image other than that of the situation which it indicates. It thus appears that, in the first case, the small form is as it were injected into the large form through the intermediary of the theatrical representation and, in the second case, that the large form is injected into the small form through the intermediary of the sculptural or plastic representation. In any case, there is no longer a direct relation between a situation and an action, an action and a situation: between the two images, or between the two elements of the image, a third intervenes to ensure the conversion of the forms. It might be said that the fundamental duality which characterised the action-image tends to go beyond itself towards a higher instance, as a 'thirdness' capable of converting the images and their elements. Take an example borrowed from Kant: the despotic State is directly presented in certain actions, such as a slave-based and mechanical organisation of labour; but the 'windmill' would be the indirect figuration in which that State is reflected.[4] Eisenstein's method in *Strike* is exactly the same: the tsarist State is presented directly in the shooting of the demonstrators, but the abattoir is the indirect image, which both reflects that State and represents this action. Whether they are theatrical or plastic, Eisenstein's attractions do not merely ensure the conversion of one form of action into the other: they carry situations and actions to an extreme limit; they raise them to a third which goes beyond their constitutive duality. The authorities controlling Soviet cinema were not necessarily receptive to these indirect images and could even see them as a dangerous and deviationist method. Thus it is in *Que viva Mexico* that Eisenstein was able to achieve a free development of theatrical and plastic representations which reflect the idea of life and death in Mexico, combining the stages and the frescos, the sculptures and dramatic effects, the pyramids and the gods: the crucifixion, the bull-fight, the crucified bull, the great dance of death. . . .

Figures are these new attractive, attractional images, which circulate through the action-image. Indeed, when Fontanier attempted his great classification of 'figures of discourse' at the start of the nineteenth century, these figures are presented in four forms: in the first case, tropes strictly speaking, a word taken in a figurative sense replaces another word (metaphors, metonymies, synecdoches); in the second case, imperfect tropes, it is a group of words, a proposition, which has the figurative sense (allegory, personification, etc.); in the third case, there *is* substitution, but it is in their strictly literal sense that the words are subjected to exchanges and transformations (reversal is one of these procedures); the last case is that of figures of thought which do not pass through any modification of words (deliberation, concession, support, prosopopoeia, etc.).[5] At this level of our analysis, we are not posing any general problem about the relationship of the cinema and language, of images and words; we are simply noting that cinematographic images have figures proper to them which correspond in their own way to Fontanier's four types. Eisenstein's sculptural or plastic representations are images which represent another image, and have a value one by one even when they are taken in series. But theatrical representations proceed in sequence, and it is the sequence of images which has the figural role. We can recognise the first two of the four above cases. The other cases are of a different nature. Literal figures – operating for example through reversal – have always been widely developed in the cinema, notably in the burlesque parody. But, as we have seen, it is in Hawks that the mechanisms of reversal reach the state of an autonomous and generalised figure. As for the figures of thought – which are already present in Chaplin's talkies – we will not be able to discover their nature and function until a later chapter because they are no longer content to play on the limits of the action-image, but evolve in a new type of image which is only promised by the preceding figures.

2   *The figures of the Large and the Small in Herzog*

As Ideas, the Small and the Large designate both two forms and two
conceptions. These are distinct, but capable of passing into one
another. They have yet a third sense and designate Visions which
deserve even more to be called Ideas. And, although this is true of all
the directors that we are studying, we should like to consider
Herzog's action cinema as an extreme case in this respect. For his
work divides up according to two obsessive themes, which are like
visual and musical motifs.[6] In one, a man who is larger than life
frequents a milieu which is itself larger than life, and dreams up an
action as great as the milieu. It is an SAS′ form, but a very special one:
the action, in effect, is not required by the situation, it is a crazy
enterprise, born in the head of a visionary, which seems to be the only
one capable of rivalling the milieu in its entirety. Or rather, the action
divides in two: there is the sublime action, always beyond, but which
itself engenders another action, a heroic action which confronts the
milieu on its own account, penetrating the impenetrable, breaching
the unbreachable. There is thus both a hallucinatory dimension,
where the acting spirit raises itself to boundlessness in nature and a
hypnotic dimension where the spirit runs up against the limits which
Nature opposes to it. And the two are different, they have a figural
relationship. In *Aguirre, Wrath of God* the heroic action, the descent
of the rapids, is subordinated to the sublime action, the only one
which is equal to the vast, virgin forest: Aguirre's plan to be the only
Traitor, to betray everyone at once – God, the King, men – in order
to found a pure race in an incestuous union with his daughter, in
which History will become the 'opera' of Nature. And, in
Fitzcarraldo the heroic is even more directly the means of the sublime
(the crossing of the mountain by the heavy boat); the whole virgin
forest becomes the temple of Verdi's opera and Caruso's voice.
Finally, in *Heart of Glass*, the Bavarian landscape harbours the
hypnotic creation of the glass ruby, but goes still further beyond
itself into hallucinatory landscapes which summon to the search for
the great abyss of the Universe. Hence the Large is realised as pure
Idea, in the double nature of the landscapes and the actions.

But in the other theme, or following the other facet of Herzog's
work, it is the Small which becomes the Idea, and is realised, firstly, in
dwarves who 'also started small', and is extended in men who have
similarly not ceased to be dwarves. No longer are they 'conquerors of
the useless', but beings incapable of being used. No longer are they
visionaries, but weaklings and idiots. The landscapes are dwarfed or

flattened, they turn sad and dismal, even tend to disappear. The beings who frequent them no longer have Visions at their disposal but instead seem reduced to an elementary sense of touch, like the deaf mutes of *Land of Silence and Darkness*, and walk close to the earth, following an uncertain line which only allows them a pause, a remnant of vision between two torments, to the rhythm of their steps or their monstrous feet. This is the tread of *Kaspar Hauser* in the professor's garden. This is *Stroszek*, with his dwarf and his whore, and his line of flight [*ligne de fuite*] from Germany towards a pitiable America. This is *Nosferatu*, who is treated in the opposite way to Murnau's character, caught in a uterine regression, a foetus reduced to its feeble body and to what it touches and sucks, who will only propagate himself in the universe in the form of his successor, a tiny point fleeing towards the horizon of a flat earth. This is *Woyzeck*, always reduced to his own Passion, where the earth, the red moon, the black pool are now inferred only from staccato indices instead of grandiose synsigns.[7] Thus, on this occasion, it is the small form ASA', but reduced in its turn to its most feeble aspect. For, in both cases – the sublimation of the large form and the enfeeblement of the small form – Herzog is a metaphysician. He is the most metaphysical of cinema directors (although German Expressionism had already been imbued with metaphysics, this was within the confines of a problem of Good and Evil to which Herzog is indifferent). When Bruno asks the question: 'Where do objects go when they no longer have any use?' we might reply that they normally go in the dustbin, but that reply would be inadequate, since the question is metaphysical. Bergson asked the same question and replied metaphysically: that which has ceased to be useful simply begins to *be*. And when Herzog remarks that '*he who walks is defenceless*', we might say that the walker lacks any strength in comparison with cars and aeroplanes. But, there again, the remark was metaphysical.[8] 'Absolutely defenceless' is the definition which Bruno gave of himself. The walker is defenceless because he is he who is beginning to be, and never finishes being small. It is Kaspar's tread, the tread of the unnameable. We can see how the Small enters into a relationship with the Large such that the two Ideas communicate and form figures in interchanging. The visionary's sublime plan failed in the large form and his whole reality was enfeebled: Aguirre ended alone on his slimy raft, with only a colony of monkeys as his race; as his final performance, Fitzcarraldo provided a mediocre troupe of singers in front of a sparse audience and a black piglet; and the fire at the glass-works had no conclusion other than workmen picking up the pieces. But, conversely, the weaklings walking in the small form have such tactile relationships with the world that they inflate and inspire the image itself, as when the deaf-mute child touches a tree or a cactus, or when Woyzeck feels the powers of the Earth rising up at the touch of the wood he is cutting. And this liberation of tactile values does not merely inspire the image; it partially opens it, to insert vast hallucinatory visions of flight, ascent or passage, like the red skier in mid-jump in *Land of Silence and Darkness*, or the three great dreams of landscapes in *The Enigma of Kaspar Hauser*. Here again we therefore witness a dividing-in-two analogous to that of the sublime; and the whole sublime is rediscovered on the side of the Small. This latter, as in Plato, is no less Idea than is the Large. In both senses, Herzog will have shown that the albatross' big feet and its great white wings are the same thing.

3   The two spaces: the breath-Encompasser, and the line of the Universe

Finally, the basic domains where the small and large forms manifest both their real distinction and all their possible transformations must be determined. There is, firstly, the physico-biological domain which corresponds to the *notion of milieu*. For this, in a first sense, designates the interval between two bodies, or rather that which occupies that interval, the fluid which transmits the action of one body on the other at a distance (the action of contact thus implying an infinitely small distance). We therefore find ourselves in a characteristic ASA' form. But the milieu then designates the ambiance or the encompasser which surrounds a body and acts on it, even though the body reacts on the milieu: an SAS' form. We move easily from one sense to the other, but the combinations do not erase the distinct origin of the two ideas, the one belonging to a mechanics of fluids, the other to a bio-anthropological sphere.[9]

The mathematical domain which corresponds to the *notion of space* also gives rise to two distinct conceptions. A conception which starts off from a set whose structure is given, in order to determine a univocal place and function of the elements which belong to that set (even before its nature is known) will be called 'global'. It is an ambiance-space which can undergo certain transformations in relation to the figures which are submerged in it: SAS'. The 'local' conception, on the other hand, starts off from an infinitesimal element which forms, with its immediate surroundings, a fragment of space; but these elements, or these fragments, are not linked up to one another as long as a line of connexion by tangent vectors has not been determined (ASA'). It will be noted that the two conceptions are not opposed like the whole and the part, but rather as two ways of constituting their relationship.[10] It is a case of two spaces which are different in nature and do not have the same limit. The limit of the first would be empty space, but that of the second would be disconnected space whose parts can link together in an infinite number of ways. There are nevertheless conditions under which one can move from one space to the other and the two limits are themselves re-united in the notion of the any-space-whatever. But these are spaces which are very different in origin and conception. If the Western had a pure geometrical representation, the two aspects which we have analysed would correspond to these two spatial forms.

Thirdly, we will consider the aesthetic domain which corresponds to the *notion of landscape*. Chinese and Japanese painting invoke two fundamental principles: on one hand the primordial void and the breath of life which permeates all things in One, unites them in a whole, and transforms them according to the movement of a great circle or an organic spiral; on the other hand, the median void and the skeleton, the articulation, the joints, the wrinkle or broken stroke which moves from one being to another by taking them at the summit of their presence, following a line of the universe. In the one case it is the union which counts, diastole and systole, but in the other it is rather the separation into autonomous events, all of which are decisive. In the one case, the presence of things is in their 'appearing', but in the other presence itself lies in a 'disappearing', like a tower whose top is lost in the sky and whose base is invisible, or like the dragon concealed behind the clouds.[11] The two principles are certainly inseparable and the former is dominant: 'It is advisable that the strokes should be interrupted, without the breath being, that the forms should be discontinuous without the spirit being'. 'All the art of execution is in fragmentary notations and interruptions, although the aim is to achieve a total result. . . .' How can one paint the pike without discovering the broken line of the universe which links it to the rock it brushes in the depths of the water, and to the reeds of the bank where it lurks? But how can one paint it without animating it with the cosmic breath, of which it is only a part, an impression? Even so, under both principles, things do not have the same sign, and spaces do not have the same form: synsigns for the breath or the spiral, vectors for the lines of the universe: the 'single stroke' and the 'wrinkled stroke'.

Eisenstein was fascinated by Chinese and Japanese landscape painting, because he saw in it a prefiguration of the cinema.[12] But in the Japanese cinema itself, each of the two great directors closest to us has given priority to one of the two action spaces. Kurosawa's work is animated by a breath which fills the duels and battles. This breath is represented by a single stroke, both as synsign of the work and as Kurosawa's personal signature. Imagine a thick vertical line which runs from top to bottom of the screen, which is crossed by two thinner horizontal lines, from right to left and from left to right. In *Kagemusha* this is the envoy's magnificent descent, constantly diverted to left and right. Kurosawa is one of the greatest film-makers of rain: in *The Seven Samurai* a dense rain falls while the bandits, caught in a trap, gallop on horseback from one end of the village to the other and back again. The camera angle often forms a flattened image, which brings out the constant lateral movements. We can understand this great breath-space – whether expanded or contracted – if we refer to a Japanese topology. One does not begin with an individual, going on to indicate the number, the street, the locality, the town; one starts off, on the contrary, from the walls, the town, then one designates the large block, then the locality, finally the space in which to seek the unknown woman.[13] One does not move from an unknown woman to the givens capable of determining her: one starts off from all the givens, and one moves down from them to mark the limits within which the unknown woman is contained. This, it would seem, is an extremely pure SA formula: one must know all the givens before acting and in order to act. Kurosawa says that the most difficult time for him is 'before the character starts to act: to get to that point I need to think for several months'.[14] But, indeed, this is only difficult because it is difficult for the character himself: he first had to have all the givens. This is why Kurosawa's films often have two clearly distinct parts; the first, a long exposition and the second when senseless, brutal action begins (*Stray Dog, Heaven and Hell*). This is also why Kurosawa's space can be a contracted, theatrical space where the hero has all the givens before him and keeps them in view in order to act (*The Bodyguard*).[15] This is why, finally, the space expands and forms a great circle which joins the world of the rich and the world of the poor, the heights and the depths, heaven and hell. An exploration of the lower depths must take place at the same time as an exposition of the heights in order to trace this circle of the large form, crossed laterally by a diameter in which the hero is and moves (*Heaven and Hell*).

But, if there were nothing else, Kurosawa would merely be a

distinguished director who developed the large form and could be understood according to the Western criteria which have become classical. His exploration of the lower depths might correspond accurately to the criminal or 'miserabilist' film. His great circle of the world of the poor and the world of the rich might reflect the liberal humanist conception which Griffith was able to impose both as a given of the Universe and as a foundation of montage – and, indeed, this Griffithian version exists in Kurosawa: there are rich and poor, and they ought to understand each other, come to a mutual agreement. . . . In short, the requirement of an exposition before the action would correspond exactly to the SA formula: from the situation to the action. Within the context of this large form there are, however, several aspects which bear witness to a profound originality which can certainly be linked to Japanese traditions, but which may also be attributed to Kurosawa's own genius. In the first place, the givens, of which there must be a complete exposition, are not simply those of the situation, They are the *givens of a question* which is hidden in the situation, wrapped up in the situation, and which the hero must extract in order to be able to act, in order to be able to respond to the situation. The 'response' therefore is not merely that of the action to the situation, but, more profoundly, a response to the question, or to the problem that the situation was not sufficient to disclose. If there is a certain affinity between Kurosawa and Dostoevsky, it is precisely on this point. In Dostoevsky, the urgency of a situation, however great, is deliberately ignored by the hero, who first wants to look for a question which is still more pressing. This is what Kurosawa loves in Russian literature, the connection which he establishes between Russia and Japan. One must tear from a situation the question which it contains, discover the givens of the secret question which alone permit a response to it and without which even the action would not be a response. Kurosawa is thus in his own way a metaphysician, inventing an expansion of the large form: he goes beyond the situation towards a question and raises the givens to the status of givens of the question, no longer of the situation. Hence it matters little that the question sometimes appears disappointing, bourgeois, born of an empty humanism. What counts is this form of the extraction of an any-question-whatever, its intensity rather than its content, its givens rather than its object, which make it, in any event, into a sphinx's question, a sorceress's question.

He who does not understand, he who is in a hurry to act because he believes he possesses all the givens of a situation and is content with this, will perish, by a wretched death: in *The Castle of the Spider's*

Web, the breath-space is transformed into a spider's web which entraps Macbeth because he has not understood the question, whose secret was held by the sorceress alone. In a second case, a character believes it is enough to grasp the givens of a situation: he even proceeds to draw all their consequences, but notices that there is a hidden question, which he suddenly understands and which changes his decision. Thus, *Red Beard*'s deputy understands the situation of sick people and the givens of madness scientifically; he prepares to leave his master whose practices seem authoritarian, archaic, and barely scientific. But he meets a madwoman and in her complaint apprehends what was nevertheless already present in all the other madwomen, the echo of an insane, unfathomable question, which goes infinitely beyond any objective or objectifiable situation. He suddenly understands that the master 'understood' the question, and that his practices explored its basis; he will therefore stay with Red Beard (in any case, no flight is possible in Kurosawa's space). What was particularly in evidence here was that the givens of the question in themselves implied the dreams and nightmares, ideas and visions, impetuses and actions of the subjects involved, while the givens of the situation merely contained causes and effects against which one could only struggle by wiping out this great breath, which bore both the question and its response. In reality, there will be no response if the question is not preserved and respected, even in the terrible, senseless and puerile images in which it is expressed. This is the origin of Kurosawa's oneirism, such that the hallucinatory visions are not merely subjective images, but rather figures of the thought which discovers the givens of a transcendent question, in so far as they belong to the world, to the deepest part of the world (*The Idiot*). The respiration in Kurosawa's films does not solely consist in the alternation between epic and intimate scenes, intensity and respite, tracking-shot and close-up, realistic and unrealistic sequences, but to an even greater extent in the manner in which one is elevated from a real situation to the necessarily unreal givens of a question which haunts the situation.[16]

In a third case it is clearly necessary that the character should absorb all the givens. But, since it refers to a question rather than a situation, this respiration-absorption differs profoundly from that of the Actors Studio. Instead of absorbing a situation in order to produce a response which is merely an explosive action, it is necessary to absorb a question in order to produce an action which would truly be a considered response. Consequently, the sign of the impression had an unprecedented development. In *Kagemusha* the double must absorb everything surrounding the master, he must himself become impression and pass through the various situations (the women, the small child, and above all the horse). One might say that Western films have taken up the same theme. But, in this case, the double has to absorb all the givens of the question that only the master knows, 'fast as the wind, silent as the forest, terrible as fire, immobile as the mountain'. This is not a description of the master; it is the enigma whose response he possesses and carries off. Far from making imitation of him easier, it is this which makes him superhuman or secures for him a cosmic relevance. Here, it seems, we run up against a new limit: he who absorbs all the givens will merely be a double, a shadow in the service of the master, of the World. *Dersu Uzala*, master of the forest impressions, slips into the state of shadow himself when his eyesight fails and he can no longer hear the sublime question which the forest asks men. He will die, although a comfortable 'position' has been arranged for him. And *The Seven Samurai*: if they take so long to gather information on the situation, if they absorb not merely the physical givens of the village but the psychological givens of the inhabitants, it is because there is a higher question which can only be extracted gradually from all the situations. This question is not 'Can the village be defended?' but 'What is a samurai today, at this particular moment of History?' And the response, which comes with the question, once it is finally reached, will be that the samurai have become shadows who no longer have a place, either with the rich or with the poor (the peasants have been the true victors).

But in those very deaths, there is something appeased which allows a more complete response to be presaged. A fourth case, in effect, allows us to recapitulate the whole. *To Live*, one of Kurosawa's finest films, asks the question, 'What is a man who knows he is allowed only a few more months of life to do?' Everything depends on the givens. Should we understand it to be, 'What should one do to know pleasure at last?' The man, astonished and inept, duly does the rounds of the haunts of pleasure, bars and strip-clubs. Does this give the real givens for a question? Is it not rather a restlessness which obscures and hides it? Feeling a strong affection for a girl, the man learns from her that neither is it a question of a last-minute love affair. She cites her own example, explains that she makes little mechanical rabbits on a production-line, and is happy knowing that they will fall into the hands of unknown children, and in this way pass around the town. And the man understands: the givens of the question 'What is to be done?' are those of a useful task to be performed. He therefore takes up his plan for a public park again and before he dies overcomes all the obstacles to it. There again, one might say that Kurosawa is giving us a fairly mundane humanist message. But the film is something quite different: the dogged search for the question and its givens through the situations. And the discovery of the response, gradually as the search progresses. The only response consists in providing givens again, re-stocking the world with givens, putting something into circulation, as much as possible, however little it may be in such a way that through these new or renewed givens, questions which are less cruel arise and are disseminated, questions which are more joyful, closer to nature and to life. This is what Dersu Uzala was doing when he wanted the hut to be prepared and a little food left around, so that the next travellers might survive and circulate in their turn. Then one may be a shadow, one may die: but one will have given back some breath to space, one will have regained the breath-space, one will have become park or forest, or mechanical rabbit, in the sense in which Henry Miller said that if he had to be reincarnated, he would be reincarnated as a park.

The contrast between Kurosawa and Mizoguchi is as well known as that between Corneille and Racine (the chronological order being reversed). Kurosawa's almost exclusively masculine world is opposed to Mizoguchi's feminine universe. Mizoguchi's work belongs to the small form, as much as Kurosawa's belongs to the large; Mizoguchi's signature is not the single stroke, but the wrinkled stroke, as on the lake in *Chronicle of the May Rain*, where the wrinkles of the water occupy the whole image. The two directors provide evidence for a clear distinction between the two forms, rather than for the complementarity which converts one into the other. But Kurosawa, through his technique and his metaphysics, subjects the large form to a broadening which operates as a transformation on the spot. On the other hand, Mizoguchi subjects the small form to a lengthening, a drawing-out which transforms it in itself. It is obvious from several points of view that Mizoguchi starts off from the second principle: no longer is it the breath, but the skeleton, the little fragment of space which must be connected to the next fragment. Everything starts out from the 'background', that is, the fragment of space reserved for women, 'the part of the house which is furthest back', with its delicate framework and veils. In *A Story from Chikamatsu* the action – that is, the wife's flight – is inaugurated by events in the women's rooms. Indeed, even in the house a whole system of connexions is activated, thanks to the removable sliding partitions. But it is in relation to the street that the problem of the linking of one fragment of space to another is first established; and, more generally, many median voids are interposed between two fragments of space, a character having left the frame, or the camera having abandoned the character. A shot defines a limited area, like the visible portion of the lake covered over by the mist in *Ugetsu Monagatari*, or else a hill obstructs the horizon and the transition from one shot to the next rules out fading, affirming a contiguity which is opposed to continuity. Although it is a question of a constant separation, we will not speak of a fragmented space. But each scene, each shot, must carry a character or an event to the peak of his autonomy, of his intensive presence. This intensity must be maintained, prolonged even to the point of its fall = 0, which belongs to it in its own right and does not confuse it with any other, so that the void is a constituent of each intensity, like the 'disappearing', a mode immanent to each presence (this, as we will see, is quite different from what happens in Ozu).[17] The more the fragments thus defined are the process of constitution of the space, the less it is a fragmented space: the space is not constituted by vision, but by progression, the unit of progression being the area or the fragment. In opposition to Kurosawa – in whom lateral movement owed all its importance to the fact that it met up in both directions with the limits of a greater or lesser circle of which it was the diameter – Mizoguchi's lateral movement moves by degrees in a determined but unlimited direction, which creates the space instead of presupposing it. And the determined direction in no way implies a unity of direction, since the direction varies with each fragment, a vector being attached to each one (this variation of directions culminates in *Le Héros sacrilège* (1955)). This is not a simple change of location. It is the paradox of a successive space as space, where time is fully affirmed, but in the form of a function of the variables of that space: thus in *Ugetsu Monagatari* we see the hero bathing with a fairy, then the overflow which forms a stream in the fields, then the fields and a plain, and finally a garden where we again find the couple, having dinner, 'several months later'.[18]

Finally the problem is, beyond the linking-up step by step, that of a generalised connexion of the fragments of space. Four procedures converge to this effect, once again defining a metaphysics as much as a technique: the relatively high position of the camera, which produces the effect of a high-angle shot in perspective, ensuring the deployment of a scene in a narrow area; the maintenance of the same angle for contiguous shots, which produces a sliding effect, overlaying the cuts; the principle of distance which refuses to go beyond the medium shot and allows circular movements of the camera, not neutralising a scene but, on the contrary, maintaining and prolonging its intensity to the very end in space (for example, the woman's agony in *The Story of the Last Chrysanthemums*); finally, and most importantly, the sequence-shot as it has been analysed by Noël Burch, in the particular form which it assumes in Mizoguchi: that of a genuine 'rolling shot', which unravels the successive fragments of space, to which are nevertheless attached vectors of a different direction (the finest examples, according to Burch, being in *Sisters of the Gion*, and *The Story of the Last Chrysanthemums*).[19] And this seems to us to be the essential element in what have been called the extravagant camera-movements in Mizoguchi: the sequence-shot ensures a sort of parallelism of vectors with different orientations and thus constitutes a connexion of heterogeneous fragments of space, giving a very special homogeneity to the space thus constituted. In this unlimited lengthening or drawing-out, we touch on the ultimate nature of the space of the small form: it is indeed no longer any smaller than that of the large form. It is 'small' by its process, but its immensity derives from the connexion of the fragments which compose it, from the placing in parallel of the different vectors (which retain their differences), from the homogeneity which is only formed progressively. This is the origin of Mizoguchi's interest, at the end of his life, in cinemascope, his intuition that he might draw from it new resources, as a function of his conception of space. This conception is therefore that of the 'wrinkled stroke', or the broken stroke. And the wrinkled or broken stroke is the sign of one or several lines of the universe, the ultimate nature of this slope of space. It was Mizoguchi who attained the lines of the universe, the fibres of the universe, and who constantly traced them in all his films. In this way, he gives the small form an incomparable range.

It is not the line which unites into a whole, but the one which connects or links up the heterogeneous elements, while keeping them heterogeneous. The line of the universe links up the back rooms to the street, the street to the lake, the mountain, the forest. It links up man and woman and the cosmos. It connects desires, suffering, errors, trials, triumphs, appeasements. It connects the moments of intensity, as so many points through which it passes. It connects the living and the dead: like the visual and auditory line of the universe which binds the old emperor to the murdered empress in *Yang Kwei Fei*, like the potter's line of the universe in *Ugetsu Monagatari*, which passes through the seductive fairy to find the dead wife once more, whose 'disappearing' has become pure intensity of presence: the hero explores all the rooms of the house, emerges from them, and returns to the hallway, where the ghost, in the meantime, has appeared. Each one of us has his own line of the universe to discover, but it is only discovered through tracing it, through tracing its wrinkled stroke. Lines of the universe have both a physics – which reaches its peak in the sequence-shot and the tracking-shot – and a metaphysics, constituted by Mizoguchi's themes. But it is here that we run up against the worst obstacle: at the precise point at which metaphysics comes face to face with sociology. This confrontation is not theoretical: it takes place in the Japanese house, where the back rooms are subject to the hierarchy of the front, in the Japanese space where the connexion of the fragments must be determined according to the demands of the hierarchical system. Mizoguchi's sociological idea is, in this respect, both simple and extremely powerful: for him there is no line of the universe which does not pass through women, or even which does not issue from them; and yet the social system reduces women to a state of oppression, often to disguised or overt prostitution. The lines of the universe are feminine, but the social state is prostitutional. Threatened to the core, how could they survive, continue, or even extract themselves? In *The Story of the Last Chrysanthemums* it is indeed the woman who draws the man on to a line of the universe, and transforms the execrable actor into a great master: but she knows that the very success will shatter the line, giving her nothing but a lonely death. In *A Story from Chikamatsu* the couple, who are unaware of their love, only discover it when they both have to flee, their line of the universe already no more than a line of flight [*ligne de fuite*], necessarily doomed to failure. How splendid are these images where we are present at the birth of a line, obsessed at each moment by its own brutal termination. It is even worse in *The Life of Oharu*, in which the line of the universe which goes from mother to son is irrevocably barred by the guards who separate the unfortunate woman several times from the young prince whom she brought into the world. And, if Mizoguchi's 'geisha' films constantly conjure up lines of the universe, it is no longer even in a disappearing, which would still be a mode of their presence, but in a blocking at the source which only allows them to subsist in ancient despair or, indeed, the modern callousness of a prostitute as a last refuge. Mizoguchi thus reaches an extreme limit of the action-image: when a world of misery undoes all the lines of the universe, allowing a reality to surge forth which is no longer anything but disoriented, disconnected. Kurosawa for his part, confronted the extreme limit of the action-image's other aspect: when the world of misery rose up to such an extent that it caused the great circle to crack, revealing a chaotic reality that was no longer anything but dispersive (*Dodes' Ka-Den*, with its shanty town which has as its only unity the lateral movement of the half-wit who crosses it believing himself to be a tram).

12 The crisis of the action-image

1 Peirce's 'thirdness' and mental relations

After having distinguished between affection and action, which he calls Firstness and Secondness, Peirce added a third kind of image: the 'mental' or Thirdness. The point of thirdness was a term that referred to a second term through the intermediary of another term or terms. This third instance appeared in signification, law or relation. This may seem to be already included in action, but this is not so. An action, that is to say a duel or a pair of forces, obeys laws which make it possible, but it is never its law which makes it act. An action does have a signification, but this is not what constitutes its end; the end and the means do not include signification. An action relates two terms, but this spatio-temporal relation (for example, opposition) must not be confused with a logical relation. On the one hand, according to Peirce, there is nothing beyond thirdness: beyond, everything is reducible to combinations between 1, 2, 3. On the other hand, thirdness, that which is three by itself, will not let itself be reduced to dualities: for example, if A 'gives' B to C, it is not as if A threw B (first pair) and C picked up B (second pair); if A and B make an 'exchange', it is not as if A and B parted with, respectively, *a* and *b*, and took possession of, respectively, *b* and *a*.[1] Therefore thirdness gives birth not to actions but to 'acts' which necessarily contain the symbolic element of a law (giving, exchanging); not to perceptions, but to interpretations which refer to the element of sense; not to affections, but to intellectual feelings of relations, such as the feelings which accompany the use of the logical conjunctions 'because', 'although', 'so that', 'therefore', 'now', etc.

Thirdness perhaps finds its most adequate representation in relation; for relation is always third, being necessarily external to its terms. And philosophical tradition distinguishes two kinds of relations, natural and abstract relations – signification belonging to the first kind and law or sense belonging to the second kind. By the first kind, one passes naturally and easily from one image to another: for example from a portrait to its model, then to circumstances in which the portrait was done, then to the place where the model is now, etc. There is thus the formation of a succession or habitual series of images. This is, however, not unlimited, for the realisation of natural relations is exhausted quickly enough. The second kind of relations, abstract relation, designates on the contrary a circumstance through which one compares two images which are not naturally united in the mind (for example, two very different figures, but which have as their common circumstance being conical sections). Here there is the constitution of a whole, not the formation of a series.[2]

Peirce insists on the following point: if firstness is 'one' by itself, secondness two, and thirdness three, it is necessary that, in the two, the first term should 'recapitulate' [*reprenne*] firstness in its own way, whilst the second affirms secondness. And, in the three, there will be a representative of firstness, one of secondness, the third affirming thirdness. There is therefore not merely 1, 2, 3, but 1, 2 in 2 and 1, 2, 3 in 3. One could see here a kind of dialectic; but it is doubtful that the dialectic includes all these movements. One would say rather that it is an interpretation of it – a very inadequate interpretation.

The affection-image undoubtedly already contains something mental (a pure consciousness). And the action-image also implies it in the end of the action (conception), in the choice of means (judgement), in the set of implications (reasoning). And, of course, the 'figures' introduced the mental into the image. But this is completely different from making the mental the proper object of an image, a specific, explicit image, with its own figures. Does this amount to saying that this image ought to represent to us someone's thought, or even a pure thought and a pure thinker? Obviously not, although attempts have been made in this direction. On the one hand the image would become really too abstract, or ridiculous. And on the other hand the affection-image, the action-image, already contained quite enough thought (for example, the reasonings in the image in Lubitsch). When we speak of mental image, we mean something else: it is an image which takes as objects *of* thought, objects which have their own existence outside thought, just as the objects of perception have their own existence outside perception. *It is an image which takes as its object, relations*, symbolic acts, intellectual feelings. It can be, but is not necessarily, more difficult than the other images. It will necessarily have a new, direct, relationship with thought, a relationship which is completely distinct from that of the other images.

What has all this got to do with the cinema? When Godard says 1, 2, 3 . . . it is not merely a matter of adding images to one another, but of classifying types of images and of circulating in these types. Take the example of burlesque. If we leave aside Chaplin and Keaton, who carried the two fundamental forms of burlesque perception to perfection, we can say: 1 is Langdon, 2 Laurel and Hardy, 3 the Marx Brothers. Langdon, indeed, is the affection-image in a purer state than it is actualised in any other matter or milieu, so that it inspires in him an irresistible sleep. But in Laurel and Hardy there is the action-image, the perpetual duel with matter, the milieu, women, other people and with each other; they were able to decompose the duel, by breaking all simultaneity in space and substituting for it a succession in time, a blow for one, then a blow for the other, so that the duel propagates itself to infinity, and its effects increase by being piled on instead of being weakened by fatigue. Laurel is like the 1 of the couple, the affective representative, the one who goes crazy and unleashes practical catastrophe, but is gifted with an inspiration which enables him to get through the man-traps of matter and milieu; whilst Hardy, the 2, the man of action, so lacks intuitive resources, is so much under the sway of brute matter, that he falls into all the traps of the actions for which he takes responsibility, and into all the catastrophes that Laurel has unleashed without falling into them himself. The Marx brothers, finally, are 3. The three brothers are distributed in such a way that Harpo and Chico are most often grouped together, Groucho for his part looming up in order to enter into a kind of alliance with the two others. Caught in the indissoluble group of 3, Harpo is the 1, the representative of celestial affects, but also already of infernal impulses, voraciousness, sexuality, destruction. Chico is 2: it is he who takes on action, the initiative, the duel with the milieu, the strategy of effort and resistance. Harpo hides, in his immense raincoat, all kinds of objects, bits and pieces which can be used for any kind of action; but he himself only uses them in an affective or fetishistic way and it is Chico who uses them for organised action. Finally, Groucho is the three, the man of interpretations, of symbolic acts and abstract relations. Nevertheless each of the three equally belongs to the thirdness that they make up together. Harpo and Chico already have a relationship such that Chico throws a *word* to Harpo who has to provide the corresponding object, in a series which is constantly denatured (for example the series *flash-fish-flesh-flask-flush* . . . in *Animal Crackers*); conversely Harpo proposes to Chico the enigma of a language of gestures, in a series of mimes that Chico must constantly guess in order to extract a *proposition* from them. But Groucho pushes the art of interpretation to its final degree, because he is the master of *reasoning*, of arguments and syllogisms which find a pure expression in nonsense: 'Either this man is dead, or my watch has stopped' (he says, feeling Harpo's pulse

in *A Day at the Races*). In all these senses, the greatness of the Marx
Brothers is to have introduced the mental image into burlesque.

It was also Hitchcock's task to introduce the mental image into the
cinema and to make it the completion of the cinema, the perfection of
all the other images. As Rohmer and Chabrol say of *Dial M for
Murder*, 'the whole aim of the film is only the exposition of a
reasoning, and nevertheless the attention never wanders'.[3] And this
does not merely come at the end, it starts from the beginning: with its
famous false flash-back, *Stage Fright* begins with an interpretation,
which is presented as a memory of recent events, or even a
perception. In Hitchcock, actions, affections, perceptions, all is
interpretation, from beginning to end.[4] *The Rope* is made up of a
single shot in so far as the images are only the winding paths of a
single reasoning process. The reason for this is simple: in Hitchcock's
films an action, once it is given (in present, future or past), is literally
surrounded by a set of relations, which vary its subject, nature, aim,
etc. What matters is not who did the action – what Hitchcock calls
with contempt the *whodunit* – but neither is it the action itself: it is
the set of relations in which the action and the one who did it are
caught. This is the source of the very special sense of the frame. The
sketches for framing, the strict delimitation of the frame, the apparent
elimination of the out-of-frame, are explained by Hitchcock's
constant reference, not to painting or the theatre, but to tapestry-
making, that is, to weaving. The frame is like the posts which hold
the warp threads, whilst the action constitutes merely the mobile
shuttle which passes above and below. We can thus understand that
Hitchcock usually works with short shots, as many shots as there are
frames, each shot showing a relation or a variation of the relation. But
the theoretically single shot of *The Rope* is no exception to this rule: it
is very different from the sequence-shot of Welles or Dreyer, which
tends in two ways to subordinate the frame to a whole, whilst
Hitchcock's single shot subordinates the whole (relations) to the
frame, being content to open this frame lengthways, provided that it
remains closed breadthways, exactly as in a weaving process
producing an infinitely long tapestry. The essential point, in any
event, is that action, and also perception and affection, are framed in a
fabric of relations. It is this chain of relations which constitutes the
mental image, in opposition to the thread of actions, perceptions and
affections.

Hitchcock will, therefore, borrow a particularly striking action of
the type 'killing', 'stealing' from the detective or the spy film. As it is
engaged in a set of relations that the characters do not know (but that

the spectator already knows or will discover before them), it only appears to be a duel which governs all action: it is already something else, since the relation constitutes the thirdness which elevates it to the state of mental image. It is therefore not sufficient to define Hitchcock's schema by saying that an innocent man is accused of a crime that he has not committed; this would merely be an error of 'coupling', a false identification of the 'second'; what we called an index of equivocity. On the contrary, Rohmer and Chabrol have analysed Hitchcock's schema perfectly: the criminal has always done his crime *for* another, the true criminal has done his crime for the innocent man who, whether we like it or not, is innocent no longer. In short, the crime is inseparable from the operation by which the criminal has 'exchanged' his crime, as in *Strangers on a Train*, or even 'given' and 'delivered up' his crime to the innocent, as in *I Confess*. One does not commit a crime in Hitchcock, one delivers it up, one gives it or one exchanges it. In our view this is the strongest point in Rohmer and Chabrol's book. The relation (the exchange, the gift, the rendering . . .) does not simply surround action, it penetrates it in advance and in all its parts, and transforms it into a necessarily symbolic act. There is not only the acting and the action, the assassin and the victim, there is always a third and not an accidental or apparent third, as a suspected innocent would simply be, but a fundamental third constituted by the relation itself, the relation of the assassin, of the victim or of the action with the apparent third. This perpetual tripling also takes over objects, perceptions, affections. Each image in its frame, by its frame, must exhibit a mental relation. The characters can act, perceive, experience, but they cannot testify to the relations which determine them. These are merely the movements of the camera, and their movements towards the camera. Hence, the opposition between Hitchcock and the Actors Studio, his requirement that the actor acts in the most simple, even neutral, way, the camera attending to what remains. This remainder is the essential or the mental relation. It is the camera, and not a dialogue, which *explains* why the hero of *Rear Window* has a broken leg (photos of the racing car, in his room, broken camera). It is the camera in *Sabotage* which means that the woman, the man and the knife do not simply enter into a succession of pairs, but into a true relation (thirdness) which makes the woman deliver up her crime to the man.[5] In Hitchcock there is never duel or double: even in *Shadow of a Doubt*, the two Charlies, the uncle and the niece, the assassin and the girl, both appeal to the same state of the world which, for the one, justifies his crimes, and, for the other, cannot be justified in producing such a criminal.[6] And, in the history of the cinema Hitchcock appears as one who no longer conceives of the constitution of a film as a function of two terms – the director and the film to be made – but as a function of three: the director, the film and the public which must come into the film, or whose reactions must form an integrating part of the film (this is the explicit sense of suspense, since the spectator is the first to 'know' the relations).[7]

There are many excellent commentators on Hitchcock (for no film director has been the object of so many commentaries) and there is no need to decide between those who see him as a profound thinker, and those who see him merely as a great entertainer. There is, however, no need to make Hitchcock a Platonic and Catholic metaphysician, as do Rohmer and Chabrol, or a psychologist of the depths, as does Douchet. Hitchcock has a very sound conception of theoretical and practical relations. Not only Lewis Carroll, but the whole of English thought has shown that the theory of relations is the key element of logic and can be both the deepest and the most amusing element. If there are Christian themes in Hitchcock, beginning with original sin, it is because these themes have from the beginning posed the problem of relation, as the English logicians well knew. Hitchcock, in his turn, begins from relations, the mental image, from what he calls the postulate. It is from this basic postulate that the film is developed with a mathematical or absolute necessity, despite the improbabilities of the plot and the action. Now, if one begins from relations, what happens, by virtue of their very exteriority? It may be that the relation vanishes, suddenly disappears, without the characters changing, but leaving them in the void: the comedy *Mr and Mrs Smith* belongs to Hitchcock's oeuvre, precisely because the couple learn all of a sudden that, their marriage not being legal, they have never been married. It may be, on the contrary, that the relation proliferates and multiplies itself, according to the terms in view and the apparent thirds which arise to join up with it, subdividing it or orientating it in a new direction (*The Trouble with Harry*). Finally, it may be that the relation itself passes through variations, depending on variables which carry it out, and entailing changes in one or more characters. In this sense Hitchcock's characters are certainly not intellectuals, but have feelings that can be called intellectual feelings, rather than affects, in that they are modelled on a varied play of experienced conjunctions; because . . . although . . . since . . . if . . . even if . . . (*Secret Agent, Notorious, Suspicion*). In all these cases the relation introduces an essential instability between the characters, the roles, the actions, the set [*décor*]. The model of this instability will be that of the guilty and the innocent. But, also, the autonomous life of the relation will make it tend towards a kind of equilibrium, even though it may be devastated, desperate or even monstrous. The innocent-guilty equilibrium, the restitution to each of his role, the retribution upon each for his action, will be achieved, but at the price of a limit which risks corroding and even effacing the whole[8] – like the indifferent face of the wife who has gone crazy in *The Wrong Man*. It is in this respect that Hitchcock is a tragic director: in his work the shot, as always in the cinema, has two faces, the one turned towards the characters, the objects and the actions in movement, the other turned towards a whole which changes progressively as the film goes on. But, in Hitchcock, the whole which changes is the evolution of relations, which move from the disequilibrium that they introduce between characters to the terrible equilibrium that they attain in themselves.

Hitchcock introduces the mental image into the cinema. That is, he makes relation itself the object of an image, which is not merely added to the perception, action and affection images, but frames and transforms them. With Hitchcock, a new kind of 'figures' appear which are figures of thoughts. In fact, the mental image itself requires particular signs which are not the same as those of the action-image. It has often been noticed that the detective only has a mediocre and secondary role (except when he enters fully into the relation, as in *Blackmail*); and that indices have little importance. On the other hand, Hitchcock produces original signs, in accordance with the two types of relations, natural and abstract. In accordance with the natural relation, a term refers back to other terms in a customary series such that each can be 'interpreted' by the others: these are *marks*; but it is always possible for one of these terms to leap outside the web and suddenly appear in conditions which take it out of its series, or set it in contradiction with it, which we will refer to as the *demark*. It is therefore very important that the terms should be completely ordinary, in order that one of them, first of all, can detach itself from the series: as Hitchcock says, *The Birds* must be ordinary birds. Certain of Hitchcock's demarks are famous, like the windmill in *Foreign Correspondent* whose sails turn in the opposite direction to the wind, or the crop-spraying plane in *North by Northwest* which appears where there are no crops to spray. Similarly, the glass of milk made suspect by its internal luminosity in *Suspicion*, or the key which does not fit the lock in *Dial M for Murder*. Sometimes the demark is constituted very slowly, as in *Blackmail*, where one wonders whether the cigar buyer is, in the normal way, part of the series client–choice–preparations–lighting, or if he is a master-blackmailer who is using the cigar and its ritual in order to provoke the young couple. On the other hand and in second place, in accordance with the abstract relation, what we will call a *symbol* is not an abstraction, but a concrete object which is a bearer of various relations, or of variations of a single relation, of character with others and with himself.[9] The bracelet is such a symbol in *The Ring*, like the handcuffs in *The Thirty-Nine Steps* or the wedding ring of *Rear Window*. Demarks and symbols can converge, particularly in *Notorious*: the bottle gives rise to such emotion in one of the spies that it springs out of its natural wine–cellar–dinner series; and the key to the cellar that the heroine holds in her closed hand bears the set of relations that she maintains with her husband from whom she has stolen it, with her lover to whom she will give it, with her mission which lies in discovering what there is in the cellar. We see that a single object - a key, for example - can, according to the images in which it is caught, function as a symbol (*Notorious*) or as a demark (*Dial M for Murder*). In *The Birds*, the first gull which strikes the heroine is a demark, since it violently leaves the customary series which unites it to its species, to man and to Nature, But the thousands of birds, all species brought together, grasped in their preparations, in their attacks, in their moments of rest, are a symbol: these are not abstractions or metaphors, they are real birds, literally, but which present the inverted image of men's relationships with Nature, and the naturalised image of men's relationships between themselves. Although demarks and symbols may superficially resemble indices, they are completely different from them, and constitute the two great signs of the mental image. Demarks are clashes of natural relations (series), and symbols are nodes of abstract relations (set).

Inventing the mental image or the relation-image, Hitchcock makes use of it in order to close the set of action-images, and also of perception and affection images. Hence his conception of the frame. And the mental image not only frames the others, but transforms them by penetrating them. For this reason, one might say that Hitchcock accomplishes and brings to completion the whole of the cinema by pushing the movement-image to its limit. Including the spectator in the film, and the film in the mental image, Hitchcock brings the cinema to completion. However, some of Hitchcock's finest films give us a glimpse of a fundamental question. *Vertigo* communicates a genuine image to us; and, certainly, what is vertiginous, is, in the heroine's heart, the relation of the Same with the Same which passes through all the variations of its relations with others (the dead woman, the husband, the inspector). But we cannot forget the other, more ordinary, vertigo – that of the inspector who is incapable of climbing the bell-tower staircase, living in a strange state of contemplation which is communicated to the whole film and which is rare in Hitchcock. And in *Family Plot* the discovery of relations refers, even if jokingly, to a clairvoyant function. In a still more direct way the hero of *Rear Window* has access to the mental image, not simply because he is a photographer, but because he is in a state of immobility: he is reduced as it were to a pure optical situation. If one of Hitchcock's innovations was to implicate the spectator in the film, did not the characters themselves have to be capable – in a more or less obvious manner – of being assimilated to spectators? But then it may be that one consequence appears inevitable: the mental image would then be less a bringing to completion of the action-image, and of the other images, than a re-examination of their nature and status, moreover, the whole movement-image which would be re-examined through the rupture of the sensory-motor links in a particular character. What Hitchcock had wanted to avoid, a crisis of the traditional image of the cinema, would nevertheless happen in his wake, and in part as a result of his innovations.

2   The origin of the crisis: Italian neo-realism and the French new wave

But can a crisis of the action-image be presented as something new? Was this not the constant state of the cinema? The purest action films have always had value in episodes outside the action, or in idle periods between actions, through a whole set of extra-actions and infra-actions which cannot be cut out in montage without disfiguring the film (hence the formidable power of producers). At all times too, the cinema's potentialities, its vocation for changes of location, have caused directors to wish to limit or even to suppress the unity of action, to undo the action, the drama, the plot or the story and to carry further an ambition with which literature was already permeated. On the one hand, the SAS structure found itself called into question: there was no globalising situation which was able to concentrate itself in a decisive action, but action or plot were only to be a component in a dispersive set, in an open totality. Jean Mitry is right in this sense to show that Delluc, scriptwriter of Germaine Dulac's *La Fête espagnole*, already wanted to plunge the drama into a 'multiplicity of facts', none of which would be principal or secondary, so that it could only be reconstituted following a broken line lifted from among all the points and all the lines of the whole of the festival.[10] On the other hand, the structure ASA was subjected to an analogous critique. In the same way as there was no previous history, there was no preformed action whose consequences on a situation could be foreseen, and the cinema could not transcribe events which had already happened, but necessarily devoted itelf to reaching the event in the course of happening, sometimes by cutting across an 'actuality', sometimes by provoking or producing it. Comolli has shown this very well: however far the work of preparation in many directors goes, the cinema cannot avoid the 'detour through the direct'. There is always a moment when the cinema meets the unforeseeable or the improvisation, the irreducibility of a present living under the present of narration, and the camera cannot even begin its work without engendering its own improvisations, both as obstacles and as indispensable means[11] These two themes, the open totality and the event in the course of happening, are part of the profound Bergsonianism of the cinema in general.

Nevertheless, the crisis which has shaken the action-image has depended on many factors which only had their full effect after the war, some of which were social, economic, political, moral and others more internal to art, to literature and to the cinema in particular. We might mention, in no particular order, the war and its consequences, the unsteadiness of the 'American Dream' in all its aspects, the new consciousness of minorities, the rise and inflation of images both in the external world and in people's minds, the influence on the cinema of the new modes of narrative with which literature had experimented, the crisis of Hollywood and its old genres. . . . Certainly, people continue to make SAS and ASA films: the greatest commercial successes always take that route, but the soul of the cinema no longer does. The soul of the cinema demands increasing thought, even if thought begins by undoing the system of actions, perceptions and affections on which the cinema had fed up to that point. We hardly believe any longer that a global situation can give rise to an action which is capable of modifying it – no more than we believe that an action can force a situation to disclose itself, even partially. The most 'healthy' illusions fall. The first things to be compromised everywhere are the linkages of situation–action, action–reaction, excitation–response, in short, the sensory-motor links which produced the action-image. Realism, despite all its violence – or rather with all its violence which remains sensory-motor – is oblivious to this new state of things where the synsigns disperse and the indices become confused. We need new signs. A new kind of image is born that one can attempt to identify in the post-war American cinema, outside Hollywood.

In the first place, the image no longer refers to a situation which is globalising or synthetic, but rather to one which is dispersive. The characters are multiple, with weak interferences and become principal or revert to being secondary. It is nevertheless not a series of sketches, a succession of short stories, since they are all caught in the same reality which disperse them. Robert Altman explores this direction in *A Wedding* and particularly in *Nashville*, with the multiple sound-tracks and the anamorphic screen which allows several simultaneous stagings. The city and the crowd lose the collective and unanimist character which they have in King Vidor; the city at the same time ceases to be the city above, the upright city, with skyscrapers and low-angle shots, in order to become the recumbent city, the city as horizontal or at human height, where each gets on with his own business, on his own account.

In the second place, the line or the fibre of the universe which prolonged events into one another, or brought about the connection of portions of space, has broken. The small form ASA is therefore no less compromised than the large form SAS. Ellipsis ceases to be a mode of the tale [*récit*], a way in which one goes from an action to a partially disclosed situation: it belongs to the situation itself, and reality is lacunary as much as dispersive. Linkages, connections, or liaisons are deliberately weak. Chance becomes the sole guiding thread, as in Altman's *Quintet*. Sometimes the event delays and is lost in idle periods, sometimes it is there too quickly, but it does not belong to the one to whom it happens (even death . . .). And there are close relationships between these aspects of the event: the dispersive, the direct in the course of happening and the non-belonging. Cassavetes plays on these three aspects in *The Killing of a Chinese Bookie* and in *Too Late Blues*. We could call them white events, events which never truly concern the person who provokes or is subject to them, even when they strike him in his flesh: events whose bearer, a man internally dead, as Lumet says, is in a hurry to extricate himself. In Scorsese's *Taxi Driver*, the driver wavers between killing himself and committing a political murder and, replacing these projects by the final slaughter, is astonished by it himself, as if the carrying out concerned him no more than did the preceding whims. The actuality of the action-image, the virtuality of the affection-image can interchange, all the more easily for having fallen into the same indifference.

In the third place, the sensory-motor action or situation has been replaced by the stroll, the voyage and the continual return journey. The voyage has found in America the formal and material conditions of a renewal. It takes place through internal or external necessity, through the need for flight. But now it loses the initiatory aspect that it had in the German journey (even in Wenders' films) and that it kept, despite everything, in the beat journey (Dennis Hopper and Peter Fonda's *Easy Rider*). It has become urban voyage, and has become detached from the active and affective structure which supported it, directed it, gave it even vague directions. How could there be a nerve fibre or a sensory-motor structure between the driver of *Taxi Driver* and what he sees on the pavement in his driving mirror? And, in Lumet, everything happens in continual trips and in return journeys, at ground level, in aimless movements where characters behave like windscreen wipers (*Dog Day Afternoon*, *Serpico*). This is in fact the clearest aspect of the modern voyage. It happens in any-space-whatever – marshalling yard, disused warehouse, the undifferentiated fabric of the city – in opposition to action which most often unfolded in the qualified space-time of the old realism. As Cassavetes says, it is a question of undoing space, as well as the story, the plot or the action.[12]

In the fourth place, we ask ourselves what maintains a set [*ensemble*] in this world without totality or linkage. The answer is simple: what forms the set are *clichés*, and nothing else. Nothing but clichés, clichés everywhere. . . . The problem had already been raised by Dos Passos, and the new techniques that he began in the novel, before the cinema had ever dreamed of them: dispersive and lacunary reality, the swarming of characters with weak interferences, their capacity to become principal and revert to being secondary, events which descend on the characters and which do not belong to those who undergo or provoke them. Now, what consolidates all this, are the current clichés of an epoch or a moment, sound and visual slogans, which Dos Passos calls, with names borrowed from the cinema, 'actualities' and 'eye of the camera' (actualities are news interwoven with political or social events, interest items, interviews and light-hearted songs and the eye of the camera is the internal monologue of any third whatever, who is not an identified character). They are these floating images, these anonymous clichés, which circulate in the external world, but which also penetrate each one of us and constitute his internal world, so that everyone possesses only psychic clichés by which he thinks and feels, is thought and is felt, being himself a cliché among the others in the world which surrounds him.[13] Physical, optical and auditory clichés and psychic clichés mutually feed on each other. In order for people to be able to bear themselves and the world, misery has to reach the inside of consciousnesses and the inside has to be like the outside. It is this romantic and pessimist vision that we discover in Altman or Lumet. In *Nashville* the city locations are redoubled by the images to which they give rise – photos, recordings, television – and it is in an old song that the characters are finally brought together. This power of the sound cliché, a little song, is asserted in Altman's *A Perfect Couple*: the voyage/ballad[14] takes on its second sense here, the sung and danced poem. In Lumet's *Bye Bye Braveman*, which tells the story of the stroll through the city of four Jewish intellectuals going to the burial of a friend, one of the four wanders among the tombs reading to the dead the recent news from the newspapers. In *Taxi Driver* Scorsese makes a catalogue of all the psychic clichés which bustle about in the driver's head, but at the same time of the optical and sound clichés of the neon-city that he sees filing past along the streets: he himself, after his slaughter, will be the national hero of a day, attaining the state of cliché, without the event being his for all that. Finally, it is no longer even possible to distinguish what is physical and psychic in the universal cliché of *King of Comedy*, sucking the interchangeable characters into a single void.

The idea of one single misery, internal and external, in the world and in consciousness, had already been had by English Romanticism in its blackest form, notably in Blake or Coleridge. People would not accept the intolerable if the same 'reasons' which it imposed on them from the outside were not insinuating themselves in them in order to make them adhere, from the inside. According to Blake there was a whole *organisation of misery*, from which the American revolution could perhaps save us.[15] But we can see how America, on the contrary, raised the romantic question again, by giving it a still more radical, still more urgent, still more technical form: the reign of clichés internally as well as externally. How can one not believe in a powerful concerted organisation, a great and powerful plot, which has found the way to make clichés circulate, from outside to inside, from inside to outside? The criminal conspiracy, as organisation of Power, was to take on a new aspect in the modern world, that the cinema would endeavour to follow and to show. It is no longer the case, as in the *film noir* of American realism, of an organisation which related to a distinctive milieu, to assignable actions by which the criminals would be distinguishable (although very successful films of this kind, like *The Godfather*, are still made). There is no longer even a magic centre, from which hypnotic actions could start spreading everywhere as in Lang's first two Mabuse films. We do, it is true, see that Lang evolves in this respect: *The Testament of Dr Mabuse* no longer passes through a production of secret actions, but rather through a monopoly of reproduction. Occult power is confused with its effects, its supports, its media, its radios, its televisions, its microphones: it now only operates through the 'mechanical reproduction of images and of sounds'.[16] And this is the fifth characteristic of the new image, this is the one which inspired post-war American cinema. In Lumet, the conspiracy is the system of reception, surveillance and transmission of *The Anderson Tapes*; *Network*, also, doubles the city with all the transmissions and reception that it ceaselessly produces, whilst *The Prince of the City* records the whole city on magnetic tape. And Altman's *Nashville* fully grasps this operation which doubles the city with all the clichés that it produces, and divides in two the clichés themselves, internally and externally, whether optical or sound clichés and psychic clichés.

These are the five apparent characteristics of the new image: *the dispersive situation, the deliberately weak links, the voyage form, the consciousness of clichés, the condemnation of the plot*. It is the crisis of both the action-image and the American Dream. Everywhere there is a re-examination of the sensory-motor schema; and the Actors Studio becomes the object of severe criticism, at the same time as it undergoes an evolution and internal splits. But how can the cinema attack the dark organisation of clichés, when it participates in their fabrication and propagation, as much as magazines or television? Perhaps the special conditions under which it produces and reproduces clichés allow certain directors to attain a critical reflection which they would not have at their disposal elsewhere. It is the organisation of the cinema which means that, however great the controls which bear upon him, the creator has at his disposal at least a certain time to 'commit' the irreversible. He has the chance to extract an Image from all the clichés and to set it up against them. On the condition, however, of there being an aesthetic and political project capable of constituting a positive enterprise. Now, it is here that the American cinema finds its limits. All the aesthetic or even political qualities that it can have remain narrowly critical and in this way even less 'dangerous' than if they were being made use of in a project of positive creation. Then, either the critique swerves abruptly and attacks only a misuse of apparatuses and institutions, in striving to save the remains of the American Dream, as in Lumet; or it extends itself, but becomes empty and starts to grate, as in Altman, content to parody the cliché instead of giving birth to a new image. As Lawrence said about painting: the rage against clichés does not lead to much if it is content only to parody them; maltreated, mutilated, destroyed, a cliché is not slow to be reborn from its ashes.[17] In fact, what gave the American cinema its advantage, the fact of being born without a previous tradition to suffocate it, now rebounded against it. For the cinema of the action-image had itself engendered a tradition from which it could now only, in the majority of cases, extricate itself negatively. The great genres of this cinema, the psycho-social film, the *film noir*, the Western, the American comedy, collapse and yet maintain their empty frame. For great creators the path of emigration was thus reversed, for reasons which were not just related to McCarthyism. In fact, Europe had more freedom in this respect; and it is first of all in Italy that the great crisis of the action-image took place. The timing is something like: around 1948, Italy; about 1958 France; about 1968, Germany.

3   Towards a beyond of the movement-image

Why Italy first, before France and Germany? It is perhaps for an essential reason, but one which is external to the cinema. Under the impetus of de Gaulle, France had, at the end of the war, the historical and political ambition to belong fully to the circle of victors. The Resistance, therefore, even when underground, needed to appear as the detachment of a regular, perfectly organised army and the life of the French, even when full of conflict and ambiguities, needed to appear as a contribution to victory. These conditions were not favourable to a renewal of the cinematographic image, which found itself kept within the framework of a traditional action-image, at the service of a properly French 'dream'. The result of this was that the cinema in France was only able to break with its tradition rather belatedly and by a reflexive or intellectual detour which was that of the New Wave. The situation in Italy was completely different. It could certainly not claim the rank of victor; but, in contrast to Germany, on the one hand it had at its disposal a cinematographic institution which had escaped fascism relatively successfully, on the other hand it could point to a resistance and a popular life underlying oppression, although one without illusion. To grasp these, all that was necessary was a new type of tale [*récit*] capable of including the elliptical and the unorganised, as if the cinema had to begin again from zero, questioning afresh all the accepted facts of the American tradition. The Italians were therefore able to have an intuitive consciousness of the new image in the course of being born. This explains nothing of the genius of Rossellini's first films. But it does at least explain the reaction of certain American critics who saw in them the inordinate pretension of a defeated country, an odious form of blackmail, a way of making the conquerors ashamed.[18] And above all, it is this very special situation of Italy which made possible the enterprise of neo-realism.

It was Italian neo-realism which forged the five preceding characteristics. In the situation at the end of the war, Rossellini discovered a dispersive and lacunary reality – already in *Rome, Open City*, but above all in *Païsa* – a series of fragmentary, chopped up encounters, which call into question the SAS form of the action-image. It is the post-war economic crisis, on the other hand, which inspires De Sica, and leads him to shatter the ASA form: there is no longer a vector or line of the universe which extends and links up the events of *The Bicycle Thief*; the rain can always interrupt or deflect the search fortuitously, the voyage of the man and of the child. The Italian rain becomes the sign of idle periods and of possible interruption. And again the theft of the bicycle, or even the insignificant events of *Umberto D*, have a vital importance for the protagonists. However, Fellini's *I Vitelloni* testifies not only to the insignificance of events, but also to the uncertainty of the links between them and of their non-belonging to those who experience them in this new form of the voyage. In the city which is being demolished or rebuilt, neo-realism makes any-space-whatevers proliferate – urban cancer, undifferentiated fabrics, pieces of waste-ground – which are opposed to the determined spaces of the old realism.[19] And what rises to the horizon, what is outlined on this world, what will be imposed in a third moment, is not even raw reality, but its understudy, the reign of clichés, both internally and externally, in people's heads and hearts as much as in the whole of space. Did not *Païsa* already propose all the possible clichés of the encounters between America and Italy? And in *Strangers* Rossellini catalogues the clichés of pure Italianness, as seen by a bourgeois woman out walking; volcano, museum statues, Christian sanc-tuary. . . . In *General della Rovere* he drew out the cliché of the manufacture of a hero. In a very special way, it is Fellini who put his first films under the sign of the manufacture, the detection and the proliferation of external and internal clichés: the photo-novel of *The White Sheikh*, the photo-inquest of *Un' Agenzia matrimoniale*, the nightclubs, music halls and circuses, and all the jingles which console or despair. Should we add the great conspiracy which organised this misery, and for which Italy had a ready-made name, the Mafia? Francesco Rosi set up the faceless portrait of the bandit *Salvatore Giuliano*, by cutting up history according to the prefabricated roles which were imposed on it by a power which cannot be pinned down, which is only known by its effects.

Neo-realism already had a high technical conception of the difficulties that it would encounter and of the means that it invented; it had a no less sure intuitive consciousness of the new image in the course of being born. It is rather by way of an intellectual and reflexive consciousness that the French New Wave was able to take up this mutation on its own account. It is here that the voyage-form is freed from the spatio-temporal co-ordinates which were left over from the old Social Realism and begins to have value for itself or as the expression of a new society, of a new pure present: the return journey from Paris to the provinces and from the provinces to Paris in Chabrol (*Le beau Serge* and *Les Cousins*); wanderings which have become analytic instruments of an analysis of the soul, in Rohmer (the series of *Moral Tales*) and in Truffaut (the trilogy of *L'Amour à vingt ans*, *Baisers volés* and *Domicile conjugal*); Rivette's investigation-outing [*promenade-enquête*] (*Paris nous appartient*); the flight-outing [*promenade-fuite*] of Truffaut (*Tirez sur le pianiste*) and particularly of Godard (*A bout de souffle*, *Pierrot le fou*). In these we see the birth of a race of charming, moving characters who are hardly concerned by the events which happen to them – even treason, even death – and experience and act out obscure events which are as poorly linked as the portion of the any-space-whatever which they traverse. Rivette's film title is echoed by Péguy's song-formula, 'Paris belongs to no one.' And, in Rivette's *L'Amour fou*, forms of behaviour are replaced by the postures of the asylum, by explosive acts, which shatter the actions of characters as well as the connexions of the play which they are rehearsing. In this new kind of image the sensory-motor links tend to disappear, a whole sensory-motor continuity which forms the essential nature of the action-image vanishes. It is not only the famous scene in *Pierrot le fou*, 'I dunno what to do', where the voyage/ballad[20] imperceptibly becomes the sung and danced poem; but it is also a whole upsurge of sensory-motor disturbances, which are hardly indicated when necessary, movements which make false [*font faux*], 'slight warping of perspectives, slowing down of time, alteration of gestures' (Godard's *Les Carabiniers, Tirez sur le pianiste*, or *Paris nous appartient*).[21] Making-false [*faire-faux*] becomes the sign of a new realism, in opposition to the making-true of the old.

Clumsy fights, badly aimed punches or shots, a whole out-of-phase of action and speech replace the too perfect duels of American Realism. Eustache makes a character in *La Maman et la putain* say, 'The more you appear false like that, the farther you go, the false is the beyond.'

Under this power of the false all images become clichés, sometimes because their clumsiness is shown, sometimes because their apparent perfection is attacked. The gauche gestures of the *Carabiniers* have as a correlate the series of postcards that they bring back of the war. The external, optical and sound clichés have as their correlate internal or psychic clichés. It is perhaps in the perspectives of the new German cinema that this element finds its fullest development: Daniel Schmid invents a slowness which makes possible the dividing in two of characters, as if they were to one side of what they say and do, and chose from among the external clichés the one that they will embody from the inside, in a perpetual interchangeability of inside and outside (already in *La Paloma* but above all in *Schatten der Engel* where 'the Jew could be the fascist, the prostitute could be the pimp . . .', in a game of cards which makes each player himself a card, but a card played by another).[22] If things are like this, how is it possible not to believe in a world-wide, diffuse conspiracy, an enterprise of generalised enslavement which extends to every location of the any-space-whatever, spreading death everywhere? In Godard, *Le petit Soldat, Pierrot le fou, Made in USA, Weekend*, with their maquis of resistance to the end illustrate in different ways a plot from which escape is impossible. And Rivette, from *Paris nous appartient* to *Pont du Nord*, via *La Religieuse*, ceaselessly invokes the world-wide conspiracy which distributes roles and situations in a kind of malevolent game of snakes and ladders.

But, if everything is clichés and a plot to exchange and propagate them, the only result seems to be a cinema of parody or contempt for which Chabrol and Altman are sometimes criticised. What do the neo-realists mean, on the contrary, when they speak of the respect and the love which is necessary for the birth of the new image? Far from being satisfied with a negative or parodic critical consciousness, the cinema is engaged in its highest reflection, and has constantly deepened and developed it. We will find in Godard formulas which express the problem: if images have become clichés, internally as well as externally, how can an Image be extracted from all these clichés, 'just an image', an autonomous mental image? An image *must* emerge from the set of clichés. . . . With what politics and what consequences? What is an image which would not be a cliché? Where does the cliché end and the image begin? But, if the question has no immediate answer, it is precisely because the set of preceding characteristics do not constitute the new mental image which is being sought. The five characteristics form an envelope (including physical and psychic clichés), they are a necessary external condition, but do not constitute the image although they make it possible. And here one can assess the similarities to and the differences from Hitchcock. The New Wave could be called with good reason Hitchcocko-Marxian, rather than 'Hitchcocko-Hawksian'. Like Hitchcock it wanted to reach mental images and figures of thought (thirdness). But, whilst Hitchcock saw there a kind of complement which ought to have extended and realised the traditional 'perception–action–affection' system, it discovered there on the contrary a requirement which was enough to smash the whole system, to cut perception off from its motor extension, action, from the thread which joined it to a situation, affection from adherence or belonging to characters. The new image would therefore not be a bringing to completion of the cinema, but a mutation of it. It was necessary, on the contrary, to want what Hitchcock had constantly refused. The mental image had not to be content with weaving a set of relations, but had to form a new substance. It had to become truly thought and thinking, even if it had to become 'difficult' in order to do this. *There were two conditions.* On the one hand, it would require and presuppose a putting into crisis of the action-image, the perception-image and the affection-image, even if this entailed the discovery of 'clichés' everywhere. But, on the other hand, this crisis would be worthless by itself, it would only be the negative condition of the upsurge of the new thinking image, even if it was necessary to look for it beyond movement.

Glossary

ACTION-IMAGE: reaction of the centre to the set [*ensemble*].

AFFECTION-IMAGE: that which occupies the gap between an action and a reaction, that which absorbs an external action and reacts on the inside.

IMAGE CENTRE: gap between a received movement and an executed movement, an action and a reaction (interval).

MOVEMENT-IMAGE: the acentred set [*ensemble*] of variable elements which act and react on each other.

PERCEPTION-IMAGE: set [*ensemble*] of elements which act on a centre, and which vary in relation to it.

PERCEPTION-IMAGE (the thing):
Dicisign: term created by Peirce in order to designate principally the sign of the proposition in general. It is used here in relation to the special case of the 'free indirect proposition' (Pasolini). It is a perception in the *frame* of another perception. This is the status of solid, geometric and physical perception.
Reume: not to be confused with Peirce's 'rheme' (word). It is the perception of that which crosses the frame or flows out. The liquid status of perception itself.
Gramme (engramme or photogramme): not to be confused with a photo. It is the genetic element of the perception-image, inseparable as such from certain dynamisms (immobilisation, vibration, flickering, sweep, repetition, acceleration, deceleration, etc.). The gaseous state of a molecular perception.

AFFECTION-IMAGE (quality or power):
Icon: used by Peirce in order to designate a sign which refers to its object by internal characteristics (resemblance). Used here in order to designate the affect as *expressed* by a face, or a facial equivalent.
Qualisign (or potisign): term used by Peirce in order to designate a quality which is a sign. Used here to designate the affect as expressed (or exposed) in an *any-space-whatever*. An any-space-whatever is sometimes an emptied space, sometimes a space the linking up of whose parts is not immutable or fixed.
Dividual: that which is neither indivisible nor divisible, but is divided (or brought together) by changing qualitatively. This is the state of the entity, that is to say of that which is expressed in an expression.

IMPULSE-IMAGE (energy):

Symptom: designates the qualities or powers related to an *originary world* (defined by impulses).

Fetish: fragment torn away, by the impulse, from a real milieu, and corresponding to the originary world.

ACTION-IMAGE (the force or act):

Synsign (or encompasser): corresponds to Peirce's 'sinsign'. Set of qualities and powers as actualised in a state of things, thus constituting a real milieu around a centre, a situation in relation to a subject: spiral.

Impression: internal link between situation and action.

Index: used by Peirce in order to designate a sign which refers to its object by a material link. Used here in order to designate the link of an action (or of an effect of action) to a situation which is not given, but merely inferred, or which remains equivocal and reversible. We distinguish in this sense *indices of lack* and *indices of equivocity*: the two senses of the French word *ellipse* (ellipse and ellipsis).

Vector (or line of the universe): broken line which brings together singular points or remarkable moments at the peak of their intensity. Vectorial space is distinguished from encompassing space.

IMAGE AT TRANSFORMATION (reflection):

Figure: sign which, instead of referring to its object, reflects another *(scenographic* or *plastic image)*; or which reflects its own object, but by inverting it (inverted image); or which directly reflects its object *(discursive image)*.

MENTAL IMAGE (relation):

Mark: designates natural relations, that is, the aspect under which images are linked by a habit which takes [*fait passer*] us from one to the other. The *demark* designates an image torn from its natural relations.

Symbol: used by Peirce to designate a sign which refers to its object by virtue of a law. Used here in order to designate the support of *abstract relations*, that is to say of a comparison of terms independently of their natural relations.

Opsign and sonsign: pure optical and sound image which breaks the sensory-motor links, overwhelms relations and no longer lets itself be expressed in terms of movement, but opens directly on to time.

Notes

1 Theses on movement

1 Henri Bergson, *Creative Evolution*, trans. Arthur Mitchell, 1954; p. 322 (hereafter *CE*).
2 *Ibid.*, p. 322-3.
3 *Ibid.*, p. 349.
4 *Ibid.*, p. 355.
5 On the organic and the pathetic, cf. S. Eisenstein, *La non-indifférente Nature*, I, 10-18.
6 Arthur Knight, *Revue du cinéma*, no. 10.
7 Jean Mitry, *Histoire du cinéma muet*, III, pp. 49-51.
8 Bergson, *op. cit.*, p. 374.
9 *Ibid.*, p. 364.
10 On all these points, cf. Henri Bergson, *Matter and Memory*, 1911, Chapter IV.
11 *CE*, p. 10.
12 *Ibid.*, p. 34.
13 *Ibid.*, p. 359.
14 *Ibid.*, p. 16.
15 *Ibid.*, p. 16. The only resemblance between Bergson and Heidegger – and it is a considerable one – lies here: both base the specificity of time on a conception of the open.
16 We raise the problems of relations at this point, although it was not raised explicitly by Bergson. We know that the relation between two things is not reducible to an attribute of one thing or the other, nor, indeed, to an attribute of the set [*ensemble*]. On the other hand, it is still quite possible to relate the relations to a whole (*tout*) if one conceives the whole as a continuum, and not as a given set.
17 *CE*, p. 32.
18 *Ibid.*, p. 10.

2 Frame and shot, framing and cutting

1 Cf. P.P. Pasolini, *L'Expérience hérétique*, pp. 263-5.
2 Noël Burch, *Praxis du cinéma*, p. 86: on the black or white screen, when it no longer simply serves as 'punctuation' but takes on a 'structural value'.
3 Claude Ollier, *Souvenirs écran*, Cahiers du cinéma, p. 88. It is this which Pasolini analysed as 'obsessive framing' in Antonioni (*L'Expérience hérétique*, p. 148).
4 Dominique Villain, in an unpublished work which includes interviews with cameramen [*cadreurs*], analyses these two conceptions of framing: *Le Cadrage cinématographique*.

5   Lotte Eisner, *L'Écran démoniaque*, p. 124 (translated as *The Haunted Screen* (1969)).
6   Cf. Bouvier and Leutrat, *Nosferatu*, Cahiers du cinéma pp. 75–6.
7   Jean Mitry, *Esthétique et psychologie du cinéma*, II, pp. 78–9.
8   Pascal Bonitzer, 'Décadrage', *Cahiers du cinéma*, no. 284, January 1978.
9   R. Bresson, *Notes on Cinematography*, trans. Jonathan Griffin, 1977, p. 28: 'A sound must never come to the help of an image, nor an image to the help of a sound. . . . Image and sound must not support each other, but must work each in turn through *a sort of relay*.'
10 The most systematic study of the out-of-field was made by Noël Burch, precisely in relation to Renoir's *Nana* (*Praxis du cinéma*, pp. 30–51). And it is from this point of view that Jean Narboni contrasts Hitchcock and Renoir (*Hitchcock*, 'Visages d'Hitchcock', p. 37). But, as Narboni recalls, the cinematographic frame is always a mask in Bazin's sense: this is because Hitchcock's closed framing also has its out-of-field, although in a completely different way from Renoir (not a 'space which is continuous and homogeneous with that of the screen' but an 'off-space' 'which is discontinuous and heterogeneous to that of the screen' which defines virtualities).
11 Bergson developed all these points in *Creative Evolution*, Chap. 1. On the 'tenuous thread', cf. p. 11.
12 Bonitzer objects to Burch's view that there is no 'becoming-field of the out-of-field' and that the out-of-field remains imaginary, even when it is actualised by the effect of a continuity shot: something always remains out-of-field, and according to Bonitzer it is the camera itself which can appear on its own account, but by introducing a new duality into the image (*Le Regard et la voix*, p. 17). These remarks of Bonitzer seem to us to be solidly based. But we believe that there is an internal duality in the out-of-field itself which does not merely relate to the working implement.
13 Dreyer, quoted by Maurice Drouzy, *Carl Th. Dreyer né Nilsson*, p. 353.
14 On the separation and the reunion of fluxes, cf. H. Bergson, *Duration and Simultaneity*, Chap. III (Bergson takes as a model three fluxes; of a consciousness, of running water and of a flying bird).
15 Eric Rohmer, *L'Organisation de l'espace dans le 'Faust' de Murnau*, 10–18.
16 François Regnault, 'Système formel d'Hitchcock', in *Hitchcock*, on the composition of a movement which expresses the whole of the work, cf. p. 27.
17 Pudovkin, quoted by Lherminier, *L'Art du cinéma*, p. 192.
18 Bergson, *Matter and Memory*, Chap. 4; 'The Creative Mind', in *An Introduction to Metaphysics*, trans. M.L. Andison, 1965, pp. 71–2. We often find the same expression, 'movements of movements', in Gance.
19 Cf. André Bazin's analysis which made famous Renoir's great panorama in *The Crime of Monsieur Lange*: the camera abandons a character at the end of the yard, swerves off in the opposite direction, sweeping the empty side of the set to await the character at the other end of the yard where he is going to commit his crime (*Jean Renoir*, trans. W.W. Halsey II and W.H. Simon, 1974), p. 46: 'this stunning turn of

the camera . . . is the pure spatial expression of the entire, *"mise-en-scène"*.'

20 J. Epstein (*Ecrits I, sur le cinéma*, p. 115) wrote this text about Fernand Léger, who was undoubtedly the painter closest to the cinema. But later he applied the terms directly to the cinema (pp. 138, 178).

21 On the difference between moulding and modulation in general cf. Simondon, *L'Individu et sa genèse physico-biologique*, pp. 40–2.

22 André Bazin, *Qu'est-ce que le Cinéma*, p. 151.

23 These essential points were analysed by Noël Burch: 1) the connections of montage and the movement of the banal camera have very different origins; it was Griffith who codified the continuity, but by making exceptional use of the mobile camera (*Birth of a Nation*); it was Pastrone who used the mobile camera in an ordinary way, but neglecting continuity and placing himself under the exclusive sign of frontality characteristic of the first primitive cinema (*Cabiria*). 2) But the two processes, in Griffith and in Pastrone, come up against a single condition of spontaneously sought imperceptibility (Noël Burch, *Marcel L'Herbier*, pp. 142–5).

24 H. Bergson, *Time and Free Will*, trans. F.L. Pogson (1910) pp. 85–7.

25 These two conceptions of depth in painting, from the sixteenth to the seventeenth centuries, were studied by Wölfflin in an excellent chapter of the *Principles of Art History* (trans. M.D. Hottinger, 1932); 'Plane and Recession'. The cinema presents exactly the same evolution, as two very different aspects of depth of field which were analysed by Bazin ('Pour en finir avec la profondeur de champ', *Cahiers du cinéma*, no. 1, April 1951). Despite all his reservations about Bazin's thesis, Mitry concedes the essential point: in a primary form, depth is cut up into superimposable isolable slices each of which is valid on its own (as in Feuillade or Griffith); but, in Renoir and in Welles, another form replaces slices with a perpetual interaction, and shortcircuits the foreground and the background. The characters no longer meet on the same plane [*plan*], they are related and summon each other from one plane to another. The first example of this new depth would perhaps be Stroheim's *Greed* and would correspond exactly to Wölfflin's analysis: like the startled woman in close-up, whilst her husband enters by the door in the background, a ray of light going from one to the other.

26 Hitchcock's experiment in *The Rope* – a single sequence-shot for the whole film (only interrupted by changes of reel) – is of the same type. Bazin objected that the sequence-shot of Renoir, Welles and Wyler broke with the traditional cutting or shot, whilst Hitchcock preserved them, being content to carry out a 'perpetual succession of reframings'. Rohmer and Chabrol rightly reply that this is precisely Hitchcock's innovation, transforming the traditional frame, whilst Welles, conversely, preserves it.

27 Pascal Bonitzer has analysed all these types of shot-depth of field, shots without depth, up to modern shots which he calls 'contradictory' (in Godard, Syberberg, Marguérite Duras) in *Le Champ aveugle*, And among contemporary critics, Bonitzer is undoubtedly the one who is

most interested in the notion of the shot and its evolution. It seems to us that his very vigorous and subtle analyses should have brought him to a new conception of the shot as well-grounded unity, to a new conception of unities (for which one would find equivalents in the sciences). However, instead he draws from it doubts about the consistency of the notion of the shot whose 'composite, ambiguous and fundamentally fake character' he condemns. It is only on this point that we cannot follow him.

28 Pasolini, *L'Expérience hérétique*, pp. 197–212.
29 J. Narboni, Sylvie Pierre and J. Rivette, 'Montage', *Cahiers du cinéma*, no. 210, March 1969.

3 *Montage*

1 On the close-up and binary structure in Griffith, cf. Jacques Fieschi, 'Griffith le précurseur', *Cinématographe*, no. 24, February 1977. On Griffith's close-up and the process of miniaturisation and subjectivation, cf. Yann Lardeau, 'King David', *Cahiers du cinéma*, no. 346, April 1983.
2 S. Eisenstein's brilliant analysis consists in showing that parallel montage, in its practice as well as its conception, relates to bourgeois society in its conception of itself and in its practice: *Film Form*, 1951, 'Dickens, Griffith and the film today'.
3 Eisenstein, *La non-indifférente Nature*, 'L'organique et le pathétique'. This chapter, which revolves around *Battleship Potemkin*, analyses the organic (genesis and growth) and tackles the pathetic which completes it. The following chapter, '*La centrifugeuse et le Graal*', centred on *The General Line*, continues the analysis of the pathetic in its relation to the organic.
4 S. Eisenstein, *Mémoires*, I. pp. 283–4.
5 Bonitzer analyses this difference between Eisenstein and Griffith (absolute or relative change of dimension) in *Le Champ aveugle*, pp. 30–2.
6 For instance what Eisenstein calls 'vertical montage' in *The Film Sense*, 1968, trans. Jay Leyda, pp. 67 ff.
7 Eisenstein, in *La non-indifférente Nature*, already emphasises the formal character of the qualitative (and not merely material) jump. This character is defined by the necessary presence of a 'raising of power' of the image; 'montage by attraction' necessarily intervenes here. The many commentaries to which montage of attraction as presented by Eisenstein in *Au-delà des Étoiles* has given rise, seem interminable if the growing powers of the images are not taken into account. And, from this standpoint, the question whether Eisenstein renounced this technique does not arise: he would always need it in his concept of the qualitative leap.
8 Cf. Mitry, *L'Histoire du cinéma muet*, III, p. 306: 'Then she looks: the glass, the boots, the policeman; then hurls herself upon the glass and throws it with her full strength at the window. The old man

immediately drops down, sees the policeman and flees. By turns, a mere glass of tea, then an element of betrayal, a means of signalisation and salvation, that object . . . successively reflects an attention, a state of mind, an intention.'

9   Amengual, *Dovzhenko*, Dossiers du cinéma: 'The poetic freedom which Dovzhenko had only recently demanded from the organisation of disjointed fragments, is obtained in *Aerograd* by a cutting of extraordinary continuity.'

10 The question of ascertaining whether there is only a human dialectic, or indeed whether one can speak of a dialectic of Nature in itself (or of matter), has always troubled Marxism. Jean-Paul Sartre raises it again in *The Critique of Dialectical Reason* (1976), in affirming the human character of any dialectic.

11 Eisenstein recognised that the Vertov method might be appropriate when man had attained his full 'development'. But, until that time, man needed the pathetic, and attractions. 'It is not a cinema-eye that we need, but a cinema-fist. The Soviet cinema should split skulls', and not merely 'bring together millions of eyes', cf. *Au-delà des Étoiles*, p. 153.

12 J. Epstein, *Ecrits sur le cinéma* II, p. 67 (on L'Herbier): 'By means of a soft focus which becomes progressively intensified, the dancers gradually lose their individual differentiations, cease to be recognisable as individuals, become merged in a common visual term: the dancer, an element henceforward anonymous, impossible to distinguish from twenty or fifty equivalent elements, whose set comes to form another generality, another abstraction: not this or that fandango, but *the* fandango; that is, the structure of the musical rhythm of all fandangos made visible.'

13 Cf. Barthélemy Amengual's analyses in *René Clair*. Amengual also analyses the role of the automaton in Vigo, contrasting it with Expressionism: see his *Jean Vigo. Etudes cinématographiques*, pp. 68–72.

14 On the abstract kinetic cinema and its conceptions of rhythm, cf. Jean Mitry, *Le Cinéma expérimental*, Chs IV, V, X. Mitry poses the problem of the visual image which has not the same rhythmic possibilities as the musical image. In his own experiments, Mitry was himself to pass from the solid (*Pacific 231*) to the liquid (*Images pour Debussy*) to resolve one aspect of these problems.

15 Epstein, *op.cit.*, I, pp. 127–38.

16 Cf. the analysis of René Clair's film and his relationships with Vertov by Annette Michelson, 'L'homme à la caméra de la magie à l'epistémologie', in *Cinéma, théorie, lectures*, pp. 305–7.

17 Cf., for example, in Eisenstein (*Film Form*: 'Methods of montage'), metrical montage and its corollaries, rhythmic, tonal and harmonic montage. With Eisenstein, it is always more a case of organic proportions than of properly metrical relations.

18 Burch, *Marcel L'Herbier*, p. 139. Cf. also Amengual's remarks on light in *René Clair*, p. 56 and also in *Vigo* (p. 72): 'deconsecration of the shadows of Expressionism'. And, on Grémillon, Mireille Latil in *Cinématographe*, no. 40, October 1978.

19 Abel Gance in Pierre Lherminier *L'Art du cinéma*, pp. 163–7.
20 I. Kant, *Critique of Judgement*, para 36.
21 Epstein, *op.cit.*, I, p. 67.
22 Burch asks how *L'Argent* can convey such an impression of movement when big camera movements are relatively rare. Now the monumental character of the set (for example a large drawing-room) undoubtedly implies considerable movement by the characters, but it does no more to explain our impression of an absolute maximum of movement. Burch discovers the explanation in a multiplicity of shots for a given sequence: it is a 'supersaturation' which produces a measureless effect, taking us beyond the relations between relative magnitudes (*Marcel L'Herbier*, pp. 146–57).
23 Cf. Gance, *op.cit.*
24 Delaunay is opposed to the Futurists, for whom simultaneity is the limit of an increasingly rapid kinetic movement. For Delaunay, it has nothing to do with kinetic movement; rather it is concerned with a pure mobility of light, which creates luminous and coloured forms, and envelops them in discs and helixes which are of the nature of time. It was Blaise Cendrars who enabled French film-makers to familiarise themselves with Delaunay's ideas; cf. Gance's text, 'Le temps de l'image éclatée', in Sophie Daria, *Abel Gance hier et demain*. To move to a related area, in Messiaen there is a musical simultaneism which is defined precisely by 'rhythms of added value' and 'non-retrogradable rhythms' (Goléa, *Rencontres avec Olivier Messaien*, pp. 65 ff.).
25 Cf. Fleuri's role as analysed by Norman King through Gance's successive projects: 'Une épopée populiste', *Cinématographe*, no. 83, November 1982.
26 On light and its relationships with darkness or the opaque, the basic text is Goethe's *Theory of Colours*, trans. C. Eastlake 1970. Eliane Escoubas has made an excellent analysis of this, which can find many cinematographic applications 'L'oeil du teinturier', *Critique*, no. 418, March 1982. Expressionist light is Goethean, just as French light, closer to Delaunay, was Newtonian. It is true that Goethe's theory has another side to it which we will encounter later: the pure relationship of light with white.
27 Lotte Eisner, 'Notes sur le style de Stroheim', *Cahiers du cinéma*, no. 67, January 1957. In *The Haunted Screen* (1969) Lotte Eisner continually analyses the two processes, the striations and chiaroscuro of Expressionism: also in her *Murnau* (1973), in particular pp. 80–1 and 171–2.
28 Hermann Warm describes a set from *Fantôme*, a lost film by Murnau: an exterior, a street whose left side is effectively built up, but whose right is occupied by false façades mounted on a rail. Thus the façades moving more and more quickly cast their shadow on to the immobile houses of the other side and appear to chase the young man. Warm gives another example from the same film, where a complicated mechanism simultaneously produces a whirlwind movement, and a descent into a black hole (cf. Eisner, *Murnau*). (This reference is to an appendix not

included in the English translation, but which may be found on pp. 231-2 of the French edition, *Le Terrain vague*.)

29 Worringer, *Form in Gothic*, 1927. It was Rudolf Kurtz who particularly developed the theme of a non-organic life in the cinema in his *Expressionismus und Film*, 1926.

30 On geometry in Lang, cf. Eisner, *The Haunted Screen*: 'Architecture and landscape in the studio' and 'The handling of crowds'.

31 Cf. in particular Rohmer's analysis of scintillation in *L'Organisation de l'espace dans le 'Faust' de Murnau*, p. 48 (Eliane Escoubas, in the article cited above, studies the effects of brilliance and intensification according to Goethe's colour theory).

32 Bouvier and Leutrat, *Nosferatu*, pp. 135-6: 'Light spots which describe a white circle behind the characters, such that the forms seem to be excluded by their own movement more than they are determined by it, chased from a bottomlessness [*sans-fond*] or from a background more native than that of their rear-ground which is in this way drowned in light [. . . .] By this rupture, what is actualised in front of this spot of light, and bursts forth, a phantom divorced from the background, *is not that which normally remains hidden in the deep evanescence which is suggested by chiaroscuro, for example.* This is the source of the frequently flat character of the figures illuminated in this way, and of the feeling that they are the heirs, by their very nature, of the shadow *without romantically getting their nourishment from it* [. . .]. *This effect cannot be reduced to one which is produced by backlighting.*' (Deleuze's italics.)

33 Kant, *Critique of Judgement*, paras 26–8.

34 Cf. Worringer's text on Expressionism as 'new art', cited by Bouvier and Leutrat, *op.cit.*, pp. 175-9. Despite the reservations of certain critics, Worringer's modernist positions seem to us to be very close to those of W. Kandinsky (*Concerning the Spiritual in Art*, trans. Sadler, (1977)). Both criticise a concern – in both Goethe and Romanticism – to reconcile Spirit and Nature, which keeps art tied to an individualistic and sensualist perspective. They conceive, on the contrary, of a 'spiritual art' as a union with God, which goes beyond persons and keeps Nature in the background, relating them to a chaos from which modern man must emerge. They are not even sure that the enterprise will succeed, but there is no other choice: this is the origin of Worringer's comments on 'the cry' as the only expression of Expressionism, and one which is, however, perhaps illusory. This pessimism about a world-chaos crops up again in Expressionist cinema, where even the idea of a spiritual well-being which is attained through sacrifice remains relatively rare. It is found mainly in Murnau, more often than in Lang. But it is also the case that Murnau is the closest of all the Expressionists to Romanticism: he retains an individualism and a 'sensualism' which were to be increasingly freely displayed in his American period, with *Sunrise* and particularly with *Tabu*.

4   *The movement-image and its three varieties*

1 This is the most general theme of the first chapter and the conclusion of *Matter and Memory (MM)*.
2 M. Merleau-Ponty, *Phenomenology of Perception*, trans. Colin Smith, 1962, p. 68.
3 This is at least what appears to us in Albert Lattay's complex theory, which is phenomenologically inspired: *Logique du cinéma*.
4 *CE*, pp. 322–3.
5 *MM*, p. 20: 'I say in consequence that conscious perception must be produced.'
6 *MM*, pp. 28 and 29.
7 *MM*, pp. 9–10.
8 *MM*, p. 31: cf. atoms or lines of force.
9 *MM*, p. 5.
10 *CE*, p. 319.
11 This notion of the plane of immanence and the characteristics which we give it, seem to be a long way from Bergson. Nevertheless, we believe that we are being faithful to him. Bergson does indeed present the plane of matter as an 'instantaneous section' of becoming (*MM*, p. 86). But this is for ease of exposition for, as Bergson reminds us and will remind us later even more precisely (p. 178), it is a plane where the movements which express the changes in becoming constantly appear and reproduce themselves. It therefore includes time. It has a time as variable of movement. Moreover, the plane is itself mobile, Bergson says. In fact, to each set of movements which expresses a change there will correspond a presentation of the plane. The idea of blocs of space-time is therefore not at all contrary to Bergson's thesis.
12 We adopt the usual translation, 'machine assemblage', of the important Deleuzian term *'agencement machinique'*. See 'Rhizome', trans. P. Patton, *I and C*, no. 8, spring 1981, p. 50. *'Agencement'* can also be translated as 'ordering' or 'fitting together'.
13 *CE*, pp. 320–1.
14 *MM*, p. 32.
15 Bergson, *Duration and Simultaneity* Chap. V. The importance and the ambiguity of this book, in which Bergson confronts the theory of relativity, is well known. But though Bergson had to forbid its republication, this was not because he realised that he might have made errors. The ambiguity came rather from readers who believed that Bergson was discussing the theories of Einstein themselves. This was obviously not the case (but Bergson was not able to dispel this misunderstanding). We have just seen that he completely accepted the primacy of light and blocs of space-time. The discussion bore on something else: do these blocs prevent the existence of a universal time conceived as becoming or duration? Bergson never believed that the theory of relativity was false, but only that it was incapable of constituting the philosophy of real time which ought to correspond to it.

16 *MM*, p. 29.
17 *MM*, p. 32. There, 'The photograph of the whole is translucent: here there is wanting behind the plate the black screen on which the image could be seen'.
18 Sartre clearly noted the Bergsonian reversal in *The Imagination* (trans. F. Williams, 1962); 'There is pure light, a phosphorescence, and no illuminated matter. But this pure light, diffused on all sides, becomes actual only by reflecting off certain surfaces which serve simultaneously as the screen for other luminous zones. We have here a sort of reversal of the classical comparison: instead of consciousness being a light going from the subject to the thing, it is a luminosity which goes from the thing to the subject' (pp. 39–40). But Sartre's anti-Bergsonianism leads him to play down the impact of this reversal and to deny the novelty of the Bergsonian conception of the image.
19 D. Vertov, *Articles, journaux, projects* (this is the constant theme of Vertov's manifestos).
20 This word also conveys the idea that such images are separated or diverted (*écarté*).
21 *MM*, pp. 28–9.
22 *MM*, p. 20.
23 *MM*, p. 12.
24 *MM*, p. 27.
25 A constant theme of the first chapter of *MM*: the circular formation of the world 'around' the centre of indetermination.
26 *MM*, p. 43.
27 *MM*, p. 23.
28 *CE*, p. 320.
29 *MM*, p. 2–3.
30 *MM*, pp. 61–3.
31 Samuel Beckett, 'Film', in *Comédie et actes divers*, Ed. de Minuit, pp. 113–34. The three moments distinguished by Beckett are: the street, the staircase, the room (p. 115). We propose a different distinction: the action-image, which groups the street and the staircase; the perception-image, for the room; finally the affection-image for the hidden room and the dozing of the character in the rocking chair.
32 Beckett proposes a first schema, for the flight into the street, which presents no difficulty (cf. here, Figure 1, p. 228, which we have completed). And the climbing of the stairs merely implies a displacement of the figure on a vertical plane and a final rotation. But a general schema would be needed to represent the set of all the moments. This is Figure 2 (p. 228), proposed by Fanny Deleuze.
33 The majority of Peirce's work was published posthumously under the title *Collected Papers* (Harvard University Press) in eight volumes.
34 Eisenstein, *Au-delà des Étoiles*, 'En gros plan', pp. 263 ff. It is true that, reading the text literaliy, Eisenstein considers the close-up as a point of view which is not exactly affective, but 'professional', on the whole of the film; this is however a 'passional' point of view, which penetrates 'to the innermost being of what is happening'.

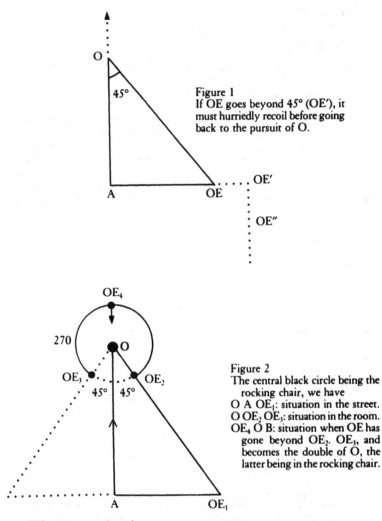

Figure 1
If OE goes beyond 45° (OE′), it must hurriedly recoil before going back to the pursuit of O.

Figure 2
The central black circle being the rocking chair, we have
O A OE$_1$: situation in the street.
O OE$_2$ OE$_3$: situation in the room.
OE$_4$ O B: situation when OE has gone beyond OE$_2$. OE$_3$, and becomes the double of O, the latter being in the rocking chair.

5   The perception-image

1   Mitry, *Esthétique et psychologie du cinéma*, II, pp. 61 ff.
2   Pasolini sets out his theory in *L'Expérience hérétique* from the standpoint of literature (in particular pp. 39–65) and from the standpoint of the cinema (in particular pp. 139–55). We refer to Bakhtine's conceptions about free indirect discourse in M. Bakhtine (V.N. Volosinov) *Marxism and the Philosophy of Language* (1973) Chaps X and XI.

3   Bergson, *L'Énergie spirituelle*, p. 920 (139) (the first page number is for the 'Centenaire' edition of Bergson's works. The second is for the current PUF edition).

4   Pasolini sketches out a very brilliant parallel between Antonioni, with his 'Paduan-Roman' aestheticism, and Godard, with his libertarian technicism: the difference between the 'heroes' of the two directors stems from this. Cf. *L'Expérience hérétique*, pp. 150-1.

5   Cf. Pasolini, *Etudes cinématographiques*, in particular Jean Semolué's study, 'Après *le Décameron* et *Les Contes de Canterbury*; réflexions sur le récit chez Pasolini'.

6   Eric Rohmer seems to have been dogged by the problem of indirect discourse. As early as the *Moral Tales*, the dialogues, carefully composed in an indirect style, are related to a 'commentary'. We refer to an article by Rohmer; 'Le film et les trois plans du discours, indirect, direct, hyperdirect' (*Cahiers Renaud-Barrault*, no. 96, 1977). But it is strange that, at least to our knowledge, Rohmer never invokes free indirect discourse, and does not seem to be aware of Pasolini's theories, However, it is indeed that special form of indirect discourse which he has in mind: cf. what he says in his article about *The Marquise of O*, on Kleist's indirect style, and about *Perceval* on the characters who talk about themselves in the third person. And, most importantly, it is not the presentation of the text in free indirect discourse, but the presentation of visual images or scenes in a corresponding mode: hence the obsessive framings of *The Marquise of O* and in particular the treatment of the image as miniature in *Perceval*.

7   Cf. Lotte Eisner's description in *The Haunted Screen*.

8   Cf. Henri Langlois' commentary, cited by Noël Burch in *Marcel L'Herbier*, p. 68.

9   Mitry, *Le Cinéma expérimental*, pp. 211-17.

10 Paul Virilio has shown the maritime origin and model of the proletariat in a text which might well be applied to Grémillon's cinema in *Vitesse et politique*, p. 50.

11 We are using an unpublished text of J.P. Bamberger on *L'Atalante*.

12 Amengual puts the question clearly: why does Vigo present the bourgeoisie in its biological rather than political and economic aspects? He answers by invoking a function of clairvoyance, and of 'objectivity' of the bodies. Cf. *Vigo. Etudes cinématographiques* (Amengual also analyses the high-angle shots in Vigo).

13 In his classification of signs, what Peirce distinguishes from the 'dicisign' (proposition) is the 'rheme' (word). Pasolini takes up Peirce's term, but introduces a very general idea of flowing into it: the cinematographic shot 'should flow', thus it is a 'rheme' (*L'Expérience hérétique*, p. 271). But here Pasolini makes an etymological mistake. In Greek, that which flows is a rheume (or reume). We will therefore use this term to designate not a general characteristic of the shot, but a special sign of the perception-image.

14 Vertov, *Articles, journaux, projets*, pp. 126-7.

15 Mitry, *Histoire du cinéma muet*, III, p. 256: 'One cannot defend montage

and simultaneously uphold the integrity of the real. There is a blatant contradiction between the two.'

16 Vertov, *op.cit.*: 'The rapid shot, the micro-shot (*micro-prise de vue*), the backward shot, the animation shot (*prise de vue d'animation*), the mobile shot, shots with the most unexpected camera-angles are not considered to be trick shots, but normal procedures, to be widely used.'

17 Abramov, *Dziga Vertov*, pp. 40–2.

18 Cf. the definition of the category of 'community' in I. Kant, *Critique of Pure Reason*.

19 Annette Michelson, 'L'homme à la caméra, de la magie à l'epistémologie', in *Cinéma, théorie, lectures* analysed all these themes: the elaboration of the theory of the interval and of reversal, the theme of the sleeping town, the role of the photogramme in Vertov (and his increasing points of contact with René Clair).

20 Cf. Marcorelles, *Eléments pour un nouveau cinéma*, 'How many colours are there in a field for a crawling baby, unconscious of green?'

21 Snow films a 'dehumanised landscape', without any human presence, and puts the camera under the control of an automatic apparatus which continually varies its movements and angles. He thus frees the eye from the condition of relative immobility and of dependence on co-ordinates. Cf. *Cahiers du cinéma*, no. 296, January 1979 (Marie-Christine Questerbert: 'Operated by the machine, regulated by sound, the camera's line of vision no longer centres on the frontal, perspective vision. [The vision] remains that of one eye only, but it is an empty, hyper-mobile eye'.)

22 P.A. Sitney's article 'Le film structurel' in *Cinéma, théorie, lectures* analyses all these aspects in the principal directors of American experimental cinema; notably the formation of the 'photogramme-shot' and the loop; flickering in Markopoulos, Conrad, Sharits; speed in Robert Breer; granulation in Gehr, Jacobs, Landow.

23 Castanéda, *Voir*.

24 Sitney, *op.cit.*, p. 348.

6 *The affection-image Face and close-up*

1 On these two techniques of the portrait, cf. Wölfflin, *Principles of Art History*, trans. M.D. Hottinger (1932) pp. 41–3.

2 Descartes, *Les Passions de l'âme*, § 54: 'To admiration is joined esteem or contempt, depending on whether it is the greatness of an object or its pettiness that we are admiring.' On the conception of admiration in Descartes and the painter Le Brun, the reader is referred to an excellent analysis by Henri Souchon, *Etudes philosophiques*, 1, 1980.

3 In English in the original.

4 Cf. G.W. Pabst, *Pandora's Box*, Classic Film Scripts, pp. 133–5.

5 Eisenstein, *Film Form*, pp. 195ff.

6 J. Fieschi, 'Griffith le précurseur', *Cinématographe*, no. 24, February, 1977, p. 10 (*Cinématographe* devoted two issues to the close-up, 24 and 25, with articles on Griffith, Eisenstein and Bergman).

7 Goethe, *Theory of Colours*, § 495.
8 English in the original.
9 Ollier, *Souvenir écran*, pp. 274–95.
10 Cf. J. von Sternberg, *Souvenirs d'un montreur d'ombres* (1965), Chap. 12, in which Sternberg sets out his theory of light. The *Cahiers du cinéma* (no. 63, October 1956) published a more complete version of this text, under the Goethean title 'Plus de lumière'.
11 B. Balázs, *Le cinéma* p. 57.
12 J. Epstein, *Ecrits sur le cinéma* I, pp. 146–7.
13 Eisenstein, *Film Form*, pp. 241–2. Eisenstein shows, on the other hand, that that which extends beyond space and time should not be considered 'supra-historical': cf. *La non-indifférente Nature*, I, pp. 391–3.
14 Cf. Peirce, *Ecrits sur le signe*. The reader is referred to the index of this edition, and Gérard Deledalle's commentaries, regarding these two notions.
15 Cf. Maine de Biran, *Mémoire sur la décomposition de la pensée* (1804). This is a very important and strange aspect of Maine de Biran's thought. Deledalle stresses the influence of Biran on Peirce. Biran is not only the first theoretician of the 'force-resistance' relation of action, which corresponds to Peirce's secondness, but the inventor of the concept of pure affection which corresponds to firstness.
16 Here we might make another comparison. Phenomenology, primarily with Max Scheler, has produced the notion of a *material and affective a priori*. Then Mikel Dufrenne gave this notion a detailed extension and status in a series of books (*Phénoménologie de l'expérience esthétique* II. *La notion d'A-priori, L'inventaire des A-priori*, by posing the problem of the relation of these *a-prioris* with history and with the work of art: in what sense are there aesthetic a-prioris, in what sense are they nevertheless created, like a particular nuance of colour in a painter? Phenomenology and Pierce have not yet been properly compared. It nevertheless seems to us that Pierce's Firstness and Dufrenne's material or affective *A-priori* coincide in many respects.
17 Bergman, in *Cahiers du cinéma*, October, 1959.
18 Denis Marion, *Ingmar Bergman* p. 37.
19 Kafka, *Lettres à Milena*, p. 260.
20 Cf. Kafka's pressing suggestions in his *Lettres à Félice*, I, p. 299.
21 An unpublished text by Michel Couthial, *Le Visage*, analyses the notion of entity, and all the aspects of the face which derive from it, primarily as a function of the Old Testament (effacement and turning aside, the closed and the open), but also with reference to art, literature, painting and the cinema.

7 *The affection-image Qualities, powers, any-space-whatevers*

1 B. Balázs, *L'Esprit du cinéma*, p. 131.
2 M. Blanchot, *L'Espace littéraire*, 1955 p. 161.

3   Roger Leenhardt, quoted by Lherminier, *L'Art du cinéma*, p. 174.
4   'Hylé', the Greek word for 'matter' or 'content'.
5   On this aspect of the close-up in Bergman, cf. Claude Roulet, 'Une épure tragique', *Cinématographe*, no. 24, February 1977.
6   Peirce, *Ecrits sur le signe*, p. 43. 'There are certain sensible qualities like the value of magenta, the smell of essence of rose, the sound of a locomotive whistle, the taste of quinine, the quality of emotion felt in contemplating a beautiful mathematical proof, the quality of the feeling of love, etc. . . . I do not mean the impression of having the experience of these feelings at the present moment, whether directly or in the memory or the imagination; that is to say something which implies these qualities as one of its elements. But I do mean the qualities themselves which, in themselves are pure *perhaps* not necessarily realised.'
7   On all these points, framing, cutting and montage in Dreyer, cf. Philippe Parrain, *Dreyer, cadres et mouvements*, *Etudes cinématographiques*, and *Cahiers du cinéma*, no. 65, 1956: 'Reflexions sur mon metier', where Dreyer demands the 'suppression' of the notions of foreground, medium shot and background [*premier plan, plan moyen* and *arrière plan*].
8   Cf. the articles by Jean Semolué and Michel Estève in *Jeanne d'Arc à l'écran*, *Etudes cinématographiques*.
9   Bresson, *Notes on Cinematography* (trans. Jonathan Griffin, 1977), p. 46, 'ON FRAGMENTATION: This is indispensable if one does not want to fall into REPRESENTATION. To see beings and things in their separate parts. To isolate these parts. Render them independent in order to give them a new dependence.'
10   This is one of the essential theses of Bonitzer's book, *Le Champ aveugle*; as soon as the over-simple distinctions are transcended, and shots become 'ambiguous' or even 'contradictory' (which is already eminently the case in Dreyer), the cinema conquers a new system, not only of perception, but of emotion.
11   M.-A Sechehaye, *Journal d'une schizophrène*, pp. 3–5.
12   Balázs, *Le Cinéma*, p. 167 (and *L'Esprit du cinéma*, p. 205).
13   Bouvier and Leutrat have analysed these different procedures used by Murnau in *Nosferatu*, pp. 56–8, 135–7, 149, 151. On the role of shadows in expressionism, cf. Lotte Eisner, *The Haunted Screen*, Chap. VIII (she analyses *Warning Shadows* in particular).
14   The reader is referred in this regard to the article on Jacques Tourneur in the dictionary *Les Classiques du cinéma fantastique* by J.-M Sabatier. This 'alternative' tendency of the horror cinema, as opposed to the Gothic tendency, is not independent of the producer Lewton and of the RKO (cf. Sabatier).
15   In his article in *Arts*, 30 December 1959, Louis Malle insisted on the sensual elements of Bresson's work, notably in *Pickpocket*. Conversely, Sternberg could be given a spiritual interpretation, notably in terms of *Shanghai Express* (cf. the great scene of the prayer).
16   On alternations, and on the spiritual alternative, we find many elements of the analysis in Philippe Parrain in relation to Dreyer (*op.cit.*), and in Michel Estève in relation to Bresson (*Robert Bresson*).

17 In the second half of the nineteenth century philosophy not only strove
    to renew its content, but to conquer new means and forms of expression,
    in very different thinkers, whose only common feature is that they feel
    themselves to be the first representatives of a philosophy of the future.
    This is clearly true of Kierkegaard. (In France this search for new forms
    appeared around Renouvier and Lequier, in an unjustly forgotten
    group, one of whose principal themes is the idea of choice.) Remaining
    with Kierkegaard, one of his particular methods is to introduce into his
    meditation something that the reader has difficulty in identifying
    formally: is this an example, or a fragment of an intimate journal, or a
    tale, an anecdote, a melodrama, etc.? For example, in *The Concept of
    Dread* (trans. Walter Laurie (1944)), it is the story of the bourgeois who
    takes his breakfast and reads his newspaper with his family and
    suddenly rushes to the window shouting, 'I must have the possible, or
    else I will suffocate.' In *Stages on Life's Way* (trans. Walter Laurie
    (1940)), it is the story of the accountant who goes mad for one hour a
    day, and seeks a law which could capitalise and fix resemblance: one day
    he was in a brothel, but retains no memory of what happened there, it is
    'the possibility which makes him mad. . .'. In *Fear and Trembling*
    (trans. Walter Laurie (1968)), it is the tale, 'Agnes and the triton' as an
    animated drawing, of which Kierkegaard gives several versions. There
    are many other examples. But the modern reader has perhaps the
    wherewithal to classify these bizarre passages: in each case it is already a
    kind of script, a veritable synopsis, which thus appears for the first time
    in philosophy and theology.
18 Ollier, *Souvenirs écran*, pp. 211-18 (and p. 217: 'alienation by colour').
19 In the report on Minnelli in the *Dossiers du cinéma*, Tristan Renaud
    constantly invokes a phenomenon of absorption: 'The unexpected
    shock of two worlds, their struggle and the triumph, or the absorption
    of the one by the other. . . .' We refer to Jean Douchet's articles which
    analyse the theme of destruction and of devouring in Minnelli: *Objectif*,
    64, February 1964 and *Cahiers du cinéma*, no. 150, January 1964:
    'poisonous or carniverous flowers. . . .'
20 Bonitzer, *op.cit.*, p. 88 (Bonitzer sets up a comparison with Bergman).
21 On neo-realist space, cf. two important articles by Sylvie Trosa and by
    Michel Devillers, in *Cinématographe*, nos. 42 and 43, December 1978
    and January 1979.
22 Jean Narboni, 'La'; Serge Daney, 'Le plan straubien', *Cahiers du cinéma*,
    no. 275, April 1977 and no. 305, November 1979.
23 Cf. an analysis of space without reference points or co-ordinates in
    Cassavetes by Phillipe de Lara, *Cinématographe*, no. 38, May 1978. In
    general, it has been the contributors to this review who have taken
    furthest the discovery and the analysis of these disconnected spaces, to
    the non-connected and non-orientated parts: for Rossellini, for
    Cassavetes, but also for Lumet (Dominique Rinieri, no. 74), for Schmid
    (Nadine Tasso, no. 43). The *Cahiers du cinéma* have chosen in preference
    the other pole, the analysis of emptied spaces.
24 Sitney (*op.cit.*) describes and comments on this film, as 'the structural

film': 'this intuition of space and, implicitly, of the cinema as potentiality, is an axiom of structural film. The room is always the place of the pure possible' (p. 342).

8   *From affect to action The impulse image*

1   Pasolini's *Pig Pen*, for example, separates the originary cannibalistic world, and the derived milieu of the pig-sty in two clearly defined parts: such a work is not naturalistic (and Pasolini hated naturalism, of which he had a very dull conception). On the other hand, in the field of cinema, as elsewhere, the originary world may constitute by itself the derived milieu which is assumed to be real: this is the case of prehistoric films, like Annaud's *La Guerre du feu*, and many horror or science-fiction films. Such films are part of naturalism. In literature, it was the elder Rosny, author of *La Guerre du feu*, who opened naturalism up in the duel direction of prehistoric novel and science-fiction novel.

2   Erich von Stroheim, *Poto-Poto*, p. 132. We know that Stroheim published three cine-novels, plus scripts and works other than novels properly speaking, to compensate to some small extent for the position in which he had been placed, where it was impossible to make films: *Poto-Poto*, *Paprika* and *Les Feux de Saint-Jean*. *Poto-Poto* seems to be the autonomous development of what was to have been the *Queen Kelly* series, the African series that Stroheim had begun (it is the 'eleventh reel' of *Queen Kelly*).

3   We refer to the analysis of these two films by Maurice Drouzy, *Louis Buñuel, architecte du rêve*.

4   Oblivion frequently crops up in Buñuel. One of the most striking examples is the end of *Susana* where, for all the characters, it is as if nothing had happened. Thus oblivion reinforces the impression of dream or hallucination. But it seems to us to have a more important function, that of marking the end of a cycle, after which it can begin again (thanks to the oblivion). Sabatier also emphasised, in Terence Fisher, the existence of false happy endings, in which all the decent characters forget all the horrors through which they have passed (*Les Classiques du cinéma fantastique*, p. 144).

5   Here again a contrast with Pasolini is possible. For the film *Theorem* also shows a family milieu literally exhausted by the arrival of an external character. But, in Pasolini, it is primarily a case of an 'exhaustion' of logic, for example, in the sense that a demonstration exhausts the set of possible cases of a figure. This is indeed Pasolini's originality; whence the title *Theorem* and the role of the external character as supernatural agent or spiritual demonstrator. On the other hand, in Buñuel, and in naturalism, the external character is the representative of the impulses, who proceeds to the physical exhaustion of the milieu under consideration (hence *Susana*).

6   Drouzy, *op.cit.*, pp. 74–5.

7   After *Queen Kelly*, Stroheim made one more film, his only talkie, which

was to have been called *Walking down Broadway*, but which was changed beyond recognition and appeared under the title *Hello Sister*, and under another director's name. Using eye-witness accounts and documents, Michel Ciment has analysed in detail the scenes attributed to Stroheim (*Les Conquérants d'un nouveau monde*, pp. 78–94). But the episodes which are genuinely attributable, and Stroheim's synopsis itself, seem to remain on the lines of his earlier work. The elements of a possible evolution perhaps appear more in *Honeymoon*, the sequel of *The Wedding March*, which was taken away from Stroheim. Here there was to have been a spiritual conversion of the heroine, which undoubtedly opened up new horizons for Stroheim. Other elements of evolution appear in the cine-novels, whether in the African world of *Poto-Poto*, and the way in which the two lovers are saved by love, or in the gipsy world of *Paprika*, and the lovers' death in the field of flowers.

8   Michel Butor analyses and compares the theme of repetition in Kierkegaard and Roussel: *Répertoire I*.

9   Maurice Drouzy analyses the shots of *The Milky Way*, in which Christ appears and raises the question of the way in which Buñuel conceived of a possible liberation (*La Voie lactée*, pp. 174 ff.).

10   Pierre Domeyne, *Dossiers du cinéma*: 'In one of his most cherished projects, *Cain and Abel*, Fuller wants to enumerate the birth of the emotions (the first lie, the first attack of jealousy, etc.), and he added the natural complement, the birth of evil. This project, like most of his films, reveals the primitive roots of Fuller's work, a film-maker of the instinct, of the return to natural and elemental impulses, of physical violence.'

11   Christian Viviani, 'La garce ou le côté pile', *Positif*, no. 163, November 1974. This same issue contains an article by Michel Henry ('Le blé, l'acier et la dynamite'), which analyses this period of Vidor's work, 1947–53: he shows how Vidor's 'lack of moderation' then changes direction, by abandoning the themes of the collectivity and regeneration central to the action-image of American realism. And the opposition dear to Vidor between the *country girl* and the *city girl* takes on a new aspect, the first becoming a violent and voracious woman, the second weak and exhausted.

12   Cf. François Truchaud, *Nicholas Ray*. This book is a model analysis of a director's evolution. Truchaud distinguishes three periods which he defines in relation to violence, and as a function of the concept of 'choice' which each presents: (1) in the first films, youthful violence and the contradictory choice which it implies; (2) in a second period, which began as early as *Johnny Guitar*, instinctual, internal violence and the alternative between a choice for evil and an effort to exceed violence; (3) finally, the violence overcome in his last films, and the choice of love and acceptance. Truchaud often points out an inspiration which is close to that of Rimbaud in Ray, who wanted to devote a film to him: a certain relationship between beauty and 'upheaval'.

13   Francis Bacon, *L'art de l'impossible*, pp. 30–2; Jean Genêt, *Journal du voleur*, pp. 14ff.

14 Speaking about *The Servant*, Losey declared: 'For me the film is only a film about servility, the servility of our society, servility of the master, servility of the servant and servility in the attitude of all sorts of people in different classes and positions [. . . .] It is a society of fear, and the reaction in the face of fear is in the majority of cases not resistance and combat, but servility, and servility is a state of mind' (*Présence du cinéma*, no. 20, March 1964). Cf. also Michel Ciment, *Le Livre de Losey*, pp. 275 ff.; and on *Don Giovanni*, pp. 408 ff.

15 This is also the theme of one of Arthur Miller's best novels, *Focus*: an average American, believed wrongly to be Jewish, persecuted by the KKK, deserted by his wife and friends, begins by protesting and trying to prove that he is a pure Aryan. Then he gradually recognises that these persecutions would be no less odious if he were really a Jew, and he ends up by voluntarily identifying himself with the Jew which he is not. Losey's film seems very close in spirit to Miller's novel.

16 Quoted by Pierre Rissient, *Losey*, pp. 122–3.

9 *The action-image The large form*

1 Noël Burch puts forward this term to characterise the structure of Lang's *M*: 'Le travail de Fritz Lang', in *Cinéma, théorie, lectures*.

2 Peirce writes 'sinsign' in order to emphasise the individuality of the state of things. But the individuality of the state of things, and of the agent, must not be confused with the singularity which already belongs to pure powers and qualities. This is why we prefer the prefix 'syn' which indicates, in line with Peirce's analysis, that there are always several qualities or powers actualised in a state of things. We therefore write 'synsign'.

3 Cf. A.J. Toynbee, *A Study of History* (1962).

4 English in the original.

5 According to J. Mitry (*Ford*) Ford is much more tragic than epic, and tends to construct a closed space, without real time or movement: it is like an 'idea of movement' suggested by static and slow images. Henri Agel takes up this point of view again, in conformity with his 'closed–open', 'expanded–contracted' alternative (*L'Espace cinématographique*, pp. 50–1, 139–41).

6 Cf. Bernard Dort, in *Le Western*. The (pastoral) epic is defined by the equivalence of the soul and the world, of the hero and the milieu; even the Indians are only evil powers, but ones who do not call into question the cosmos and its order any more than do a disaster, a fire or a flood; and the work of the hero does not modify the milieu, but re-establishes it, rather as one has to remake a road.

7 J. Mitry, *Cahiers du cinéma*, nos. 19–21, January–March 1953.

8 A scrupulous analysis of *Two Rode Together* can be found in Jean Roy, *Pour John Ford*. He emphasises the 'spiral' character of the film, and shows that this form of the spiral is common in Ford (p. 120). See also his excellent analysis of *Wagonmaster*, pp. 56–9.

9 Jack London, *Le Cabaret de la dernière chance* 10–18, pp. 283ff. And John Ford's 'I believe in the American Dream' (Andrew Sinclair, *John Ford*, p. 124).

10 F. Nietzsche, *Untimely Meditations* (trans. R.J. Hollingdale (1983)), 'On the Uses and Disadvantages of History for Life', 2 and 3. This text, on history in Germany in the nineteenth century, seems to us still valid today, and applies in particular to a whole category of historical films, from the Italian antiquity-film to the American cinema.

11 On the plan for a 'triptych of the struggle of man for water' (Tamburlane–tsarism–kolhozes), cf. Eisenstein, *La non-indifférente Nature*, I, p. 325.

12 Eisenstein, *Film Form*, p. 235. 'Naturally, the montage concept of Griffith, as a primarily parallel montage, appears to be a copy of his dualistic picture of the world, running in two parallel lines of poor and rich towards some hypothetical "reconciliation" [. . . .] Thus, it was to be expected that our concept of montage had to be born from an entirely different "image" of an understanding of phenomena which was opened to us by a world view both monistic and dialectic.' This is equally valid for the plan for a universal history: Eisenstein's triptych must be based on a dialectic of social formations, that Eisenstein compares to a three-stage rocket. As the three stages had to be despotic formation – capitalism – socialism it is understandable that the project was stopped (Stalin detesting all historical reference to despotic formations).

13 We would need to ask the same question for each great current of the historical cinema – what is the implicit conception of history? The analysis of the cinema–history relationship is already very advanced, thanks to the work of Marc Ferro (*Cinéma et Histoire*) and to the studies of *Cahiers du cinéma* (nos. 254, 257, 277, 278, notably Jean-Louis Comolli's articles). But the problem raised is more fundamental than that which we have indicated here, and concerns the relationship between historical utterances and statements on the one hand, and cinematographic utterances and images on the other. Our question would only be a part of this latter problem.

14 Bazin, *Qu'est-ce que le cinéma?*, p. 59.

15 M. Merleau-Ponty, *Sense and non-Sense*, trans. Hubert and Patricia Dreyfus (1964), 'Cinema and the new psychology'.

16 *CE*, Chap. II.

17 On all these points relating to Kazin (both aesthetic problems of structuring and personal problems of delation which react on the oeuvre), we refer to Roger Tailleur's analysis, *Kazin*. We have seen how the American cinema, and notably the historical film, gave great prominence to the theme of the traitor. But after the war, and with McCarthyism, it took on an even greater importance. We find in Fuller an original treatment of this theme of the traitor: cf. Jacques Courcelles: 'Thème du traitre et du héros', *Présence du cinéma*, no. 20, March 1964.

18 On the development of a behaviourist psychology which takes internal behavioural factors increasingly into account, cf. Tilquin, *Le Behaviorisme*.

19 On the inner, the contact and the affective memory cf. C. Stanislavsky,

The Actor Prepares, trans. E.R. Hapgood (1967); Lee Strasberg, *Le travail à l'Actors Studio*, Gallimard, pp. 96–142. On the Actors Studio and its successors, Odette Aslan, *L'Acteur au XXe siècle*, pp. 258ff.

20   Tailleur, *op.cit.*, p. 94.

21   Michel Ciment, by the questions that he puts to Kazan, brings out this type of image that tends to replace the close-up: *Kazan par Kazan*, pp. 74ff.

10   The action-image The small form

1   The French word '*ellipse*' has two senses; one corresponding to the rhetorical 'ellipsis', the other to the geometrical figure ('an ellipse'). In this chapter, Deleuze plays on both senses of the word.

2   Charles Chaplin, *My Autobiography* (1964) (see also the collection on *Public Opinion* in *Cinématographe*, no. 64, January 1981, particularly the article by Jean Tedesco, a contemporary of the film, and the analysis by Jacques Fieschi).

3   Lubitsch had a professional knowledge of cloths and of 'tailoring' which was as great as Sternberg's in relation to laces and haberdashery. Lotte Eisner, despite her severity towards Lubitsch's costume films, recognised that he introduces a new element into Expressionism and its love of depths: the play of light on fabrics, on the surface of the image. This would later also be one of Murnau's dazzling successes in *Tartuffe*; cf. *The Haunted Screen*.

4   On the two previous points, cf. Michel Devillers' article in *Cinématographe*, no. 36, March 1978: 'Quatre études sur Howard Hawks'.

5   *Positif*, no. 195, July 1977: on the theme of the outside and the inside in Hawks, we refer to the articles by Eyquem, Legrand, Masson and Ciment, and to the one by Bourget which introduces many nuances into this same theme. In *Cinématographe*, Emmanuel Decaux and Jacques Fieschi lay great emphasis on the general mechanisms of the reversals in Hawks.

6   Jacques Rivette: 'Génie de Howard Hawks', *Cahiers du cinéma*, no. 23, May 1953.

7   On the vegetable and the mineral in relation to *The Man of the West*, cf. *Jean-Luc Godard par Jean-Luc Godard*, pp. 199–200.

8   Benayoun, *Peckinpah*, Dossiers du cinéma.

9   Philippe Demonsablon, 'Le plus court chemin', *Cahiers du cinéma*, no. 48, June 1955, pp. 52–3. In this short seminal text, the author analyses Mann's *The Far Country*. For a fuller analysis of Mann and Daves in this respect, one can refer to the texts by Claude-Jean Philippe and Christian Ledieu, *Etudes cinématographiques, le Western*.

10   A. Bazin and E. Rohmer, *Charlie Chaplin*, pp. 28–32.

11   Mireille Latil le Dantec, 'Chaplin, ou le poids d'un mythe', *Cinématographe*, no. 35, February 1978: 'Verdoux the impostor moves the rich woman by lamenting the final illness of his wife, while he contemplates the garden full of roses, from which shortly before smoke had been rising,

the trace of his crime. But this conjugal fiction recalls in an abominable way the reality of his love for his true wife and the flowery setting of his house.'

12 Cf. the final speech of *The Great Dictator*, part of which is printed in Bazin and Rohmer, *op.cit.*

13 Benayoun, *Le Regard de Buster Keaton.*

14 Cited by David Robinson, 'Buster Keaton', *La Revue du cinéma*, no. 234, December 1969; on *Steamboat Bill Junior*, see p. 74.

15 We refer to David Robinson's analyses (see note 14), which are often compiled shot by shot: not just for *The Three Ages* and *Sherlock Junior*, but also for the great scene of the rapids and waterfalls in *Our Hospitality* (pp. 46–8). Likewise in relation to the fixed position of the character against a change of scenery and the geometrical problems this raised (in the absence of the transparency procedure), see p. 53.

16 Robinson, *op.cit.*: 'A young, rich couple, who have never learned to get by on their own, go adrift on a deserted liner. The ordinary difficulties of existence are increased by the fact that all the ship's facilities are geared not to individuals, but to thousands [. . .] They have to cope with household equipment generally used by hundreds of people' (pp. 54–6).

11 Figures, or the transformation of forms

1 Mikhail Romm in *Cahiers du cinéma*, no. 219, April 1970.

2 Pudovkin, cited by George Sadoul, *Histoire générale du cinéma*, VI, p. 487.

3 Eisenstein's very detailed commentary can be found in the chapter 'La centrifugeuse et le Graal', *La non-indifférente Nature*, I.

4 I. Kant, *Critique of Judgement*, para 59. (This is what Kant calls 'symbol'.)

5 P. Fontanier, *Les Figures du discours* (1968).

6 Cf. M.-L. Potrel-Dorget, 'Dialectique du surhomme et du sous-homme dans quelques films d'Herzog', *Revue du cinéma*, no. 342.

7 In a very fine book, *Werner Herzog*, Emmanuel Carrère has analysed this absence of landscape in *Woyzeck*, just as he analysed the existence of the great visions in the other case.

8 Herzog puts forward this idea as self-evident in a circumlocution at the end of his walker's diary, *Sur le Chemin des glaces*, Hachette, p. 114: '. . . and, since she knew I was one of those who walk, and leaving, defenceless, she understood me.'

9 Georges Canguilhem, *La Connaissance de la vie*, 'Le vivant et son milieu'.

10 On these two conceptions, cf. Albert Lautman, *Essai sur les notions de structure et d'existence en mathématiques*, I, Chaps I and II. Lautman makes two Platonic ideas correspond to them.

11 Henri Maldiney, *Regard, parole, espace*, pp. 167ff. and Francis Cheng, *Vide et plein, le langage pictural chinois* (from which we borrow the two following quotations from Chinese painters).

12 Cf. in particular, *La non-indifférente Nature*, II, pp. 71–107. However, Eisenstein is interested less in different spaces than in the form of the 'rolling pictures', which he compares to a pan shot. But he notes that the first rolling pictures constitute a linear space, and evolve in the direction of a tonal organisation of surfaces, animated by a breath. There is even a form where it is no longer the surface which is rolled up, but the image which is rolled on to the surface in such a way as to constitute a whole. Thus we rediscover the two spaces. And Eisenstein presents the cinema as the synthesis of the two forms.

13 Akira Mizubayashi, 'Autour du bain', *Critique*, no. 418, January 1983, p. 5.

14 Kurosawa, 'Entretien avec Shimizu', *Etudes cinématographiques Kurosawa*, p. 7.

15 Luigi Martelli, p. 112: 'All the episodes are placed in view of the main character [. . .] [Kurosawa] has sought to give priority to camera angles which contribute to flattening the image, and in the absence of depth of field, to inducing an impression of transversal movement. These technical processes play a fundamentally important role to the extent that they tend to represent a critical judgement, that of the hero who follows history through eyes with which we identify.'

16 Cf. Michel Estève, pp. 52–3 and Alain Jourdat (*Cinématographe*, no. 67, May 1981), who analyse some of the great scenes of *The Idiot* in this connexion: the snow, the skaters' carnival, the eyes and the ice, where the oneirism does not alternate with, but is extracted from, the realism of the situation.

17 On intensity and its prolongation to the brink of the void in Mizoguchi, cf. Hélène Bokanowski, 'L'espace de Mizoguchi', *Cinématographe*, no. 41, November 1948.

18 Cf. the analysis of this sequence by Godard, *Jean-Luc Godard par Jean-Luc Godard*, pp. 113–14.

19 Noël Burch (*Pour un Observateur lointain*, pp. 223–50) analyses all these aspects, and shows how the rolling-shot integrates them all. Burch emphasises the specificity of this type of sequence-shot. And, indeed, there are many kinds of irreducible sequence-shots in different directors. In his very rigorous choice of films by Mizoguchi, Burch considers that after the war, around 1948, his work starts to decline and returns to a 'classical code', and a 'sequence-shot à la Wyler' (p. 249). However, it seems to us that Mizoguchi's sequence-shot does not cease to have the specific function of tracing lines of the universe: an echo of this – and only a distant one at that – would be found only in certain examples of the American neo-Western.

12   The crisis of the action-image

1   Cf. Peirce, *Ecrits sur le signe*, Peirce believed that 'thirdness' was one of his principal discoveries.

2   Peirce does not refer explicitly to these two kinds of relations, the

distinction between which goes back to Hume. But his theory of the 'interpretant', and his own distinction between a 'dynamic interpretant' and a 'final interpretant', partially coincides with that between the two types of relations.

3 E. Rohmer and C. Chabrol, *Hitchcock*, p. 124.

4 Cf. Narboni, 'Visages d'Hitchcock', in *Alfred Hitchcock*, Cahiers du cinéma.

5 On these two examples, cf. F. Truffaut, *Le Cinéma selon Hitchcock*, pp. 165 and 79–82. And p. 15: 'Hitchcock is the only film-maker to be able to film and to make perceptible to us the thoughts of one or several characters without the help of dialogue.'

6 Rohmer and Chabrol, *op.cit.*, pp. 76–8, in this respect complete the work of Truffaut, who had only emphasised the importance of the figure 2 in *Shadow of a Doubt*. They show that, even there, there is a relation of exchange.

7 Truffaut, *op.cit.*, p. 14: 'The art of creating suspense is at the same time that of putting the public in the know by making it participate in the film. In the sphere of the spectacle, making a film is no longer a game played by two (the director and his film) but by three (the director and his film and the public).' Jean Douchet in particular has emphasised this inclusion of the spectator in the film in his *Alfred Hitchcock*. And Douchet often discovers a ternary structure in the very content of Hitchcock's films (p. 49): for example, with *North by Northwest*, 1, 2, 3 in such conditions that the first is himself 1 (the head of the FBI), the second, 2 (the couple), and third, 3 (the trio of spies). This is completely in line with Peirce's thirdness.

8 This is why one finds commentaries both on an 'essential instability of the image' in Hitchcock (Bazin) and on 'a strange equilibrium', as a limit, 'and which defines the constitutive defect' of human nature (Rohmer and Chabrol, *op.cit.*, p. 117).

9 The mark, or demark, does not appear in Peirce's classification of signs. On the other hand, the symbol appears, but in an entirely different sense from that which we are proposing: for Peirce, it is a sign which refers to its object by virtue of a law, sometimes associative and habitual, sometimes conventional (the mark would therefore be merely a particular case of the symbol).

10 Mitry, *Esthétique et psychologie du cinéma*, II, p. 397.

11 Jean-Louis Comolli, 'Le détour par le direct', *Cahiers du cinéma*, nos. 209 and 211, February and April 1969. Marcel L'Herbier is among those who have spoken best of the part of improvisation on the inevitable and 'admirable' plateau of the presence of a documentary in every film, and of the encounter with actualities: 'In *El Dorado* I made effective use of the procession, which I had not organised, in order to enrich the drama. I let my actors loose there.' In Noël Burch, *Marcel L'Herbier*, p. 76.

12 On all these points, we refer particularly to the journal, *Cinématographe*: on Altman, no. 45, March 1979 (Maraval's article) and no. 54, January 1980 (Fieschi, Carassonne); on Lumet, no. 74, January 1982 (Rinieri,

Cebe, Rieschi); on Cassavetes, no. 38, May 1978 (Lara) and no. 77, April 1982 (Sylvie Trosa, Prades); on Scorsese, no. 45, March 1979 (Cuel).

13 Claude-Edmonde Maguy has analysed all these points in Dos Passos: *L'Âge du roman américain*, pp. 125-37. Dos Passos' novels have influenced Italian neo-realism; conversely he himself was subject to a certain influence of Vertov's 'cine-eye'.

14 'Bal(l)ade': an untranslatable pun on the words *'ballade'* (ballad) and *'balade'* (voyage).

15 On the importance of this theme in English Romanticism, cf. Paul Rozenberg, *Le Romantisme anglais*.

16 Cf. Pascal Kane, 'Mabuse et le pouvoir', *Cahiers du cinéma*, no. 309, March 1980.

17 D.H. Lawrence, *Eros et les chiens*, Bourgois, p. 253-7.

18 Cf. R.S. Warshow's violent text reproduced in *Le Néo-réalisme italien, Etudes cinématographiques*, pp. 140-2. There will always be a grudge, coming from a part of America, against Italian neo-realism, which 'dared' to instigate another conception of the cinema. The Ingrid Bergman scandal also had this aspect: having become the adoptive daughter of America, she did not simply abandon her family for Rossellini, she abandoned the cinema of the conquerors.

19 Cf. the two issues of *Cinématographe* on neo-realism, 42 and 43, December 1978 and January 1979, notably the articles by Sylvie Trosa and Michel Devillers.

20 See note 14.

21 Ollier, *Souvenirs écran*, p. 58. It is Alain Robbe-Grillet who insists on the importance of the detail which 'makes' false, seeing here a sign of reality as opposed to verism; see his *Pour un nouveau Roman*, p. 140.

22 Cf. *Dossier Daniel Schmid*, pp. 78-86 (notably what Schmid calls 'papier mâché clichés'). But Schmid is perfectly conscious of the danger of leaving to the cinema only a parodic function (p. 78): therefore clichés only proliferate in order for something to come out of them. In *Schatten der Engel*, two characters emerge from the clichés which assail them from the outside and inside, the Jew and the prostitute, because they knew how to keep the feeling of 'fear'.

Index